ABOUT THIS PUBLICATION

FOR SERVICE ASSISTANCE

Customer Service
1.704.898.0770

North Carolina General Statues is published by The Muliti-Media Group of Greater Charlotte in Charlotte, North Carolina. Copyright 2015 by the Multi-Media Group of Greater Charlotte. This book or parts thereof may not be reproduced in any form, stored in a retrieval system, or transmitted in any form by any means—electronic, mechanical, photocopy, recording or otherwise—without prior written permission of the publisher, except as provided by United States of America copyright law.

The records required by U.S. Code 2257(a) through (c) and the pertinent regulations 28 C.F.R. Cli. 1, Part 75 with respect to this publication and all materials associated with such records are maintained by The Multi-Media Group of Greater Charlotte, Publisher and available for review by Attorney General.

www.visionbooks.org

Copyright © 2015 by MMGGC
All rights reserved!

TID: 5107770
ISBN (10) digit: 1503243443
ISBN (13) digit: 978-1503243446

123-4-56789-01239-Paperback
123-4-56789-01239-Hardback

First Edition

090520140547

Printed in the United States of America

2015 EDITION

North Carolina Criminal Law And Procedure-Pamphlet # 74

Printed In conjunction with the Administration of the Courts

North Carolina Criminal Law and Procedure
Pamphlet Reference Guide

Chapters	Pamphlet
Chapter 1 Civil Procedure	1
Chapter 1 Civil Procedure (Continue)	2
Chapter 1A Rules of Civil Procedure	2
Chapter 1B Contribution.	2
Chapter 1C Enforcement of Judgments.	2
Chapter 1D Punitive Damages.	2
Chapter 1E Eastern Band of Cherokee Indians.	2
Chapter 1F North Carolina Uniform Interstate Depositions and Discovery Act.	2
Chapter 2 - Clerk of Superior Court [Repealed and Transferred.]	3
Chapter 3 - Commissioners of Affidavits and Deeds [Repealed.]	3
Chapter 4 - Common Law	3
Chapter 5 - Contempt [Repealed.]	3
Chapter 5A - Contempt	3
Chapter 6 - Liability for Court Costs	3
Chapter 7 - Courts [Repealed and Transferred.]	3
Chapter 7A – Judicial Department	3
Chapter 7A – Continuation (Judicial Department)	4
Chapter 7A – Continuation (Judicial Department)	5
Chapter 7B - Juvenile Code	5
Chapter 8 - Evidence	6
Chapter 8A - Interpreters for Deaf Persons [Recodified.]	6
Chapter 8B - Interpreters for Deaf Persons	6
Chapter 8C - Evidence Code	6
Chapter 9 - Jurors	6
Chapter 10 - Notaries [Repealed.]	6
Chapter 10A - Notaries [Recodified.]	6
Chapter 10B - Notaries	6
Chapter 11 - Oaths	6
Chapter 12 - Statutory Construction	6
Chapter 13 - Citizenship Restored	6
Chapter 14 - Criminal Law	7
Chapter 14 –Criminal Law (Continuation)	8
Chapter 15 - Criminal Procedure	9
Chapter 15A - Criminal Procedure Act (Continuation)	10
Chapter 15A - Criminal Procedure Act (Continuation)	11
Chapter 15B - Victims Compensation	11
Chapter 15C - Address Confidentiality Program	11
Chapter 16 - Gaming Contracts and Futures	11
Chapter 17 - Habeas Corpus	11

Chapter 17A - Law-Enforcement Officers [Recodified.]	11
Chapter 17B - North Carolina Criminal Justice Education and Training System [Recodified.] Chapter 17C - North Carolina Criminal Justice Education and Training Standards Commission	11 11
Chapter 17D - North Carolina Justice Academy	11
Chapter 17E - North Carolina Sheriffs' Education and Training Standards Commission	11
Chapter 18 - Regulation of Intoxicating Liquors [Repealed.]	12
Chapter 18A - Regulation of Intoxicating Liquors [Repealed.]	12
Chapter 18B - Regulation of Alcoholic Beverages	12
Chapter 18C - North Carolina State Lottery	12
Chapter 19 - Offenses against Public Morals	12
Chapter 19A - Protection of Animals	12
Chapter 20 - Motor Vehicles	13
Chapter 20 - Motor Vehicles (Continuation)	14
Chapter 20 - Motor Vehicles (Continuation)	15
Chapter 20 - Motor Vehicles (Continuation)	16
Chapter 21 - Bills of Lading	17
Chapter 22 - Contracts Requiring Writing	17
Chapter 22A - Signatures	17
Chapter 22B - Contracts Against Public Policy	17
Chapter 22C - Payments to Subcontractors	17
Chapter 23 - Debtor and Creditor	17
Chapter 24 – Interest	17
Chapter 25 – Uniform Commercial Code	18
Chapter 25 – Uniform Commercial Code (Continuation)	19
Chapter 25A – Retail Installment Sales Act	20
Chapter 25B - Credit	20
Chapter 25C - Sales of Artwork	20
Chapter 26 - Suretyship	20
Chapter 27 - Warehouse Receipts [Repealed.]	20
Chapter 28 - Administration [Repealed.]	20
Chapter 28A - Administration of Decedents' Estates	20
Chapter 28B - Estates of Absentees in Military Service	20
Chapter 28C - Estates of Missing Persons	20
Chapter 29 - Intestate Succession	21
Chapter 30 - Surviving Spouses	21
Chapter 31 - Wills	21
Chapter 31A - Acts Barring Property Rights	21
Chapter 31B - Renunciation of Property and Renunciation of Fiduciary Powers Act	21
Chapter 31C - Uniform Disposition of Community Property Rights at Death Act	21
Chapter 32 - Fiduciaries	21
Chapter 32A - Powers of Attorney	21
Chapter 33 - Guardian and Ward [Repealed and Recodified.]	21

Chapter 33A - North Carolina Uniform Transfers to Minors Act	21
Chapter 33B - North Carolina Uniform Custodial Trust Act	21
Chapter 34 - Veterans' Guardianship Act	22
Chapter 35 - Sterilization Procedures	22
Chapter 35A - Incompetency and Guardianship	22
Chapter 36 - Trusts and Trustees [Repealed.]	22
Chapter 36A - Trusts and Trustees	22
Chapter 36B - Uniform Management of Institutional Funds Act [Repealed.]	22
Chapter 36C - North Carolina Uniform Trust Code	22
Chapter 36D - North Carolina Community Third Party Trusts, Pooled Trusts	23
Chapter 36E - Uniform Prudent Management of Institutional Funds Act	23
Chapter 37 - Allocation of Principal and Income [Repealed.]	23
Chapter 37A - Uniform Principal and Income Act	23
Chapter 38 - Boundaries	23
Chapter 38A - Landowner Liability	23
Chapter 39 - Conveyances	23
Chapter 39A - Transfer Fee Covenants Prohibited	23
Chapter 40 - Eminent Domain [Repealed.]	23
Chapter 40A - Eminent Domain	23
Chapter 41 - Estates	23
Chapter 41A - State Fair Housing Act	23
Chapter 42 - Landlord and Tenant	23
Chapter 42A - Vacation Rental Act	23
Chapter 43 - Land Registration	23
Chapter 44 - Liens	24
Chapter 44A - Statutory Liens and Charges	24
Chapter 45 - Mortgages and Deeds of Trust	24
Chapter 45A - Good Funds Settlement Act	24
Chapter 46 - Partition	24
Chapter 47 - Probate and Registration	25
Chapter 47A - Unit Ownership	25
Chapter 47B - Real Property Marketable Title Act	25
Chapter 47C - North Carolina Condominium Act	25
Chapter 47D - Notice of Settlement Act [Expired.]	25
Chapter 47E - Residential Property Disclosure Act	25
Chapter 47F - North Carolina Planned Community Act	25
Chapter 47G - Option to Purchase Contracts	25
Chapter 47H - Contracts for Deed	25
Chapter 48 - Adoptions	26
Chapter 48A - Minors	26
Chapter 49 - Bastardy	26
Chapter 49A - Rights of Children	26
Chapter 50 - Divorce and Alimony	26
Chapter 50A - Uniform Child-Custody Jurisdiction and	

Chapter	Page
Enforcement Act	26
Chapter 50B - Domestic Violence	26
Chapter 50C - Civil No-Contact Orders	26
Chapter 51 - Marriage	26
Chapter 52 - Powers and Liabilities of Married Persons	27
Chapter 52A - Uniform Reciprocal Enforcement of Support Act [Repealed.]	27
Chapter 52B - Uniform Premarital Agreement Act	27
Chapter 52C - Uniform Interstate Family Support Act	27
Chapter 53 - Banks	27
Chapter 53A - Business Development Corporations and North Carolina Capital Resource Corporations	28
Chapter 53B - Financial Privacy Act	28
Chapter 54 - Cooperative Organizations	28
Chapter 54A - Capital Stock Savings and Loan Associations [Repealed.]	28
Chapter 54B - Savings and Loan Associations	29
Chapter 54C - Savings Banks	29
Chapter 55 - North Carolina Business Corporation Act	30
Chapter 55A - North Carolina Nonprofit Corporation Act	31
Chapter 55B - Professional Corporation Act	31
Chapter 55C - Foreign Trade Zones	31
Chapter 55D - Filings, Names, and Registered Agents for Corporations, Nonprofit Corporations, and Partnerships	31
Chapter 56 - Electric, Telegraph and Power Companies [Repealed.]	31
Chapter 57 - Hospital, Medical and Dental Service Corporations [Recodified.]	31
Chapter 57A - Health Maintenance Organization Act [Recodified.]	31
Chapter 57B - Health Maintenance Organization Act [Recodified.]	31
Chapter 57C - North Carolina Limited Liability Company Act.	31
Chapter 58 - Insurance.	32
Chapter 58 - Insurance (Continuation)	33
Chapter 58 - Insurance (Continuation)	34
Chapter 58 - Insurance (Continuation)	35
Chapter 58 - Insurance (Continuation)	36
Chapter 58 - Insurance (Continuation)	37
Chapter 58 - Insurance (Continuation)	38
Chapter 58A - North Carolina Health Insurance Trust Commission [Recodified.]	38
Chapter 59 - Partnership.	39
Chapter 59B - Uniform Unincorporated Nonprofit Association Act.	39
Chapter 60 - Railroads and Other Carriers [Repealed and Transferred.]	39
Chapter 61 - Religious Societies	39
Chapter 62 - Public Utilities	39

Chapter 62 - Public Utilities (Continuation)	40
Chapter 62A - Public Safety Telephone Service And Wireless Telephone Service	40
Chapter 63 - Aeronautics	40
Chapter 63A - North Carolina Global TransPark Authority	40
Chapter 64 - Aliens	40
Chapter 65 – Cemeteries	40
Chapter 66 - Commerce and Business	41
Chapter 67 - Dogs	41
Chapter 68 - Fences and Stock Law	41
Chapter 69 - Fire Protection	41
Chapter 70 - Indian Antiquities, Archaeological Resources and Unmarked Human Skeletal Remains Protection	42
Chapter 71 - Indians [Repealed.]	42
Chapter 71A - Indians	42
Chapter 72 - Inns, Hotels and Restaurants	42
Chapter 73 - Mills	42
Chapter 74 - Mines and Quarries	42
Chapter 74A - Company Police [Repealed.]	42
Chapter 74B - Private Protective Services Act [Repealed.]	42
Chapter 74C - Private Protective Services	42
Chapter 74D - Alarm Systems	42
Chapter 74E - Company Police Act	42
Chapter 74F - Locksmith Licensing Act	42
Chapter 74G - Campus Police Act	42
Chapter 75 - Monopolies, Trusts and Consumer Protection	42
Chapter 75A - Boating and Water Safety	43
Chapter 75B - Discrimination in Business	43
Chapter 75C - Motion Picture Fair Competition Act	43
Chapter 75D - Racketeer Influenced and Corrupt Organizations	43
Chapter 75E - Unlawful Activities in Connection With Certain Corporate Transactions	43
Chapter 76 - Navigation	43
Chapter 76A - Navigation and Pilotage Commissions	43
Chapter 77 - Rivers, Creeks, and Coastal Waters	43
Chapter 78 - Securities Law [Repealed.]	43
Chapter 78A - North Carolina Securities Act	43
Chapter 78B - Tender Offer Disclosure Act [Repealed.]	43
Chapter 78C - Investment Advisers	43
Chapter 78D - Commodities Act	43
Chapter 79 - Strays [Repealed.]	43
Chapter 80 - Trademarks, Brands, etc.	44
Chapter 81 - Weights and Measures [Recodified.]	44
Chapter 81A - Weights and Measures Act of 1975.	44
Chapter 82 - Wrecks [Repealed.]	44
Chapter 83 - Architects [Recodified.]	44

Chapter 83A - Architects	44
Chapter 84 - Attorneys-at-Law	44
Chapter 84A - Foreign Legal Consultants	44
Chapter 85 - Auctions and Auctioneers [Repealed.]	44
Chapter 85A - Bail Bondsmen and Runners [Recodified.]	44
Chapter 85B - Auctions and Auctioneers	44
Chapter 85C - Bail Bondsmen and Runners [Recodified.]	44
Chapter 86 - Barbers [Recodified.]	44
Chapter 86A - Barbers	44
Chapter 87 - Contractors	44
Chapter 88 - Cosmetic Art [Repealed.]	44
Chapter 88A - Electrolysis Practice Act	44
Chapter 88B - Cosmetic Art	45
Chapter 89 - Engineering and Land Surveying [Recodified.]	45
Chapter 89A - Landscape Architects	45
Chapter 89B - Foresters	45
Chapter 89C - Engineering and Land Surveying	45
Chapter 89D - Landscape Contractors	45
Chapter 89E - Geologists Licensing Act	45
Chapter 89F - North Carolina Soil Scientist Licensing Act	45
Chapter 89G - Irrigation Contractors	45
Chapter 90 - Medicine and Allied Occupations	45
Chapter 90 - Medicine and Allied Occupations (Continuation)	46
Chapter 90 - Medicine and Allied Occupations (Continuation)	47
Chapter 90 - Medicine and Allied Occupations (Continuation)	48
Chapter 90A - Sanitarians and Water and Wastewater Treatment Facility Operators	48
Chapter 90B - Social Worker Certification and Licensure Act	48
Chapter 90C - North Carolina Recreational Therapy Licensure Act	48
Chapter 90D - Interpreters and Transliterators	48
Chapter 91 - Pawnbrokers [Repealed.]	48
Chapter 91A - Pawnbrokers Modernization Act of 1989	48
Chapter 92 - Photographers [Deleted.]	48
Chapter 93 - Certified Public Accountants	48
Chapter 93A - Real Estate License Law	49
Chapter 93B - Occupational Licensing Boards	49
Chapter 93C - Watchmakers [Repealed.]	49
Chapter 93D - North Carolina State Hearing Aid Dealers and Fitters Board.	49
Chapter 93E - North Carolina Appraisers Act	49
Chapter 94 - Apprenticeship	49
Chapter 95 - Department of Labor and Labor Regulations	49
Chapter 95 - Department of Labor and Labor Regulations (Continuation)	50
Chapter 96 - Employment Security	50
Chapter 97 - Workers' Compensation Act	50
Chapter 97 - Workers' Compensation Act (Continuation)	51

Chapter 98 - Burnt and Lost Records	51
Chapter 99 - Libel and Slander	51
Chapter 99A - Civil Remedies for Criminal Actions	51
Chapter 99B - Products Liability	51
Chapter 99C - Actions Relating to Winter Sports Safety and Accidents	51
Chapter 99D - Civil Rights	51
Chapter 99E - Special Liability Provisions	51
Chapter 100 - Monuments, Memorials and Parks	51
Chapter 101 - Names of Persons	51
Chapter 102 - Official Survey Base	51
Chapter 103 - Sundays, Holidays and Special Days	51
Chapter 104 - United States Lands	51
Chapter 104A - Degrees of Kinship	51
Chapter 104B - Hurricanes or Other Acts of Nature	51
Chapter 104C - Atomic Energy, Radioactivity and Ionizing Radiation [Repealed and Recodified.]	51
Chapter 104D - Southern States Energy Compact	51
Chapter 104E - North Carolina Radiation Protection Act	51
Chapter 104F - Southeast Interstate Low-Level Radioactive Waste Management Compact [Repealed]	51
Chapter 104G - North Carolina Low-Level Radioactive Waste Management Authority Act of 1987 [Repealed]	51
Chapter 105 - Taxation	51
Chapter 105 - Taxation (Continuation)	52
Chapter 105 - Taxation (Continuation)	53
Chapter 105 - Taxation (Continuation)	54
Chapter 105A - Setoff Debt Collection Act	55
Chapter 105B - Defaulted Student Loan Recovery Act	55
Chapter 106 - Agriculture	55
Chapter 106 - Agriculture (Continue)	56
Chapter 106 - Agriculture (Continue)	57
Chapter 107 - Agricultural Development Districts [Repealed.]	57
Chapter 108 - Social Services [Repealed and Recodified.]	57
Chapter 108A - Social Services	57
Chapter 108B - Community Action Programs	58
Chapter 108C Medicaid and Health Choice Provider Requirements.	58
Chapter 108D Medicaid Managed Care for Behavioral Health Services.	58
Chapter 109 - Bonds [Recodified.]	58
Chapter 110 - Child Welfare	58
Chapter 111 - Aid to the Blind	58
Chapter 112 - Confederate Homes and Pensions [Repealed.]	58
Chapter 113 - Conservation and Development	58
Chapter 113 - Conservation and Development (Continuation)	59

Chapter	Page
Chapter 113A - Pollution Control and Environment	59
Chapter 113A - Pollution Control and Environment (Continuation)	60
Chapter 113B - North Carolina Energy Policy Act of 1975	60
Chapter 114 - Department of Justice	60
Chapter 115 - Elementary and Secondary Education [Repealed.]	60
Chapter 115A - Community Colleges, Technical Institutes, and Industrial Education Centers [Repealed.]	60
Chapter 115B - Tuition and Fee Waivers	60
Chapter 115C - Elementary and Secondary Education	60
Chapter 115C - Elementary and Secondary Education (Continuation)	61
Chapter 115C - Elementary and Secondary Education (Continuation)	62
Chapter 115C - Elementary and Secondary Education (Continuation)	63
Chapter 115D - Community Colleges	63
Chapter 115E - Private Educational Facilities Finance Act [Recodified]	63
Chapter 116 - Higher Education	63
Chapter 116 - Higher Education (Continuation)	63
Chapter 116A - Escheats and Abandoned Property [Repealed.]	64
Chapter 116B - Escheats and Abandoned Property	64
Chapter 116C - Continuum of Education Programs	64
Chapter 116D - Higher Education Bonds	64
Chapter 116E -Education Longitudinal Data System	64
Chapter 117 - Electrification	64
Chapter 118 - Firemen's and Rescue Squad Workers' Relief and Pension Funds [Recodified.]	64
Chapter 118A - Firemen's Death Benefit Act [Repealed.]	64
Chapter 118B - Members of a Rescue Squad Death Benefit Act [Repealed.]	64
Chapter 119 - Gasoline and Oil Inspection and Regulation	64
Chapter 120 - General Assembly	65
Chapter 120 - General Assembly (Continuation)	66
Chapter 120 - General Assembly (Continuation)	67
Chapter 120C - Lobbying	67
Chapter 121 - Archives and History	67
Chapter 122 - Hospitals for the Mentally Disordered [Repealed.]	67
Chapter 122A - North Carolina Housing Finance Agency	67
Chapter 122B - North Carolina Agricultural Facilities Finance Act [Repealed.]	67
Chapter 122C - Mental Health, Developmental Disabilities, and Substance Abuse Act of 1985	67
Chapter 122C - Mental Health, Developmental Disabilities, and Substance Abuse Act of 1985 (Continuation)	68

Chapter	Page
Chapter 122D - North Carolina Agricultural Finance Act	68
Chapter 122E - North Carolina Housing Trust and Oil Overcharge Act	68
Chapter 123 - Impeachment	69
Chapter 123A - Industrial Development [Repealed.]	69
Chapter 124 - Internal Improvements	69
Chapter 125 - Libraries	69
Chapter 126 - State Personnel System	69
Chapter 127 - Militia [Repealed.]	69
Chapter 127A - Militia	69
Chapter 127B - Military Affairs	69
Chapter 127C - Advisory Commission on Military Affairs	69
Chapter 128 - Offices and Public Officers	69
Chapter 128 - Offices and Public Officers (Continuation)	70
Chapter 129 - Public Buildings and Grounds	70
Chapter 130 - Public Health [Repealed.]	70
Chapter 130A - Public Health	70
Chapter 130A - Public Health (Continuation)	71
Chapter 130A - Public Health (Continuation)	72
Chapter 130B - Hazardous Waste Management Commission [Repealed.]	72
Chapter 131 - Public Hospitals [Repealed.]	72
Chapter 131A - Health Care Facilities Finance Act	72
Chapter 131B - Licensing of Ambulatory Surgical Facilities [Repealed.]	72
Chapter 131C - Charitable Solicitation Licensure Act [Repealed.]	72
Chapter 131D - Inspection and Licensing of Facilities	72
Chapter 131E - Health Care Facilities and Services	72
Chapter 131E - Health Care Facilities and Services (Continuation)	73
Chapter 131F - Solicitation of Contributions	73
Chapter 132 - Public Records	73
Chapter 133 - Public Works	74
Chapter 134 - Youth Development [Recodified.]	74
Chapter 134A - Youth Services [Repealed.]	74
Chapter 135 - Retirement System for Teachers and State Employees; Social Security; Health Insurance Program for Children	74
Chapter 135 - Retirement System for Teachers and State Employees; Social Security; Health Insurance Program for Children	75
Chapter 136 - Transportation	75
Chapter 136 - Transportation (Continuation)	76
Chapter 137 - Rural Rehabilitation [Repealed.]	76
Chapter 138 - Salaries, Fees and Allowances	76
Chapter 138A - State Government Ethics Act	76

Chapter 139 - Soil and Water Conservation Districts	76
Chapter 140 - State Art Museum; Symphony and Art Societies	76
Chapter 140A - State Awards System	76
Chapter 141 - State Boundaries	76
Chapter 142 - State Debt	76
Chapter 143 - State Departments, Institutions, and Commissions	77
Chapter 143 - State Departments, Institutions, and Commissions (Continuation)	78
Chapter 143 - State Departments, Institutions, and Commissions (Continuation)	79
Chapter 143 - State Departments, Institutions, and Commissions (Continuation)	80
Chapter 143A - State Government Reorganization	80
Chapter 143B - Executive Organization Act of 1973	80
Chapter 143B - Executive Organization Act of 1973 (Continuation)	81
Chapter 143B - Executive Organization Act of 1973 (Continuation)	82
Chapter 143C - State Budget Act	83
Chapter 143D - The State Governmental Accountability and Internal Control Act	83
Chapter 144 - State Flag, Official Governmental Flags, Motto, and Colors	83
Chapter 145 - State Symbols and Other Official Adoptions.	83
Chapter 146 - State Lands	83
Chapter 147 - State Officers	83
Chapter 148 - State Prison System	84
Chapter 149 - State Song and Toast	84
Chapter 150 - Uniform Revocation of Licenses [Repealed.]	84
Chapter 150A - Administrative Procedure Act [Recodified.]	84
Chapter 150B - Administrative Procedure Act	84
Chapter 151 - Constables [Repealed.]	84
Chapter 152 - Coroners	84
Chapter 152A - County Medical Examiner [Repealed.]	84
Chapter 152A - County Medical Examiner [Repealed.] (Continuation)	84
Chapter 153 - Counties and County Commissioners [Repealed.]	84
Chapter 153A - Counties	84
Chapter 153A - Counties (Continuation)	85
Chapter 153B - Mountain Resources Planning Act	85
Chapter 153C - Uwharrie Regional Resources Act	85
Chapter 154 - County Surveyor [Repealed.]	85
Chapter 155 - County Treasurer [Repealed.]	85

Chapter 156 - Drainage	85
Chapter 156 – Drainage (Continuation)	86
Chapter 157 - Housing Authorities and Projects	86
Chapter 157A - Historic Properties Commissions [Transferred.]	86
Chapter 158 - Local Development	86
Chapter 159 - Local Government Finance	86
Chapter 159 - Local Government Finance (Continuation)	87
Chapter 159A - Pollution Abatement and Industrial Facilities Financing Act [Unconstitutional.]	87
Chapter 159B - Joint Municipal Electric Power and Energy Act	87
Chapter 159C - Industrial and Pollution Control Facilities Financing Act	87
Chapter 159D - The North Carolina Capital Facilities Financing Act	87
Chapter 159E - Registered Public Obligations Act	87
Chapter 159F - North Carolina Energy Development Authority [Repealed.]	87
Chapter 159G - Water Infrastructure	87
Chapter 159H - [Reserved.]	87
Chapter 159I - Solid Waste Management Loan Program and Local Government Special Obligation Bonds	87
Chapter 160 - Municipal Corporations [Repealed And Transferred.]	87
Chapter 160A - Cities and Towns	88
Chapter 160A - Cities and Towns (Continuation)	89
Chapter 160B - Consolidated City-County Act	89
Chapter 160C - Baseball Park Districts [Repealed.]	90
Chapter 161 - Register of Deeds	90
Chapter 162 - Sheriff	90
Chapter 162A - Water and Sewer Systems	90
Chapter 162B Continuity of Local Government in Emergency.	90
Chapter 163 Elections and Election Laws.	90
Chapter 163 Elections and Election Laws. (Continuation)	91
Chapter 164 Concerning the General Statutes of North Carolina.	92
Chapter 165 Veterans.	92
Chapter 166 Civil Preparedness Agencies [Repealed.]	92
Chapter 166A North Carolina Emergency Management Act.	92
Chapter 167 State Civil Air Patrol [Repealed.]	92
Chapter 168 Persons with Disabilities.	92
Chapter 168A Persons With Disabilities Protection Act.	92

Chapter 133.

Public Works.

Article 1.

General Provisions.

§ 133-1. Employment of architects, etc., on public works when interested in use of materials prohibited.

It shall be unlawful for any architect, engineer, or other individual, firm, or corporation providing design services for any city, county or State work supported wholly or in part with public funds, knowingly to specify any building materials, equipment or other items which are manufactured, sold or distributed by any firm or corporation in which such designer or specifier has a financial interest by reason of being a partner, officer, employee, agent or substantial stockholder. (1933, c. 66, s. 1; 1977, c. 730.)

§ 133-1.1. Certain buildings involving public funds to be designed, etc., by architect or engineer.

(a) In the interest of public health, safety and economy, every officer, board, department, or commission charged with the duty of approving plans and specifications or awarding or entering into contracts involving the expenditure of public funds in excess of:

(1) Three hundred thousand dollars ($300,000) for the repair of public buildings where such repair does not include major structural change in framing or foundation support systems, or five hundred thousand dollars ($500,000) for the repair of public buildings by The University of North Carolina or its constituent institutions where such repair does not include major structural change in framing or foundation support systems,

(1a) One hundred thousand dollars ($100,000) for the repair of public buildings affecting life safety systems,

(2) One hundred thirty-five thousand dollars ($135,000) for the repair of public buildings where such repair includes major structural change in framing or foundation support systems, or

(3) One hundred thirty-five thousand dollars ($135,000) for the construction of, or additions to, public buildings or State-owned and operated utilities, shall require that such plans and specifications be prepared by a registered architect, in accordance with the provisions of Chapter 83A of the General Statutes, or by a registered engineer, in accordance with the provisions of Chapter 89C of the General Statutes, or by both architect and engineer, particularly qualified by training and experience for the type of work involved, and that the North Carolina seal of such architect or engineer together with the name and address of such architect or engineer, or both, be placed on all these plans and specifications.

(b) (1) On all projects requiring the services of an architect, an architect shall conduct frequent and regular inspections or such inspections as required by contract and shall issue a signed and sealed certificate of compliance to the awarding authority that:

a. The inspections of the construction, repairs or installations have been conducted with the degree of care and professional skill and judgment ordinarily exercised by a member of that profession; and

b. To the best of his knowledge and in the professional opinion of the architect, the contractor has fulfilled the obligations of such plans, specifications, and contract.

(2) On all projects requiring the services of an engineer, an engineer shall conduct frequent and regular inspections or such inspections as required by contract and shall issue a signed and sealed certificate of compliance to the awarding authority that:

a. The inspections of the construction, repairs, or installations have been conducted with the degree of care and professional skill and judgment ordinarily exercised by a member of that profession; and

b. To the best of his knowledge and in the professional opinion of the engineer, the contractor has fulfilled the obligations of such plans, specifications, and contract.

(3) No certificate of compliance shall be issued until the architect and/or engineer is satisfied that the contractor has fulfilled the obligations of such plans, specifications, and contract.

(c) The following shall be excepted from the requirements of subsection (a) of this section:

(1) Dwellings and outbuildings in connection therewith, such as barns and private garages.

(2) Apartment buildings used exclusively as the residence of not more than two families.

(3) Buildings used for agricultural purposes other than schools or assembly halls which are not within the limits of a city or an incorporated village.

(4) Temporary buildings or sheds used exclusively for construction purposes, not exceeding 20 feet in any direction, and not used for living quarters.

(5) Pre-engineered garages, sheds, and workshops up to 5,000 square feet used exclusively by city, county, public school, or State employees for purposes related to their employment. For pre-engineered garages, sheds, and workshops constructed pursuant to this subdivision, there shall be a minimum separation of these structures from other buildings or property lines of 30 feet.

(d) On projects on which no registered architect or engineer is required pursuant to the provisions of this section, the governing board or awarding authority shall require a certificate of compliance with the State Building Code from the city or county inspector for the specific trade or trades involved or from a registered architect or engineer, except that the provisions of this subsection shall not apply to projects where any of the following apply:

(1) The plans and specifications are approved by the Department of Administration, Division of State Construction, and the completed project is inspected by the Division of State Construction and the State Electrical Inspector.

(2) The project is exempt from the State Building Code.

(3) The project has a total projected cost of less than $100,000 and does not alter life safety systems.

(e) All plans and specifications for public buildings of any kind shall be identified by the name and address of the author thereof.

(f) Neither the designer nor the contractor involved shall receive his final payment until the required certificate of compliance shall have been received by the awarding authority.

(g) On all facilities which are covered by this Article, other than those listed in subsection (c) of this section and which require any job-installed finishes, the plans and specifications shall include the color schedule. (1953, c. 1339; 1957, c. 994; 1963, c. 752; 1973, c. 1414, s. 2; 1979, c. 891; 1981, c. 687; 1983 (Reg. Sess., 1984), c. 970, s. 1; 1989, c. 24; 1997-412, s. 11; 1998-212, s. 11.8(e); 2001-496, ss. 6, 8(e); 2003-305, s. 1; 2005-300, s. 1; 2007-322, s. 1.)

§ 133-2. Drawing of plans by material furnisher prohibited.

It shall be unlawful for any architect, engineer, designer or draftsman, employed on county, State, or city works, to employ or allow any manufacturer, his representatives or agents, to write, plan, draw, or make specifications for such works or any part thereof. (1933, c. 66, s. 2.)

§ 133-3. Specifications to carry competitive items; substitution of materials.

All architects, engineers, designers, or draftsmen, when providing design services, or writing specifications, directly or indirectly, for materials to be used in any city, county or State work, shall specify in their plans the required performance and design characteristics of such materials. However, when it is impossible or impractical to specify the required performance and design characteristics for such materials, then the architect, engineer, designer or draftsman may use a brand name specification so long as they cite three or more examples of items of equal design or equivalent design, which would establish an acceptable range for items of equal or equivalent design. The specifications shall state clearly that the cited examples are used only to denote the quality standard of product desired and that they do not restrict bidders to a specific brand, make, manufacturer or specific name; that they are used only to set forth and convey to bidders the general style, type, character and quality of product desired; and that equivalent products will be acceptable. Where it is impossible to specify performance and design characteristics for such materials and impossible to cite three or more items due to the fact that there are not that many items of similar or equivalent design in competition, then as many items as are available shall be cited. On all city, county or State works, the maximum interchangeability and compatibility of cited items shall be required. The brand of product used on a city, county or State work shall not limit competitive bidding on future works. Specifications may list one or more preferred brands as an alternate to the base bid in limited circumstances. Specifications containing a preferred brand alternate under this section must identify the performance standards that support the preference. Performance standards for the preference must be approved in advance by the owner in an open meeting. Any alternate approved by the owner shall be approved only where (i) the preferred alternate will provide cost savings, maintain or improve the functioning of any process or system affected by the preferred item or items, or both, and (ii) a justification identifying these criteria is made available in writing to the public. Substitution of materials, items, or equipment of equal or equivalent design shall be submitted to the architect or engineer for approval or disapproval; such approval or disapproval shall be made by the architect or engineer prior to the opening of bids. The purpose of this statute is to mandate and encourage free and open competition on public contracts. (1933, c. 66, s. 3; 1951, c. 1104, s. 5; 1993, c. 334, s. 7.1; 2002-107, s. 5; 2002-159, s. 64(c).)

§ 133-4. Violation of Chapter made misdemeanor.

Any person, firm, or corporation violating the provisions of this Chapter shall be guilty of a Class 3 misdemeanor and upon conviction, license to practice his profession in this State shall be withdrawn for a period of one year and he shall only be subject to a fine of not more than five hundred dollars ($500.00). (1933, c. 66, s. 4; 1993, c. 539, s. 969; 1994, Ex. Sess., c. 24, s. 14(c).)

§ 133-4.1. Guaranteed energy savings contracts.

Except for G.S. 133-1 and [G.S.] 133-1.1, the provisions of this Article shall not apply to energy conservation measures undertaken as part of a guaranteed energy savings contract entered into pursuant to the provisions of Part 2 of Article 3B of Chapter 143 of the General Statutes. (1993 (Reg. Sess., 1994), c. 775, s. 8; 2002-161, s. 11.1.)

Article 2.

Relocation Assistance.

§ 133-5. Short title.

This Article shall be cited as "The Uniform Relocation Assistance and Real Property Acquisition Policies Act." (1971, c. 1107, s. 1.)

§ 133-6. Declaration of purpose.

The purpose of this Article is to establish a uniform policy for the fair and equitable treatment of persons displaced as a result of public works programs in order that such persons shall not suffer disproportionate injuries as a result of programs designed for the benefit of the public as a whole and to insure continuing eligibility for federal aid funds to the State and its agencies and subdivisions. (1971, c. 1107, s. 1.)

§ 133-7. Definitions.

As used in this Article:

(1) "Agency" means the State of North Carolina or any board, bureau, commission, institution, or other agency of the State, or any board or governing body of a political subdivision of the State, or an agency, commission, or authority of a political subdivision of the State.

(2) "Business" means any lawful activity, excepting a farm operation, conducted primarily:

a. For the purchase, sale, lease and rental of personal and real property, and for the manufacture, processing, or marketing of products, commodities, or any other personal property;

b. For the sale of services to the public;

c. By a nonprofit organization; or

d. Solely for the purposes of G.S. 133-8(a), for assisting in the purchase, sale, resale, manufacture, processing, or marketing of products, commodities, personal property, or services by the erection and maintenance of an outdoor advertising display or displays, whether or not such display or displays are located on the premises on which any of the above activities are conducted.

(3) a. "Displaced person" means, except as provided in subdivision (a)(ii)-

(i) Any person who moves from real property, or moves his personal property from real property - (A) as a direct result of a written notice of intent to acquire or the acquisition of such real property in whole or in part for a program or project undertaken by an agency; or (B) on which such person is a residential tenant or conducts a small business, a farm operation, or business defined in G.S. 133-7(2)(d) as a direct result of rehabilitation, demolition, or such other displacing activity as the agency may prescribe, under a program or project undertaken by an agency in any case in which the agency determines that such displacement is permanent; and

(ii) Solely for the purposes of G.S. 133-8(a) and (b) and G.S. 133-11, any person who moves from real property, or moves his personal property from real property - (A) as a direct result of a written notice of intent to acquire or the acquisition of other real property, in whole or in part, on which such person conducts a business or farm operation, for a program or project undertaken by an agency; or (B) as a direct result of rehabilitation, demolition, or such other displacing activity as the agency may prescribe, of other real property on which such person conducts a business or farm operation, under a program or project undertaken by an agency where the agency determines that such displacement is permanent.

b. The term "displaced person" does not include -

(i) A person who has been determined, according to criteria established by the agency, to be either unlawfully occupying the displacement dwelling or to have occupied such dwelling for the purpose of obtaining assistance under this Article;

(ii) In any case in which the agency acquires property for a program or project, any person (other than a person who was an occupant of such property at the time it was acquired) who occupies such property on a rental basis for a short term or a period subject to termination when the property is needed for the program or project.

(4) "Farm operation" means any activity conducted solely or primarily for the production of one or more agricultural products or commodities, including timber, for sale or home use, and customarily producing such products or commodities in sufficient quantity to be capable of contributing materially to the operator's support.

(5) "Person" means any individual, partnership, corporation or association.

(6) "Program or project" for the purpose of this Article shall mean any construction or rehabilitation project undertaken by an agency, as herein defined or the utilization of real property by an agency for any other public purposes, and to which program or project the agency makes this Article applicable.

(7) "Relocation officer" means the head of the department delegated the authority to carry out relocation policies by the agency.

(8) "Comparable replacement dwelling" means any dwelling that is (i) decent, safe, and sanitary; (ii) adequate in size to accommodate the occupants; (iii) within the financial means of the displaced person; (iv) functionally equivalent; (v) in an area not subject to unreasonably adverse environmental conditions; and (vi) in a location generally not less desirable than the location of the displaced person's dwelling with respect to public utilities, facilities, services, and the displaced person's place of employment.

(9) "Appraisal" means a written statement independently and impartially prepared by a qualified appraiser setting forth an opinion of defined value of an adequately described property as of a specific date, supported by the presentation and analysis of relevant market information.

(10) "Lead agency" means the North Carolina Department of Transportation. The lead agency shall issue such rules and regulations as may be necessary to carry out this Article and to comply with federal aid regulations. (1971, c. 1107, s. 1; 1989, c. 28, s. 1.)

§ 133-8. Moving and related expenses.

(a) Whenever the acquisition of real property for a program or project undertaken by an agency will result in the displacement of any person, such agency shall make a payment to any displaced person, upon application as approved by the head of the agency for:

(1) Actual reasonable expenses in moving himself, his family, business, farm operation, or other personal property;

(2) Actual direct losses of tangible personal property as a result of moving or discontinuing a business or farm operation, but not to exceed an amount equal to the reasonable expenses that would have been required to relocate such property, as determined by the relocation officer; and

(3) Actual reasonable expenses in searching for a replacement business or farm in accordance with criteria established by the lead agency, but not to exceed two thousand five hundred dollars ($2,500); and

(4) Actual reasonable expenses necessary to reestablish a displaced farm, nonprofit organization, or small business at its new site, in accordance with criteria to be established by the lead agency, but not to exceed ten thousand dollars ($10,000).

(b) Any displaced person eligible for payments under subsection (a) of this section who is displaced from a dwelling and who elects to accept the payments authorized by this subsection in lieu of the payments authorized by subsection (a) of this section may receive an expense and dislocation allowance, which shall be determined according to a schedule established by the lead agency.

(c) Any displaced person eligible for payments under subsection (a) of this section who is displaced from the person's place of business or farm operation and who is eligible under criteria established by the lead agency may elect to accept the payment authorized by this subsection in lieu of the payment authorized by subsection (a) of this section. Such payment shall consist of a fixed payment in an amount to be determined according to criteria established by the lead agency, except that such payment shall not be less than one thousand dollars ($1,000) nor more than twenty thousand dollars ($20,000). A person whose sole business at the displacement dwelling is the rental of such property to others shall not qualify for a payment under this subsection. (1971, c. 1107, s. 1; 1989, c. 28, s. 2; 2005-331, s. 1.)

§ 133-9. Replacement housing for homeowners.

(a) In addition to payments otherwise authorized by this Article and subject to the provisions of G.S. 133-10.1 the agency shall make an additional payment not in excess of twenty-two thousand five hundred dollars ($22,500) to any displaced person who is displaced from a dwelling actually owned and occupied by such displaced person for not less than 180 days prior to the initiation of negotiations for the acquisition of the property. Such additional payment shall include the following elements:

(1) The amount, if any, which when added to the acquisition cost of the dwelling acquired by the agency, equals the reasonable cost of a comparable replacement dwelling. All determinations required to carry out this section shall be made in accordance with standards established by the lead agency.

(2) The amount, if any, which will compensate such displaced person for any increased interest costs and other debt service costs which such person is required to pay for financing the acquisition of any such comparable replacement dwelling. Such amount shall be paid only if the dwelling acquired by the agency was encumbered by a bona fide mortgage which was a valid lien on such dwelling for not less than 180 days immediately prior to the initiation of negotiations for the acquisition of such dwelling in accordance with criteria to be established by the lead agency.

(3) Reasonable expenses incurred by such displaced person for evidence of title, recording fees, and other closing costs incident to the purchase of the replacement dwelling, but not including prepaid expenses.

(b) The additional payment authorized by this section shall be made only to a displaced person who purchases and occupies a comparable replacement dwelling within one year after the date on which such person receives final payment from the agency for the acquired dwelling, except that the agency may extend such period for good cause. If such period is extended, the payment under this section shall be based on the costs of relocating the person to a comparable replacement dwelling within one year of such date.

(c) The agency may, in cooperation with any federal agency upon application by a mortgagee, insure any mortgage (including advances during construction) on a comparable replacement dwelling executed by a displaced person assisted under this section, which mortgage is eligible for insurance under any federal law administered by such agency notwithstanding any requirements under such law relating to age, physical condition, or other personal characteristics of eligible mortgagors, and may make commitments for the insurance of such mortgage prior to the date of execution of the mortgage. (1971, c. 1107, s. 1; 1981, c. 101, s. 1; 1989, c. 28, s. 3.)

§ 133-10. Replacement housing for tenants and certain others.

(a) In addition to amounts otherwise authorized by this Article, the agency shall make a payment to or for any displaced person displaced from any dwelling not eligible to receive a payment under G.S. 133-9 which dwelling was actually and lawfully occupied by such displaced person for not less than 90 days immediately prior to (1) the initiation of negotiations for acquisition of such dwelling, or (2) in any case in which displacement is not a direct result of acquisition, such other event as the agency shall prescribe. Such payment shall consist of the amount necessary to enable such person to lease or rent for a period not to exceed 42 months, a comparable replacement dwelling, but not to exceed five thousand two hundred fifty dollars ($5,250). At the discretion of the agency, a payment under this subsection may be made in periodic installments. Computation of a payment under this subsection to a low-income displaced person for a comparable replacement dwelling shall take into account such person's income.

(b) Any person eligible for a payment under subsection (a) of this section may elect to apply such payment to a down payment on, and other incidental expenses pursuant to, the purchase of a comparable replacement dwelling. Any such person may, at the discretion of the agency, be eligible under this subsection for the maximum payment allowed under subsection (a), except that, in the case of a displaced homeowner who has owned and occupied the displacement dwelling for at least 90 days but not more than 180 days immediately prior to the initiation of negotiations for the acquisition of such dwelling, such payment shall not exceed the payment such person would otherwise have received under G.S. 133-9(a) had the person owned and occupied the displacement dwelling 180 days prior to the initiation of such negotiations. (1971, c. 1107, s. 1; 1981, c. 101, s. 2; 1989, c. 28, s. 4.)

§ 133-10.1. Authorization for replacement housing.

(a) As a last resort, if a project cannot proceed to actual construction because of the lack of availability of comparable sale or rental housing, or because required federal-aid payments are in excess of those otherwise authorized by this Article, the State of North Carolina and its agencies may:

(1) Undertake through private contractors, after competitive bidding, to provide for the construction and renovation of the necessary housing,

(2) Purchase sites and improvements after publishing in a newspaper of general circulation in the county in which such sites are located a public notice of the proposed transaction, including a description of the sites and improvements to be purchased, the owner or owners thereof, the terms of the transaction including the price and date of the proposed purchase, and a brief description of the factors upon which the agency has based its determination that such housing is not otherwise available, and

(3) Sell or lease the premises to the displaced person upon such terms as the agency deems necessary.

(4) Exceed the limitation in G.S. 133-9(a) and 133-10.

(b) Cities, counties and other local governments and agencies may comply with and provide assistance authorized under the Federal Uniform Relocation and Real Property Acquisition Policy Act of 1970, as amended, for last resort housing. (1975, c. 515; 1981, c. 101, ss. 3, 4; 1989, c. 28, s. 5.)

§ 133-11. Relocation assistance advisory services.

(a) Programs or projects undertaken by an agency shall be planned in a manner that (1) recognizes, at any early stage in the planning of such programs or projects and before the commencement of any actions which will cause displacements of individuals, families, businesses, and farm operations, and (2) provides for the resolution of such problems in order to minimize adverse impacts on displaced persons and to expedite program or project advancement and completion.

(b) Agencies shall ensure that the relocation assistance advisory services described in subsection (c) of this section are made available to all persons displaced by such agency. If such agency determines that any person occupying property immediately adjacent to the property where the displacing activity occurs suffers substantial economic injury as a result thereof, the agency may make such advisory services available to that person.

(c) Each relocation assistance advisory program required by subsection (b) of this section shall include such measures, facilities, or services as may be necessary or appropriate in order to:

(1) Determine, and make timely recommendations on, the needs and preferences, if any, of displaced persons for relocation assistance;

(2) Provide current and continuing information on the availability, sales prices, and rental charges of comparable replacement dwellings for displaced homeowners and tenants and suitable locations for businesses and farm operations;

(3) Assist a person displaced from a business or farm operation in obtaining and becoming established in a suitable replacement location;

(4) Supply (i) information concerning federal, State, and local programs which may be of assistance to displaced persons, and (ii) technical assistance to such persons in applying for assistance under such programs;

(5) Provide other advisory services to displaced persons in order to minimize hardships to such persons in adjusting to relocation; and

(6) The agency shall coordinate relocation activities performed by such agency with other federal, State, or local governmental actions in the community which could affect the efficient and effective delivery of relocation assistance and related services.

(d) Notwithstanding G.S. 133-7(3)b, in any case in which a displacing agency acquires property for a program or project, any person who occupies such property on a rental basis for a short term or a period subject to termination when the property is needed for the program or project shall be eligible for advisory services to the extent determined by the agency. (1971, c. 1107, s. 1; 1989, c. 28, s. 6.)

§ 133-12. Expenses incidental to transfer of property.

(a) In addition to amounts otherwise authorized by this Article, the agency is authorized to reimburse or to pay on behalf of the owners of real property acquired for a program or project for reasonable and necessary expenses incurred for:

(1) Recording fees, transfer taxes, and similar expenses incidental to conveying such property;

(2) Penalty costs for prepayment of any preexisting mortgage recorded and entered into in good faith encumbering such real property; and

(3) The pro rata portion of real property taxes paid which are allocable to a period subsequent to vesting of title in the agency, or the effective date of possession of such real property by the agency, whichever is earlier.

(b) Local taxing authorities shall accept prepayment of the agency's estimate of the amount of any taxes not levied but constituting a lien against real estate acquired by the agency, or the agency's estimate of its pro rata portion of such taxes, and such prepayment shall be applied to such taxes upon levy being made. (1971, c. 1107, s. 1.)

§ 133-13. Administration.

(a) The agency may enter into contracts with any individual, firm, association or corporation for services in connection with relocation assistance programs.

(b) The agency shall in carrying out relocation assistance activities utilize, whenever practicable, the services of other State or local agencies having experience in the administration or conduct in similar housing assistance activities.

(c) In acquisition of right-of-way for any State highway project, a municipality making the acquisition shall be vested with the same authority to render such services and to make such payments as is given the Board of Transportation in this Article. Such municipalities furnishing right-of-way are authorized to enter into contracts with any other municipal corporation, or State or federal agency, rendering such services. (1971, c. 1107, s. 1; 1973, c. 507, s. 5.)

§ 133-14. Regulations and procedures.

The agency is authorized to adopt such rules and regulations as it deems necessary and appropriate to carry out the provisions of this Article. The agency is authorized and empowered to adopt all or any part of applicable federal rules and regulations which are necessary or desirable to implement this Article. Such rules and regulations shall include, but not be limited to, provisions relating to:

(1) Payments authorized by this Article to assure that such payments shall be fair and reasonable and as uniform as possible on those projects to which this Article is applicable;

(2) Prompt payment after a move to displaced persons who make proper application and are entitled to payment, or, in hardship cases, payment in advance;

(3) Moving expense and allowances as provided for in G.S. 133-8;

(4) Standards for decent, safe and sanitary dwelling;

(5) Eligibility of displaced persons for relocation assistance payments, the procedure for such persons to claim such payments, and the amounts thereof;

(6) Procedure for an aggrieved displaced person to have his determination of eligibility or amount of payment reviewed by the agency head or its administrative officer;

(7) Projects or classes of projects on which payments as herein provided will be made. (1971, c. 1107, s. 1; 1973, c. 1446, s. 8.)

§ 133-15. Payments not to be considered as income.

No payment received under this Article shall be considered as income for the purposes of the State income tax law; nor shall such payments be considered as income or resources to any recipient of public assistance and such payment shall not be deducted from the amount of aid to which the recipient would otherwise be entitled under the provisions of Chapter 108 of the General Statutes. (1971, c. 1107, s. 1.)

§ 133-16. Real property furnished to the federal government.

Whenever real property is acquired by an agency and furnished as a required contribution to a federal project, the agency has the authority to make all payments and to provide all assistance in the same manner and to the same extent as in cases of acquisition by the agency of real property for a federal aid project. (1971, c. 1107, s. 1.)

§ 133-17. Administrative payments.

Nothing contained in this Article shall be construed as creating in any condemnation proceedings brought under the power of eminent domain, any element of damages not in existence on the date of enactment of this Article. Payments made and services rendered under this Article are administrative payments and in addition to just compensation as provided by the law of eminent domain. Nothing contained in this Article shall be construed as creating any right enforceable in any court and the determination of the agency under the procedure provided for in G.S. 133-14 shall be conclusive and not subject to judicial review. (1971, c. 1107, s. 1.)

§ 133-18. Additional payments by political subdivision.

The additional payments required under G.S. 133-8, 133-9, and 133-10 shall not be mandatory for political subdivisions of the State unless federal law makes such payments a condition of federal funding. (1989, c. 28, s. 7.)

§§ 133-19 through 133-22. Reserved for future codification purposes.

Article 3.

Regulation of Contractors for Public Works.

§ 133-23. Definition.

(a) The term "governmental agency" shall include the State of North Carolina, its agencies, institutions, and political subdivisions, all municipal corporations and all other public units, agencies and authorities which are authorized to enter into public contracts for construction or repair or for procurement of goods or services.

(b) The term "person" shall mean any individual, partnership, corporation, association, or other entity formed for the purpose of doing business as a contractor, subcontractor, or supplier.

(c) The term "subsidiary" shall mean a corporation with respect to which another corporation by virtue of its shareholdings alone has legal power, either directly or indirectly through another corporation or series of other corporations, domestic or foreign, to elect a majority of the directors. A corporation is a subsidiary of each such corporation, including any corporation through which this legal power may be indirectly exercised. (1981, c. 764, s. 1; 1991 (Reg. Sess., 1992), c. 1030, s. 38.)

§ 133-24. Government contracts; violation of G.S. 75-1 and 75-2.

Every person who shall engage in any conspiracy, combination, or any other act in restraint of trade or commerce declared to be unlawful by the provisions of

G.S. 75-1 and 75-2 shall be guilty of a felony under this section where the combination, conspiracy, or other unlawful act in restraint of trade involves:

(1) A contract for the purchase of equipment, goods, services or materials or for construction or repair let or to be let by a governmental agency;

(2) A subcontract for the purchase of equipment, goods, services or materials or for construction or repair with a prime contractor or proposed prime contractor for a governmental agency. (1981, c. 764, s. 1.)

§ 133-25. Conviction; punishment.

(a) Upon conviction of violating G.S. 133-24, any person shall be punished as a Class H felon. The court may also impose a fine of up to one hundred thousand dollars ($100,000) on any convicted individual and a fine of up to one million dollars ($1,000,000) on any convicted corporation. Any fine imposed pursuant to this section shall not be deductible on a State income tax return for any purpose.

(b) For a period of up to three years from the date of conviction, said period to be determined in the discretion of the court, no person shall be eligible to enter into a contract with any governmental agency, either directly as a contractor or indirectly as a subcontractor, if that person has been convicted of violating G.S. 133-24.

(c) In the event an individual is convicted of violating G.S. 133-24, the court may, in its discretion, for a period of up to three years from the date of conviction, provide that the individual shall not be employed by a corporation as an officer, director, employee or agent, if that corporation engages in public construction or repair contracts with a governmental agency, either directly as a contractor or indirectly as a subcontractor.

(d) The court shall also have authority to direct the appropriate contractor's licensing board to suspend the license of any contractor convicted of violating G.S. 133-24 for a period of up to three years from the date of conviction. (1981, c. 764, s. 1.)

§ 133-26. Individuals convicted may not serve on licensing boards.

No individual shall be eligible to serve as a member of any contractor's licensing board who has been convicted of criminal charges involving either:

(1) A conspiracy in restraint of trade in the courts of this State in violation of G.S. 75-1, 75-2, or 133-24, or similar charges in any federal court or in any other state court; or

(2) Bribery or commercial bribery in violation of G.S. 14-218 or 14-353 in the courts of this State, or of similar charges in any federal court or the court of any other state. (1981, c. 764, s. 1.)

§ 133-27. Suspension from bidding.

Any governmental agency shall have the authority to suspend for a period of up to three years from the date of conviction any person and any subsidiary or affiliate of any person from further bidding to the agency and from being a subcontractor to a contractor for the agency and from being a supplier to the agency if that person or any officer, director, employee or agent of that person has been convicted of charges of engaging in any conspiracy, combination, or other unlawful act in restraint of trade or of similar charges in any federal court or a court of any other state.

A governmental agency may order a temporary suspension of any contractor, subcontractor, or supplier or subsidiary or affiliate thereof charged in an indictment or an information with engaging in any conspiracy, combination, or other unlawful act in restraint of trade or of similar charges in any federal court or a court of this or any other state until the charges are resolved.

The provisions of this section are in addition to and not in derogation of any other powers and authority of any governmental agency. (1981, c. 764, s. 1.)

§ 133-28. Civil damages; liability; statute of limitations.

(a) Any governmental agency entering into a contract which is or has been the subject of a conspiracy prohibited by G.S. 75-1 or 75-2 shall have a right of action against the participants in the conspiracy to recover damages, as provided herein. The governmental agency shall have the option to proceed jointly and severally in a civil action against any one or more of the participants for recovery of the full amount of the damages. There shall be no right to contribution among participants not named defendants by the governmental agency.

(b) At the election of the governmental agency, the measure of damages recoverable under this section shall be either the actual damages or ten percent (10%) of the contract price which shall be trebled as provided in G.S. 75-16.

(c) The cause of action shall accrue at the time of discovery of the conspiracy by the governmental agency which entered into the contract. The action shall be brought within six years of the date of accrual of the cause of action. (1981, c. 764, s. 1; 1993, c. 441.)

§ 133-29. Reporting of violations of G.S. 75-1 or 75-2.

Any person having knowledge of acts committed in violation of G.S. 75-1 or 75-2 involving a contract with a governmental agency who reports the same to that governmental agency and assists in any resulting proceedings may receive a reward as set forth herein. The governmental agency is authorized to pay to the informant up to twenty-five percent (25%) of any civil damages that it collects from the violator named by the informant by reason of the information furnished by the informant. The information and knowledge to be reported includes but is not limited to any agreement or proposed agreement or offer or request for agreement among contractors, subcontractors or suppliers to rotate bids, to share the profits with a contractor not the low bidder, to sublet work in advance of bidding as a means of preventing competition, to refrain from bidding, to submit prearranged bids, to submit complimentary bids, to set up territories to restrict competition, or to alternate bidding. (1981, c. 764, s. 1.)

§ 133-30. Noncollusion affidavits.

Noncollusion affidavits may be required by rule of any governmental agency from all prime bidders. Any such requirement shall be set forth in the invitation to bid. Failure of any bidder to provide a required affidavit to the governmental agency shall be grounds for disqualification of his bid. The provisions of this section are in addition to and not in derogation of any other powers and authority of any governmental agency. (1981, c. 764, s. 1.)

§ 133-31. Perjury; punishment.

Any person who shall willfully commit perjury in any affidavit taken pursuant to this Article or rules pursuant thereto shall be guilty of a felony and shall be punished as a Class I felon. (1981, c. 764, s. 1; 1993, c. 539, s. 1307; 1994, Ex. Sess., c. 24, s. 14(c).)

§ 133-32. Gifts and favors regulated.

(a) It shall be unlawful for any contractor, subcontractor, or supplier who:

(1) Has a contract with a governmental agency; or

(2) Has performed under such a contract within the past year; or

(3) Anticipates bidding on such a contract in the future

to make gifts or to give favors to any officer or employee of a governmental agency who is charged with the duty of:

(1) Preparing plans, specifications, or estimates for public contract; or

(2) Awarding or administering public contracts; or

(3) Inspecting or supervising construction.

It shall also be unlawful for any officer or employee of a governmental agency who is charged with the duty of:

(1) Preparing plans, specifications, or estimates for public contracts; or

(2) Awarding or administering public contracts; or

(3) Inspecting or supervising construction

willfully to receive or accept any such gift or favor.

(b) A violation of subsection (a) shall be a Class 1 misdemeanor.

(c) Gifts or favors made unlawful by this section shall not be allowed as a deduction for North Carolina tax purposes by any contractor, subcontractor or supplier or officers or employees thereof.

(d) This section is not intended to prevent a gift a public servant would be permitted to accept under G.S. 138A-32, or the gift and receipt of honorariums for participating in meetings, advertising items or souvenirs of nominal value, or meals furnished at banquets. This section is not intended to prevent any contractor, subcontractor, or supplier from making donations to professional organizations to defray meeting expenses where governmental employees are members of such professional organizations, nor is it intended to prevent governmental employees who are members of professional organizations from participation in all scheduled meeting functions available to all members of the professional organization attending the meeting. This section is also not intended to prohibit customary gifts or favors between employees or officers and their friends and relatives or the friends and relatives of their spouses, minor children, or members of their household where it is clear that it is that relationship rather than the business of the individual concerned which is the motivating factor for the gift or favor. However, all such gifts knowingly made or received are required to be reported by the donee to the agency head if the gifts are made by a contractor, subcontractor, or supplier doing business directly or indirectly with the governmental agency employing the recipient of such a gift. (1981, c. 764, s. 1; 1987, c. 399, s. 1; 1993, c. 539, s. 970; 1994, Ex. Sess., c. 24, s. 14(c); 2007-348, s. 18.)

§ 133-33. Cost estimates; bidders' lists.

Any governmental agency responsible for letting public contracts may promulgate rules concerning the confidentiality of:

(1) The agency's cost estimate for any public contracts prior to bidding; and

(2) The identity of contractors who have obtained proposals for bid purposes for a public contract.

If the agency's rules require that such information be kept confidential, an employee or officer of the agency who divulges such information to any unauthorized person shall be subject to disciplinary action. This section shall not be construed to require that cost estimates or bidders' lists be kept confidential. (1981, c. 764, s. 1.)

Article 4.

Purchase of Contaminated Property by Public Entities.

§ 133-40. Purchase of contaminated property by public entities.

(a) For purposes of this Article, the term "public entity" means the State and the Community College System.

(b) No public entity, as defined in subsection (a) of this section, shall purchase or otherwise acquire an ownership interest in any real property with known contamination, as that term is defined in G.S. 130A-310.65(5), without approval of the Governor and the Council of State. A public entity seeking to purchase or otherwise acquire an ownership interest in such property shall petition the Governor and Council of State for approval of the transaction, with sufficient information to identify the property, the nature and extent of the contamination present, and a plan of paying for the project and for remediation of any contamination without the use of General Fund appropriations. The approval of such a transaction by the Governor and Council of State may be evidenced by a duly certified copy of excerpt of minutes of the meeting of the Governor and Council of State, attested by the private secretary to the Governor or the Governor, reciting such approval, affixed to the instrument of acquisition or transfer, and said certificate may be recorded as a part thereof, and the same shall be conclusive evidence of review and approval of the subject transaction by the Governor and Council of State. The Governor, acting with the approval of the Council of State, may delegate the review and approval of such transactions as the Governor deems advisable.

(c) This Article shall not apply to situations in which a public entity acquires ownership or control of real property involuntarily, including having obtained the property through bankruptcy, tax delinquency, abandonment, or other circumstances in which the public entity involuntarily acquires title by virtue of its function as a sovereign. (2013-413, s. 40(a).)

Chapter 134.

Youth Development.

§§ 134-1 through 134-39. Recodified as §§ 134A-1 to 134A-39.

Chapter 134A.

Youth Services.

§§ 134A-1 through 134A-39: Repealed by Session Laws 1998-202, s. 1(a).

Chapter 135.

Retirement System for Teachers and State Employees; Social Security; State Health Plan for Teachers and State Employees.

Article 1.

Retirement System for Teachers and State Employees.

§ 135-1. Definitions.

The following words and phrases as used in this Chapter, unless a different meaning is plainly required by the context, shall have the following meanings:

(1) "Accumulated contributions" shall mean the sum of all the amounts deducted from the compensation of a member and accredited to his individual account in the annuity savings fund, together with regular interest thereon as provided in G.S. 135-8.

(2) "Actuarial equivalent" shall mean a benefit of equal value when computed upon the basis of such mortality tables as shall be adopted by the Board of Trustees, and regular interest.

(3) "Annuity" shall mean payments for life derived from that "accumulated contribution" of a member. All annuities shall be payable in equal monthly installments.

(4) "Annuity reserve" shall mean the present value of all payments to be made on account of any annuity or benefit in lieu of any annuity, computed upon the basis of such mortality tables as shall be adopted by the Board of Trustees, and regular interest.

(4a) "Authorized representatives who are assisting the Retirement Systems Division staff" means only other staff of the Department of State Treasurer, staff of the Department of Justice, or persons providing internal auditing assistance required under G.S. 143-746(b).

(5) "Average final compensation" shall mean the average annual compensation of a member during the four consecutive calendar years of membership service producing the highest such average; but shall not include any compensation, as determined by the Board of Trustees, for the reimbursement of expenses or payments for housing or any other allowances whether or not classified as salary and wages. In the event a member is or has been in receipt of a benefit under the provisions of G.S. 135-105 or G.S. 135-106, the compensation used in the calculation of "average final compensation" shall be the higher of compensation of the member under the provisions of this Article or compensation used in calculating the payment of benefits under Article 6 of this Chapter as adjusted for percentage increases in the post disability benefit.

(6) "Beneficiary" shall mean any person in receipt of a pension, an annuity, a retirement allowance or other benefit as provided by this Chapter.

(7) "Board of Trustees" shall mean the Board provided for in G.S. 135-6 to administer the Retirement System.

(7a) a. "Compensation" shall mean all salaries and wages prior to any reduction pursuant to sections 125, 401(k), 403(b), 414(h)(2), and 457 of the Internal Revenue Code, not including any terminal payments for unused sick leave, derived from public funds which are earned by a member of the Retirement System for service as an employee or teacher in the unit of the Retirement System for which he is performing full-time work. In addition to the foregoing, "compensation" shall include:

1. Performance-based compensation (regardless of whether paid in a lump sum, in periodic installments, or on a monthly basis);

2. Conversion of additional benefits to salary (additional benefits such as health, life, or disability plans), so long as the benefits are other than mandated by State law or regulation;

3. Payment of tax consequences for benefits provided by the employer, so long as they constitute an adjustment or increase in salary and not a "reimbursement of expenses";

4. Payout of vacation leave so long as such payouts are permitted by applicable law and regulation;

5. Employee contributions to eligible deferred compensation plans; and

6. Effective July 1, 2009, payment of military differential wages.

b. "Compensation" shall not include any payment, as determined by the Board of Trustees, for the reimbursement of expenses or payments for housing or any other allowances whether or not classified as salary and wages. "Compensation" includes all special pay contribution of annual leave made to a 401(a) Special Pay Plan for the benefit of an employee. Notwithstanding any other provision of this Chapter, "compensation" shall not include:

1. Supplement/allowance provided to employee to purchase additional benefits such as health, life, or disability plans;

2. Travel supplement/allowance (nonaccountable allowance plans);

3. Employer contributions to eligible deferred compensation plans;

4. Employer-provided fringe benefits (additional benefits such as health, life, or disability plans);

5. Reimbursement of uninsured medical expenses;

6. Reimbursement of business expenses;

7. Reimbursement of moving expenses;

8. Reimbursement/payment of personal expenses;

9. Incentive payments for early retirement;

10. Bonuses paid incident to retirement;

10a. Local supplementation as authorized under G.S. 7A-300.1 for Judicial Department employees;

11. Contract buyout/severance payments; and

12. Payouts for unused sick leave.

c. In the event an employer reports as "compensation" payments not specifically included or excluded as "compensation", such payments shall be "compensation" for retirement purposes only if the employer pays the Retirement System the additional actuarial liability created by such payments.

(8) "Creditable service" shall mean the total of "prior service" plus "membership service" plus service, both noncontributory and purchased, for which credit is allowable as provided in G.S. 135-4. In no event, however, shall "creditable service" be deemed "membership service" for the purpose of determining eligibility for benefits accruing under this Chapter.

(9) "Earnable compensation" shall mean the full rate of the compensation that would be payable to a teacher or employee if he worked in full normal working time. In cases where compensation includes maintenance, the Board of Trustees shall fix the value of that part of the compensation not paid in money.

(10) "Employee" shall mean all full-time employees, agents or officers of the State of North Carolina or any of its departments, bureaus and institutions other than educational, whether such employees are elected, appointed or employed: Provided that the term "employee" shall not include any person who is a member of the Consolidated Judicial Retirement System, any member of the General Assembly or any part-time or temporary employee. Notwithstanding any other provision of law, "employee" shall include all employees of the General Assembly except participants in the Legislative Intern Program, pages, and beneficiaries in receipt of a monthly retirement allowance under this Chapter who are reemployed on a temporary basis. "Employee" also includes any participant whose employment is interrupted by reason of service in the Uniformed Services, as that term is defined in section 4303(16) of the

Uniformed Services Employment and Reemployment Rights Act, Public Law 103-353, if that participant was an employee at the time of the interruption; if the participant does not return immediately after that service to employment with a covered employer in this System, then the participant shall be deemed "in service" until the date on which the participant was first eligible to be separated or released from his or her involuntary military service. In all cases of doubt, the Board of Trustees shall determine whether any person is an employee as defined in this Chapter. "Employee" shall also mean every full-time civilian employee of the North Carolina National Guard who is employed pursuant to section 709 of Title 32 of the United States Code and paid from federal appropriated funds, but held by the federal authorities not to be a federal employee: Provided, however, that the authority or agency paying the salaries of such employees shall deduct or cause to be deducted from each employee's salary the employee's contribution in accordance with applicable provisions of G.S. 135-8 and remit the same, either directly or indirectly, to the Retirement System; coverage of employees described in this sentence shall commence upon the first day of the calendar year or fiscal year, whichever is earlier, next following the date of execution of an agreement between the Secretary of Defense of the United States and the Adjutant General of the State acting for the Governor in behalf of the State, but no credit shall be allowed pursuant to this sentence for any service previously rendered in the above-described capacity as a civilian employee of the North Carolina National Guard: Provided, further, that the Adjutant General, in the Adjutant General's discretion, may terminate the Retirement System coverage of the above-described North Carolina National Guard employees if a federal retirement system is established for such employees and the Adjutant General elects to secure coverage of such employees under such federal retirement system. Any full-time civilian employee of the North Carolina National Guard described above who is now or hereafter may become a member of the Retirement System may secure Retirement System credit for such service as a North Carolina National Guard civilian employee for the period preceding the time when such employees became eligible for Retirement System coverage by paying to the Retirement System an amount equal to that which would have constituted employee contributions if the employee had been a member during the years of ineligibility, plus interest. Employees of State agencies, departments, institutions, boards, and commissions who are employed in permanent job positions on a recurring basis and who work 30 or more hours per week for nine or more months per calendar year are covered by the provisions of this subdivision. On and after August 1, 2001, a person who is a nonimmigrant alien and who otherwise meets the requirements of this subdivision shall not be excluded from the definition of "employee" solely because the person holds a temporary or time-limited visa.

(11) "Employer" shall mean the State of North Carolina, the county board of education, the city board of education, the State Board of Education, the board of trustees of the University of North Carolina, the board of trustees of other institutions and agencies supported and under the control of the State, or any other agency of and within the State by which a teacher or other employee is paid.

(11a) "Filing" when used in reference to an application for retirement shall mean the receipt of an acceptable application on a form provided by the Retirement System.

(11b) "Fraud investigation" means an independent review or examination by Retirement Systems Division staff or authorized representatives who are assisting the Retirement Systems Division staff of activities, actions, or decisions by employers or other affiliated or associated entities having an impact on the Retirement System. The purpose of a fraud investigation is to help detect and prevent fraud and to ensure full accountability in the use of pension funds.

(11c) "Law-Enforcement Officer" means a full-time paid employee of an employer who is actively serving in a position with assigned primary duties and responsibilities for prevention and detection of crime or the general enforcement of the criminal laws of the State of North Carolina or serving civil processes, and who possesses the power of arrest by virtue of an oath administered under the authority of the State.

(12) "Medical board" shall mean the board of physicians provided for in G.S. 135-6.

(13) "Member" shall mean any teacher or State employee included in the membership of the System as provided in G.S. 135-3 and 135-4.

(14) "Membership service" shall mean service as a teacher or State employee rendered while a member of the Retirement System or membership service in a North Carolina Retirement System that has been transferred into this system.

(15) "Pension reserve" shall mean the present value of all payments to be made on account of any pension or benefit in lieu of any pension computed upon the basis of such mortality tables as shall be adopted by the Board of Trustees, and regular interest.

(16) "Pensions" shall mean payments for life derived from money provided by the State of North Carolina, and by county or city boards of education. All pensions shall be payable in equal monthly installments.

(17) "Prior service" shall mean service rendered prior to the date of establishment of the Retirement System for which credit is allowable under G.S. 135-4; provided, persons now employed by the Board of Transportation shall be entitled to credit for employment in road maintenance by the various counties and road districts prior to 1931.

(18) "Public school" shall mean any day school conducted within the State under the authority and supervision of a duly elected or appointed city or county school board, and any educational institution supported by and under the control of the State.

(19) "Regular interest" shall mean interest compounded annually at such a rate as shall be determined by the Board of Trustees in accordance with G.S. 135-7, subsection (b).

(20) "Retirement" under this Chapter means the commencement of monthly retirement benefits along with termination of employment and the complete separation from active service with no intent or agreement, express or implied, to return to service. A retirement allowance under the provisions of this Chapter may only be granted upon retirement of a member. In order for a member's retirement to become effective in any month, the member must perform no work for an employer, including part-time, temporary, substitute, or contractor work, at any time during the six months immediately following the effective date of retirement. For purposes of this subdivision, working as a member of a school board, board of trustees of a community college, board of trustees of any constituent institution of The University of North Carolina, as an unpaid bona fide volunteer in a local school administrative unit, or as an unpaid bona fide volunteer guardian ad litem in the guardian ad litem program shall not be considered service. A member who is a full-time faculty member of The University of North Carolina may effect a retirement allowance under this Chapter, notwithstanding the six-month requirement above, provided the

member immediately enters the University's Phased Retirement Program for Tenured Faculty as that program existed on May 25, 2011.

(21) "Retirement allowance" shall mean the sum of the "annuity and the pensions," or any optional benefit payable in lieu thereof.

(22) "Retirement System" shall mean the Teachers' and State Employees' Retirement System of North Carolina as defined in G.S. 135-2.

(23) "Service" shall mean service as a teacher or State employee as described in subdivision (10) or (25) of this section.

(24) "Social security breakpoint" shall mean the maximum amount of taxable wages under the Federal Insurance Contributions Act as from time to time in effect.

(25) "Teacher" shall mean (i) any teacher, helping teacher, teacher in a job-sharing position under G.S. 115C-326.5 except for a beneficiary in that position, librarian, principal, supervisor, superintendent of public schools or any full-time employee, city or county, superintendent of public instruction, or any full-time employee of the Department of Public Instruction, president, dean or teacher, or any full-time employee in any educational institution supported by and under the control of the State; (ii) who works at least 30 or more hours per week for at least nine or more months per calendar year: Provided, that the term "teacher" shall not include any part-time, temporary, or substitute teacher or employee except for a teacher in a job-sharing position, and shall not include those participating in an optional retirement program provided for in G.S. 135-5.1 or G.S. 135-5.4. In all cases of doubt, the Board of Trustees, hereinbefore defined, shall determine whether any person is a teacher as defined in this Chapter. On and after August 1, 2001, a person who is a nonimmigrant alien and who otherwise meets the requirements of this subdivision shall not be excluded from the definition of "teacher" solely because the person holds a temporary or time-limited visa. Notwithstanding the foregoing, the term "teacher" shall not include any nonimmigrant alien employed in elementary or secondary public schools (whether employed in a full-time, part-time, temporary, permanent, or substitute teacher position) and participating in an exchange visitor program designated by the United States Department of State pursuant to 22 C.F.R. Part 62 or by the United States Department of Homeland Security pursuant to 8 C.F.R. Part 214.2(q).

(26) "Year" as used in this Article shall mean the regular fiscal year beginning July 1 and ending June 30 in the following calendar year unless otherwise defined by regulation of the Board of Trustees. (1941, c. 25, s. 1; 1943, c. 431; 1945, c. 924; 1947, c. 458, s. 6; 1953, c. 1053; 1955, c. 818; c. 1155, s. 81/2; 1959, c. 513, s. 1; c. 1263, s. 1; 1963, c. 687, s. 1; 1965, c. 750; c. 780, s. 1; 1969, c. 44, s. 74; c. 1223, s. 16; c. 1227; 1971, c. 117, ss. 1-5; c. 338, s. 1; 1973, c. 507, s. 5; c. 640, s. 2; c. 1233; 1975, c. 475, s. 1; 1977, c. 574, s. 1; 1979, c. 972, s. 1; 1981, c. 557, ss. 1, 2; 1983, c. 412, ss. 1, 2; 1983 (Reg. Sess., 1984), c. 1034, s. 227; 1985, c. 649, s. 3; 1987, c. 738, ss. 29(a), 36(a); 1991, c. 51, s. 2; 1993 (Reg. Sess., 1994), c. 769, s. 7.31(c); 1998-1, s. 4(g); 2001-424, s. 32.24(b); 2001-426, ss. 2, 3; 2001-513, s. 24; 2002-110, s. 1; 2002-126, ss. 28.6(b), 28.12(a); 2002-174, s. 2; 2003-359, ss. 1, 2; 2004-81, s. 1; 2004-199, s. 34(a); 2005-276, s. 29.28(e); 2006-66, s. 22.21; 2007-143, s. 1; 2009-11, s. 1; 2009-66, s. 6(e), (i); 2009-281, s. 1; 2009-451, s. 26.22; 2010-31, s. 29.7(d); 2011-145, s. 29.24(b); 2011-183, s. 100; 2012-130, s. 6; 2012-185, s. 2(b); 2013-288, ss. 3(a), 4(a); 2013-291, s. 1.)

§ 135-1.1. Licensing and examining boards.

(a) Any State board or agency charged with the duty of administering any law relating to the examination and licensing of persons to practice a profession, trade or occupation, in its discretion, may elect on or before July 1, 1983, by an appropriate resolution of said board, to cause its employees so employed prior to July 1, 1983 to become members of the Teachers' and State Employees' Retirement System. Such Retirement System coverage shall be conditioned on such board's paying all of the employer's contributions or matching funds from funds of the board and on such board's collecting from its employees the employees' contributions, at such rates as may be fixed by law and by the regulations of the Board of Trustees of the Retirement System, all of such funds to be paid to the Retirement System and placed in the appropriate funds. Retroactive coverage of the employees of any such board may also be effected to the extent that such board requests provided the board pays all of the employer's contributions or matching funds necessary for such purpose and provided said board collects from its employees all employees' contributions necessary for such purpose, computed at such rates and in such amount as the Board of Trustees of the Retirement System determines, all of such funds to be paid to the Retirement System, together with such interest as may be due, and placed in the appropriate funds.

(b) Notwithstanding any other provision of this Chapter, any State board or agency charged with the duty of administering any law relating to the examination and licensing of persons to practice a profession, trade, or occupation, and who is subject to the provisions of the State Budget Act, Chapter 143C of the General Statutes, may make an irrevocable election by appropriate resolution of the board, on or before October 1, 2000, to become an employer in the Teachers' and State Employees' Retirement System. Retirement System coverage shall be conditioned on the board's payment of all of the employer's contributions or matching funds from funds of the board and on the board's collecting from its employees the employees' contributions, at such rates as may be fixed by law and by the rules of the Board of Trustees of the Retirement System, all of such funds to be paid to the Retirement System and placed in the appropriate funds. Any person who is an employee of the board on the date the board makes an irrevocable election to participate in the Retirement System may purchase creditable service for periods of employment with the board prior to the election by making a lump-sum payment equal to the full cost of the service credits calculated on the basis of the assumptions used for the purposes of the actuarial valuation of the system's liabilities, and shall take into account the additional retirement allowance arising on account of such additional service credit commencing at the earliest age at which a member could retire on an unreduced retirement allowance, as determined by the Board of Trustees upon the advice of the consulting actuary, plus an administrative fee to be set by the Board of Trustees. Notwithstanding the foregoing provisions of this subdivision that provide for the purchase of service credits, the terms "full cost", "full liability", and "full actuarial cost" include assumed annual postretirement allowance increases, as determined by the Board of Trustees, from the earliest age at which a member could retire on an unreduced service allowance. (1959, c. 1012; 1983, c. 412, s. 3; 2000-187, s. 1; 2006-203, s. 72.)

§ 135-2. Name and date of establishment.

A Retirement System is hereby established and placed under the management of the Board of Trustees for the purpose of providing retirement allowances and other benefits under the provisions of this Chapter for teachers and State employees of the State of North Carolina. The Retirement System so created shall be established as of the first day of July, 1941.

This Retirement System is a governmental plan, within the meaning of Section 414(d) of the Internal Revenue Code. Therefore, the nondiscrimination rules of

Sections 401(a)(5) and 401(a)(26) of the Code do not apply. This System shall have the power and privileges of a corporation and shall be known as the "Teachers' and State Employees' Retirement System of North Carolina," and by such name all of its business shall be transacted, all of its funds invested, and all of its cash and securities and other property held.

Consistent with Section 401(a)(1) of the Internal Revenue Code, all contributions from participating employers and participating employees to this Retirement System shall be made to funds held in trust through trust instruments that have the purposes of distributing trust principal and income to retired members and their beneficiaries and of paying other definitely determinable benefits under this Chapter, after meeting the necessary expenses of administering this Retirement System. Neither the trust corpus nor income from this trust can be used for purposes other than the exclusive benefit of members or their beneficiaries, except that employer contributions made to the trust under a good faith mistake of fact may be returned to an employer, where the refund can occur within less than one year after the mistaken contribution was made, consistent with the rule adopted by the Board of Trustees. The Retirement System shall have a consolidated Plan document, consisting of Article V, Section 6(2) of the North Carolina Constitution, relevant statutory provisions in this Chapter; associated regulations in the North Carolina Administrative Code, substantive and procedural information on the official forms used by the Retirement System, and policies and minutes of the Board of Trustees. (1941, c. 25, s. 2; 2012-130, s. 7(c).)

§ 135-3. Membership.

The membership of this Retirement System shall be composed as follows:

(1)   All persons who shall become teachers or State employees after the date as of which the Retirement System is established. On and after July 1, 1947, membership in the Retirement System shall begin 90 days after the election, appointment or employment of a "teacher or employee" as the terms are defined in this Chapter. On and after July 1, 1955, membership in the Retirement System shall begin immediately upon the election, appointment or employment of a "teacher or employee," as the terms are defined in this Chapter. Under such rules and regulations as the Board of Trustees may establish and promulgate, Cooperative Agricultural Extension Service employees excluded from coverage under Title II of the Social Security Act may

in the discretion of the governing authority of a county, become members of the Teachers' and State Employees' Retirement System to the extent of that part of their compensation derived from a county. On and after July 1, 1965, new extension service employees excluded from coverage under Title II of the Social Security Act in the employ of a county participating in the Local Governmental Employees' Retirement System are hereby excluded from participation in the Teachers' and State Employees' Retirement System to the extent of that part of their compensation derived from a county; provided that on and after July 1, 1965, new extension service employees excluded from coverage under Title II of the Social Security Act who are required to accept a federal civil service appointment may elect in writing, on a form acceptable to the Retirement System, to be excluded from the Teachers' and State Employees' Retirement System and the Local Retirement System; provided further, that effective July 1, 1985, an extension service employee excluded from coverage under Title II of the Social Security Act who is employed in part by a county and who is compensated in whole by the Cooperative Agricultural Extension Service pursuant to a contract where the Cooperative Agricultural Extension Service is reimbursed by the county for the county's share of the compensation shall participate exclusively in the Teachers' and State Employees' Retirement System to the extent of their full compensation. On or after July 1, 1979, upon election, appointment or employment, a legislative employee shall automatically become a member of the Teachers' and State Employees' Retirement System. At such time as Cooperative Agricultural Extension Service Employees excluded from coverage under Title II of the Social Security Act become covered by Title II of the Social Security Act, such employees shall no longer be covered by the provisions of this section, provided no accrued rights of these employees under this section prior to coverage by Title II of the Social Security Act shall be diminished.

(2) Repealed by Session Laws 2012-130, s. 8, effective July 1, 2012.

(3) Should any member in any period of six consecutive years after becoming a member be absent from service more than five years, or should he withdraw his accumulated contributions, or should he become a beneficiary or die, he shall thereupon cease to be a member: Provided that on and after July 1, 1967, should any member in any period of eight consecutive years after becoming a member be absent from service more than seven years, or should he withdraw his accumulated contributions, or should he become a beneficiary or die, he shall thereupon cease to be a member; provided further that the period of absence from service shall be computed from January 1, 1962, or later date of separation for any member whose contributions were not withdrawn

prior to July 1, 1967: Provided that on and after July 1, 1971, a member shall cease to be a member only if he withdraws his accumulated contributions, or becomes a beneficiary, or dies.

Notwithstanding the foregoing, any persons whose membership was terminated under the provisions set forth above who had five or more years of creditable service and had not effected a return of contributions may elect to receive a retirement allowance on or after age 60; provided that this member may retire only upon electronic submission or written application to the Board of Trustees setting forth at which time, not less than 30 days nor more than 90 days subsequent to the execution and filing, he desires to be retired.

(4) Notwithstanding any provisions contained in this section, any employee of the State of North Carolina who was taken over and required to perform services for the federal government, on a loan basis, and by virtue of an executive order of the President of the United States effective on or after January 1, 1942, and who on the effective date of such executive order was a member of the Retirement System and had not withdrawn all of his or her accumulated contributions, shall be deemed to be a member of the Retirement System during such period of federal service or employment by virtue of such executive order of the President of the United States. Any such employee who within a period of 12 months after the cessation of such federal service or employment, is again employed by the State or any employer as said term is defined in this Chapter, or within said period of 12 months engages in service or membership service, shall be permitted to resume active participation in the Retirement System and to resume his or her contributions as provided by this Chapter. If such member so elects, he or she may pay to the Board of Trustees for the benefit of the proper fund or account an amount equal to his or her accumulated contributions previously withdrawn with interest from date of withdrawal to time of payment and the accumulated contributions, with interest thereon, that such member would have made during such period of federal employment to the same extent as if such member had been in service or engaged in the membership service for the State or an employer as defined in this Chapter, which such payment of accumulated contributions shall be computed on the basis of the salary or earnable compensation received by such member on the effective date of such executive order.

(5) Repealed by Session Laws 2012-130, s. 8, effective July 1, 2012.

(6) Repealed by Session Laws 1981 (Regular Session, 1982), c. 1396, s. 1.

(7) The provisions of this subdivision (7) shall apply to any member whose retirement became effective prior to July 1, 1963, and who became entitled to benefits hereunder in accordance with the provisions hereof. Such benefits shall be computed in accordance with the provisions of G.S. 135-5(b) as in effect at the date of such retirement.

a. Notwithstanding any other provision of this Chapter, any member who separates from service prior to the attainment of the age of 60 years for any reason other than death or retirement for disability as provided in G.S. 135-5(d), after completing 20 or more years of creditable service, and who leaves his total accumulated contributions in said System shall have the right to retire on a deferred retirement allowance upon attaining the age of 60 years: Provided, that such member may retire only upon written application to the Board of Trustees setting forth at what time, not less than 30 days nor more than 90 days subsequent to the execution and filing thereof, he desires to be retired. Such deferred retirement allowance shall be computed in accordance with the provisions of G.S. 135-5(b), subdivisions (1), (2) and (3).

b. In lieu of the benefits provided in paragraph a of this subdivision (7) any member who separates from service on or after July 1, 1951, and prior to the attainment of the age of 60 years, for any reason other than death or retirement for disability as provided in G.S. 135-5(d), after completing 30 or more years of creditable service, and who leaves his total accumulated contributions in said System, may elect to retire on an early retirement allowance; provided that such member may so retire only upon written application to the Board of Trustees setting forth at what time, not less than 30 days nor more than 90 days subsequent to the execution and filing thereof, he desires to be retired; provided further that such application shall be duly filed within 60 days following the date of such separation. Such early retirement allowance so elected shall be the actuarial equivalent of the deferred retirement allowance otherwise payable at the attainment of the age of 60 years upon proper application therefor.

c. In lieu of the benefits provided in paragraph a of this subdivision (7), any member who separated from service before July 1, 1951, and prior to the age of 60 years for any reason other than death or retirement for disability as provided in G.S. 135-5(d), and who left his total accumulated contributions in said System, may elect to retire on an early retirement allowance; provided that such member may so retire only upon written application to the Board of Trustees setting forth at what time, subsequent to July 1, 1951, and not less than 30 days nor more than 90 days subsequent to the execution and filing thereof, he desires to be retired; provided that such application shall be duly filed not later than August 31, 1951. Such early retirement allowance so elected shall be the actuarial equivalent of the deferred retirement allowance otherwise payable at the attainment of the age of 60 years upon proper application therefor.

d.   Should a teacher or employee who retired on an early or service retirement allowance be restored to service prior to the attainment of the age of 62 years, his allowance shall cease, he shall again become a member of the Retirement System, and he shall contribute thereafter at the uniform contribution rate payable by all members. Upon his subsequent retirement, he shall be entitled to the allowance described in 1 below reduced by the amount in 2 below.

1.   The allowance to which he would have been entitled if he were retiring for the first time, calculated on the basis of his total creditable service represented by the sum of his creditable service at the time of his first retirement, and his creditable service after he was restored to service.

2.   The actuarial equivalent of the retirement benefits he previously received.

e.   Should a teacher or employee who retired on an early or service retirement allowance be restored to service after the attainment of the age of 62 years, his retirement allowance shall be reduced to the extent necessary (if any) so that the sum of the retirement allowance at the time of his retirement and earnings from employment by a unit of the Retirement System for any year (beginning January 1, and ending December 31) will not exceed the member's compensation received for the 12 months of service prior to retirement. Provided, however, that under no circumstances will the member's retirement allowance be reduced below the amount of his annuity as defined in G.S. 135-1(3).

(8)   The provisions of this subsection (8) shall apply to any member whose membership is terminated on or after July 1, 1963 and who becomes entitled to benefits hereunder in accordance with the provisions hereof.

a.   Notwithstanding any other provision of this Chapter, any member who became a member prior to August 1, 2011, and who separates from service prior to the attainment of the age of 60 years for any reason other than death or retirement for disability as provided in G.S. 135-5(c), after completing 15 or more years of creditable service, and who leaves his total accumulated contributions in said System shall have the right to retire on a deferred retirement allowance upon attaining the age of 60 years; provided that such member may retire only upon electronic submission or written application to the Board of Trustees setting forth at what time, not less than one day nor more than 120 days subsequent to the execution and filing thereof, he desires to be retired; and further provided that in the case of a member who so separates from service on or after July 1, 1967, or whose account is active on July 1, 1967, or has not withdrawn his contributions, the aforestated requirement of 15 or more years of creditable service shall be reduced to 12 or more years of creditable service; and further provided that in the case of a member who so separates from service on or after July 1, 1971, or whose account is active on July 1, 1971, the aforestated requirement of 12 or more years of creditable service shall be reduced to five or more years of creditable service. Such deferred retirement allowance shall be computed in accordance with the service retirement provisions of this Article pertaining to a member who is not a law enforcement officer or an eligible former law enforcement officer. Notwithstanding the foregoing, any member whose services as a teacher or employee are terminated for any reason other than retirement, who becomes employed by a nonprofit, nonsectarian private school in North Carolina below the college level within one year after such teacher or employee has ceased to be a teacher or employee, may elect to leave his total accumulated contributions in the Teachers' and State Employees' Retirement System during the period he is in the employment of such employer; provided that he files notice thereof in writing with the Board of Trustees of the Retirement System within five years after separation from service as a public school teacher or State employee; such member shall be deemed to have met the requirements of the above provisions of this subdivision upon attainment of age 60 while in such employment provided that he is otherwise vested.

b. In lieu of the benefits provided in paragraph a of this subdivision (8), any member who became a member prior to August 1, 2011, and who separates from service prior to the attainment of the age of 60 years, for any reason other than death or retirement for disability as provided in G.S. 135-5(c), after completing 20 or more years of creditable service, and who leaves his total accumulated contributions in said System, may elect to retire on an early retirement allowance upon attaining the age of 50 years or at any time thereafter; provided that such member may so retire only upon electronic submission or written application to the Board of Trustees setting forth at what time, not less than one day nor more than 120 days subsequent to the execution and filing thereof, he desires to be retired. Such early retirement allowance so elected shall be equal to the deferred retirement allowance otherwise payable at the attainment of the age of 60 years reduced by the percentage thereof indicated below.

Age at Retirement	Percentage Reduction
59	7
58	14
57	20
56	25
55	30
54	35
53	39
52	43
51	46
50	50

b1. In lieu of the benefits provided in paragraphs a and b of this subdivision, any member who became a member prior to August 1, 2011, and who is a law-enforcement officer at the time of separation from service prior to the attainment of the age of 50 years, for any reason other than death or disability as provided in this Article, after completing 15 or more years of creditable service in this capacity immediately prior to separation from service, and who leaves his total accumulated contributions in this System may elect to retire on a deferred early retirement allowance upon attaining the age of 50 years or at any time thereafter; provided, that the member may commence retirement only upon electronic submission or written application to the Board of Trustees setting forth at what time, as of the first day of a calendar month, not less than one day nor more than 120 days subsequent to the execution and filing thereof, he desires to commence retirement. The deferred early retirement allowance shall be computed in accordance with the service retirement provisions of this Article pertaining to law-enforcement officers.

b2. In lieu of the benefits provided in paragraphs a and b of this subdivision, any member who became a member prior to August 1, 2011, and who is a law-enforcement officer at the time of separation from service prior to the attainment of the age of 55 years, for any reason other than death or disability as provided in this Article, after completing five or more years of creditable service in this capacity immediately prior to separation from service, and who leaves his total accumulated contributions in this System may elect to retire on a deferred early retirement allowance upon attaining the age of 55 years or at any time thereafter; provided, that the member may commence retirement only upon electronic submission or written application to the Board of Trustees setting forth at what time, as of the first day of a calendar month not less than one day nor more than 120 days subsequent to the execution and filing thereof, he desires to commence retirement. The deferred early retirement allowance shall be computed in accordance with the service retirement provisions of this Article pertaining to law-enforcement officers.

b3. Vested deferred retirement allowance of members retiring on or after July 1, 1994. - In lieu of the benefits provided in paragraphs a. and b. of this subdivision, any member who became a member prior to August 1, 2011, and who separates from service prior to attainment of age 60 years, after completing 20 or more years of creditable service, and who leaves his total accumulated contributions in said System, may elect to retire on a deferred retirement allowance upon attaining the age of 50 years or any time thereafter; provided that such member may so retire only upon electronic submission or written application to the Board of Trustees setting forth at what time, not less than one day nor more than 120 days subsequent to the execution and filing thereof, he desires to be retired. Such deferred retirement allowance shall be computed in accordance with the service retirement provisions of this Article pertaining to a member who is not a law enforcement officer or an eligible former law enforcement officer.

b4. Any member who became a member on or after August 1, 2011, and who is not a law enforcement officer and (i) separates from service prior to the attainment of the age of 60 years, after completing 25 or more years of creditable service, and who leaves the member's total accumulated contributions in said System, may elect to retire on an unreduced service retirement allowance upon attaining the age of 60 years or at any time thereafter; or (ii) separates from service prior to the attainment of the age of 50 years, after completing 20 or more years of creditable service, and who leaves the member's total accumulated contributions in said System, may elect to retire on an early reduced retirement allowance upon attaining the age of 50 years or at any time thereafter; or (iii) separates from service prior to the attainment of the age of 60 years, after completing 10 or more years but less than 25 years of creditable service, and who leaves the member's total accumulated contributions in said System, may elect to retire on an early reduced retirement allowance upon attaining the age of 60 years or at any time thereafter; or (iv) separates from service prior to the attainment of the age of 65 years, after completing 10 or more years of creditable service, and who leaves the member's total accumulated contributions in said System, may elect to retire on an unreduced retirement allowance upon attaining the age of 65 years or at any time thereafter; provided that such member may so retire only upon electronic submission or written application to the Board of Trustees setting forth at what time, not less than one day nor more than 120 days subsequent to the execution and filing thereof, the member desires to be retired.

b5. Any member who became a member on or after August 1, 2011, who is a law enforcement officer and (i) separates from service prior to attainment of age 50 years, after completing 15 or more years of creditable service in this capacity, and who leaves the member's total accumulated contributions in said System, may elect to retire on an early reduced retirement allowance upon attaining the age of 50 years or any time thereafter; or (ii) separates from service prior to attainment of age 55 years, after completing 10 or more years of creditable service in this capacity, and who leaves the member's total accumulated contributions in said System, may elect to retire on an unreduced retirement allowance upon attaining the age of 55 years or any time thereafter; provided that such member may so retire only upon electronic submission or written application to the Board of Trustees setting forth at what time, not less than one day nor more than 120 days subsequent to the execution and filing thereof, the member desires to be retired.

c. Should a beneficiary who retired on an early or service retirement allowance under this Chapter be reemployed by, or otherwise engaged to perform services for, an employer participating in the Retirement System on a part time, temporary, interim, or on a fee for service basis, whether contractual or otherwise, and if such beneficiary earns an amount during the 12 month period immediately following the effective date of retirement or in any calendar year which exceeds fifty percent (50%) of the reported compensation, excluding terminal payments, during the 12 months of service preceding the effective date of retirement, or twenty thousand dollars ($20,000), whichever is greater, as hereinafter indexed, then the retirement allowance shall be suspended as of the first day of the month following the month in which the reemployment earnings exceed the amount above, for the balance of the calendar year, except when the reemployment earnings exceed the amount above in the month of December, in which case the retirement allowance shall not be suspended. The retirement allowance of the beneficiary shall be reinstated as of January 1 of each year following suspension. The amount that may be earned before suspension shall be increased on January 1 of each year by the ratio of the Consumer Price Index to the Index one year earlier, calculated to the nearest tenth of a percent (1/10 of 1%).

c1.   Within 90 days of the end of each month in which a beneficiary is reemployed under the provisions of sub-subdivision c. of this subdivision, each employer shall provide a report for that month on each reemployed beneficiary, including the terms of the reemployment, the date of the reemployment, and the amount of the monthly compensation. If such a report is not received within the required 90 days, the Board may assess the employer with a penalty of ten percent (10%) of the compensation of the unreported reemployed beneficiaries during the months for which the employer did not report the reemployed beneficiaries, with a minimum penalty of twenty-five dollars ($25.00). If after being assessed a penalty, an employer provides clear and convincing evidence that the failure to report resulted from a lack of oversight or some other event beyond the employer's control and was not a deliberate attempt to omit the reporting of reemployed beneficiaries, the Board may reduce the penalty to not less than two percent (2%) of the compensation of the unreported reemployed beneficiaries during the months for which the employer failed to report, with a minimum penalty of twenty-five dollars ($25.00). Upon receipt by the employer of notice that a penalty has been assessed under this sub-subdivision, the employer shall remit the payment of the penalty to the Retirement System, in one lump sum, no later than 90 days from the date of the notice.

d.   Should a beneficiary who retired on an early or service retirement allowance under this Chapter be restored to service as an employee or teacher, then the retirement allowance shall cease as of the first of the month following the month in which the beneficiary is restored to service and the beneficiary shall become a member of the Retirement System and shall contribute thereafter as allowed by law at the uniform contribution payable by all members.

Upon his subsequent retirement, he shall be paid a retirement allowance determined as follows:

1. For a member who earns at least three years' membership service after restoration to service, creditable service earned while in receipt of disability benefits under Article 6 of this Chapter shall count as membership service for this purpose only, and the retirement allowance shall be computed on the basis of his compensation and service before and after the period of prior retirement without restrictions; provided, that if the prior allowance was based on a social security leveling payment option, the allowance shall be adjusted actuarially for the difference between the amount received under the optional payment and what would have been paid if the retirement allowance had been paid without optional modification. In the alternative, the member may receive a refund of the member's accumulated contributions for the period of service after restoration to service in accordance with G.S. 135-5(f).

2. For a member who does not earn three years' membership service after restoration to service, the retirement allowance shall be equal to the sum of the retirement allowance to which he would have been entitled had he not been restored to service, without modification of the election of an optional allowance previously made, and the retirement allowance that results from service earned since being restored to service; provided, that if the prior retirement allowance was based on a social security leveling payment option, the prior allowance shall be adjusted actuarially for the difference between the amount that would have been paid for each month had the payment not been suspended and what would have been paid if the retirement allowance had been paid without optional modification. In the alternative, the member may receive a refund of the member's accumulated contributions for the period of service after restoration to service in accordance with G.S. 135-5(f), or the member may allow this new account to remain inactive.

e. Any beneficiary who retired on an early or service retirement allowance as an employee of any State department, agency or institution under the Law Enforcement Officers' Retirement System and becomes employed as an employee by a State department, agency, or institution as an employer participating in the Retirement System shall become subject to the provisions of G.S. 135-3(8)c and G.S. 135-3(8)d on and after January 1, 1989.

(8a) Notwithstanding the provisions of paragraphs c and d of subdivision (8) to the contrary, a beneficiary who was a beneficiary retired on an early or service retirement with the Law Enforcement Officers' Retirement System at the time of the transfer of law enforcement officers employed by the State and beneficiaries last employed by the State to this Retirement System on January 1, 1985, and who also was a contributing member of this Retirement System on

January 1, 1985, shall continue to be paid his retirement allowance without restriction and may continue as a member of this Retirement System with all the rights and privileges appendant to membership.

(9) Members who are participating in an intergovernmental exchange of personnel under the provisions of Article 10 of Chapter 126 may retain their membership status and receive all benefits provided by this Chapter during the period of the exchange provided the requirements of Article 10 of Chapter 126 are met; provided further, that a member participating in an intergovernmental exchange of personnel under Article 10 of Chapter 126 shall, notwithstanding whether he and his employer are making contributions to the member's account during the exchange period, be entitled to the death benefit if he otherwise qualifies under the provisions of this Article and provided further that no duplicate benefits shall be paid. (1941, c. 25, s. 3; 1945, c. 799; 1947, c. 414; c. 457, ss. 1, 2; c. 458, s. 5; c. 464, s. 2; 1949, c. 1056, s. 1; 1951, c. 561; 1955, c. 1155, s. 91/2; 1961, c. 516, ss. 1, 2; 1963, c. 687, s. 2; 1965, c. 780, s. 1; c. 1187; 1967, c. 720, ss. 1, 2, 15; c. 1234; 1969, c. 1223, ss. 1, 2, 14; 1971, c. 117, ss. 6-8; c. 118, ss. 1, 2; 1973, c. 241, s. 1; c. 994, s. 5; c. 1363; 1977, c. 783, s. 3; 1979, c. 396; c. 972, s. 2; 1981, c. 979, s. 1; 1981 (Reg. Sess., 1982), c. 1396, ss. 1, 2; 1983, c. 556, ss. 1, 2; 1983 (Reg. Sess., 1984), c. 1034, ss. 228, 229, 236; c. 1106, ss. 1, 2, 4; 1985, c. 520, s. 1; c. 649, ss. 2, 11; 1987, c. 513, s. 1; c. 738, s. 38(b); 1989, c. 791; 1993 (Reg. Sess., 1994), c. 769, ss. 7.30(e), (f), 7.31(d), (e); 1995, c. 509, s. 73.1; 1998-212, s. 28.24(a); 1998-217, s. 67; 2000-67, s. 8.24(a); 2001-424, s. 32.25(a); 2002-126, ss. 28.10(a), (b), (d), 28.13(a); 2004-124, s. 31.18A(a), (b); 2004-199, s. 57(a); 2005-144, ss. 7A.1, 7A.2, 7A.4; 2005-276, ss. 29.28(a)-(d); 2005-345, s. 43; 2006-226, s. 25(a); 2007-145, s. 7(a), (b), (d)-(f); 2007-326, ss. 1, 3(a), (b), (d)-(f); 2007-431, s. 9; 2009-66, ss. 8(a), 12(a), (b); 2009-137, s. 1; 2010-72, s. 4(a); 2011-232, s. 1; 2011-294, s. 2(a); 2012-130, s. 8; 2013-405, s. 5.)

§§ 135-3.1 through 135-3.2: Repealed by Session Laws 1961, c. 516, s. 9.

§ 135-4. Creditable service.

(a) Under such rules and regulations as the Board of Trustees shall adopt, each member who was a teacher or State employee at any time during the five years immediately preceding the establishment of the System and who became a member prior to July 1, 1946, shall file a detailed statement of all North Carolina service as a teacher or State employee rendered by him prior to the date of establishment for which he claims credit; provided, that, notwithstanding the foregoing, any member retiring on or after July 1, 1965, with credit for not less than 10 years of membership service shall file such detailed statement of service as a teacher or State employee rendered by him prior to July 1, 1941, for which he claims credit; provided, that any member who retired on a service retirement allowance prior to July 1, 1965, who at the time of his retirement did not qualify for credit for his service as a teacher or State employee prior to July 1, 1941, may request on and after July 1, 1971, that his original benefit be recalculated, in accordance with the formula prevailing at the time of his retirement, to include credit for such service with the new benefit to become effective on the first of the month following certification of the prior service.

(b) The Board of Trustees shall fix and determine by appropriate rules and regulations how much service in any year is equivalent to one year of service, but in no case shall more than one year of service be creditable for all services in one year. Service rendered for the regular school year in any district shall be equivalent to one year's service. Service rendered by a school employee in a job-sharing position shall be credited at the rate of one-half year for each regular school year of employment.

(c) Subject to the above restrictions and to such other rules and regulations as the Board of Trustees may adopt, the Board of Trustees shall verify, as soon as practicable after the filing of such statements of service, the service therein claimed.

In lieu of a determination of the actual compensation of the members that was received during such period of prior service the Board of Trustees may use for the purpose of this Chapter the compensation rates which will be determined by the average salary of the members for five years immediately preceding the date this System became operative as the records show the member actually received.

(d) Any member may, up to his date of retirement and within one year thereafter, request the Board of Trustees to modify or correct his prior service credit.

(e) Creditable service at retirement on which the retirement allowance of a member shall be based shall consist of the membership service rendered by him since he last became a member, and also if he has a prior service certificate which is in full force and effect, the amount of service certified on his prior service certificate; and if he has sick leave standing to his credit upon retirement on or after July 1, 1971, one month of credit for each 20 days or portion thereof, but not less than one hour; sick leave shall not be counted in computing creditable service for the purpose of determining eligibility for disability retirement or for a vested deferred allowance. Creditable service for unused sick leave shall be allowed only for sick leave accrued monthly during employment under a duly adopted sick leave policy and for which the member may be able to take credits and be paid for sick leave without restriction. However, in no instance shall unused sick leave be credited to a member's account at retirement if the member's last day of actual service is more than five years prior to the effective date of the member's retirement. Further, any agency with a sick leave policy that is more generous than that of all State agencies subject to the rules of the Office of State Human Resources shall proportionately adjust each of its retiring employees' sick leave balance to the balance that employee would have had under the rules of the Office of State Human Resources.

On and after July 1, 1971, a member whose account was closed on account of absence from service under the provisions of G.S. 135-3(3) and who subsequently returns to service for a period of five years, may thereafter repay in a lump sum the amount withdrawn plus regular interest thereon from the date of withdrawal through the year of repayment and thereby increase his creditable service by the amount of creditable service lost when his account was closed.

On and after July 1, 1973, a member whose account in the North Carolina Local Governmental Employees' Retirement System was closed on account of absence from service under the provisions of G.S. 128-24(1a) and who subsequently became or becomes a member of this System with credit for five years of service, may thereafter repay in a lump sum the amount withdrawn from the North Carolina Local Governmental Employees' Retirement System plus regular interest thereon from the date of withdrawal through the year of repayment and thereby increase his creditable service in this System by the amount of creditable service lost when his account was closed.

On or after July 1, 1979, a member who has obtained 60 months of aggregate service, or five years of membership service, as an employee of the North Carolina General Assembly, except legislators, participants in the Legislative Intern Program and pages, may make a lump sum payment together with interest, and an administrative fee for such service, to the Teachers' and State

Employees' Retirement System of an amount equal to what he would have contributed had he been a member on his first day of employment.

On and after January 1, 1985, the creditable service of a member who was a member of the Law-Enforcement Officers' Retirement System at the time of the transfer of law-enforcement officers employed by the State from that System to this Retirement System and whose accumulated contributions are transferred from that System to this Retirement System, shall include service that was creditable in the Law-Enforcement Officers' Retirement System; and membership service with that System shall be membership service with this Retirement System; provided, notwithstanding any provision of this Article to the contrary, any inchoate or accrued rights of such a member to purchase creditable service for military service, withdrawn service and prior service under the rules and regulations of the Law-Enforcement Officers' Retirement System shall not be diminished and may be purchased as creditable service with this Retirement System under the same conditions which would have otherwise applied.

(f) Armed Service Credit. -

(1) Teachers and other State employees who entered the Armed Forces of the United States on or after September 16, 1940, and prior to February 17, 1941, and who returned to the service of the State within a period of two years after they were first eligible to be separated or released from the Armed Forces of the United States under other than dishonorable conditions shall be entitled to full credit for all prior service. Pursuant to 38 U.S.C. § 4318(b)(1), when a member who has been on military leave returns to work consistent with the provisions of this subdivision, then the member's employer must remit to the System all the employer contributions for the full period of that member's military service.

(2) Teachers and other State employees who entered the Armed Forces of the United States on or after September 16, 1940, and who returned to the service of the State prior to October 1, 1952, or who devote not less than 10 years of service to the State after they are separated or released from the Armed Forces of the United States under other than dishonorable conditions, shall be entitled to full credit for all prior service, and, in addition they shall receive membership service credit for the period of service in the Armed Forces of the United States up to the date they were first eligible to be separated or released therefrom, occurring after the date of establishment of the Retirement System.

(3) Teachers and other State employees who enter the Armed Forces of the United States on or after July 1, 1950, or who engage in active military service on or after July 1, 1950, and who return to the service of the State within a period of two years after they are first eligible to be separated or released from such active military service under other than dishonorable conditions shall be entitled to full membership service credit for the period of such active service in the Armed Forces of the United States.

(4) Under such rules as the Board of Trustees shall adopt, credit will be provided by the Retirement System with respect to each such teacher or other State employee in the amounts that he or she would have been paid during such service in the Armed Forces of the United States on the basis of his or her earnable compensation when such service commenced. Such contributions shall be credited to the individual account of the member in the annuity savings fund, in such manner as the Board of Trustees shall determine, but any such contributions so credited and any regular interest thereon shall be available to the member only in the form of an annuity, or benefit in lieu thereof, upon the member's retirement on a service, disability or special retirement allowance; and in the event of cessation of membership or death prior thereto, any such contributions so credited and regular interest thereon shall not be payable to the member or on the member's account, but shall be transferred from the annuity savings fund to the pension accumulation fund. If any payments were made by a member on account of such service as provided by subdivision (5) of subsection (b) of G.S. 135-8, the Board of Trustees shall refund to or reimburse such member for such payments.

(5) The provisions of this subsection shall also apply to members of the North Carolina National Guard with respect to teachers and State employees who are called into federal service or who are called into State service, to the extent that such persons fail to receive compensation for performance of the duties of their employment other than for service in the North Carolina National Guard.

(6) Repealed by Session Laws 1981, c. 636, s. 1. For proviso as to inchoate or accrued rights, see Editor's Note below.

(7) Notwithstanding any other provision of this Chapter, any member and any retired member as herein described may purchase creditable service in the Armed Forces of the United States, not otherwise allowed, by paying a total lump sum payment determined as follows:

a. For members who completed 10 years of membership service, and retired members who completed 10 years of membership service prior to retirement, whose membership began on or prior to July 1, 1981, and who make this purchase within three years after first becoming eligible, the cost shall be an amount equal to the monthly compensation the member earned when the member first entered membership service times the employee contribution rate at that time times the months of service to be purchased, with sufficient interest added thereto so as to equal one-half of the cost of allowing this service, plus an administrative fee to be set by the Board of Trustees.

b. For members who complete five years of membership service, and retired members who complete five years of membership service prior to retirement, and eligible members and retired members covered by paragraph a. of this subdivision, whose membership began on or before July 1, 1981, but who did not or do not make this purchase within three years after first becoming eligible, the cost shall be an amount equal to the full liability of the service credits calculated on the basis of the assumptions used for the purposes of the actuarial valuation of the System's liabilities and shall take into account the retirement allowance arising on account of the additional service credits commencing at the earliest age at which the member could retire on an unreduced allowance, as determined by the Board of Trustees upon the advice of the consulting actuary, plus an administrative fee to be set by the Board of Trustees. Notwithstanding the foregoing provisions of this subsection that provide for the purchase of service credits, the term "full liability" includes assumed post-retirement allowance increases, as determined by the Board of Trustees, from the earliest age at which a member could retire on an unreduced service retirement allowance.

Creditable service allowed under this subdivision shall be only for the initial period of "active duty", as defined in 38 U.S. Code Section 101(21), in the Armed Forces of the United States up to the date the member was first eligible to be separated and released and for subsequent periods of "active duty", as defined in 38 U.S. Code Section 101(21), as required by the Armed Forces of the United States up to the date of first eligibility for separation or release, but shall not include periods of active duty in the Armed Forces of the United States creditable in any other retirement system except the National Guard or any reserve component of the Armed Forces of the United States, and shall not include periods of "active duty for training", as defined in 38 U.S. Code Section 101(22), or periods of "inactive duty training", as defined in 38 U.S. Code Section 101(23), rendered in any reserve component of the Armed Forces of the United States. Provided, creditable service may be allowed only for active duty in the Armed Forces of the United States of a member that resulted in a general or honorable discharge from duty. The member shall submit satisfactory evidence of the service claimed. For purposes of this subsection, membership service may include any membership or prior service credits transferred to this Retirement System pursuant to G.S. 135-18.1.

(g) Teachers and other State employees who served in the uniformed services as defined in the Uniformed Services Employment and Reemployment Rights Act of 1994, 38 U.S.C. § 4303, and who, after being honorably discharged, returned to the service of the State within a period of two years from date of discharge shall be credited with prior service for such period of service in the uniformed services for the maximum period that they are entitled to reemployment under the Uniformed Services Employment and Reemployment Rights Act of 1994, 38 U.S.C. § 4301, et seq., or other federal law, and the salary or compensation of such a teacher or State employee during that period of service is deemed to be that salary or compensation the employee would have received but for the period of service had the employee remained continuously employed, if the determination of that salary or compensation is reasonably certain. If the determination of the salary or compensation is not reasonably certain, then it is deemed to be that employee's average rate of compensation during the 12-month period immediately preceding the period of service.

(h) During periods when a member is on leave of absence and is receiving less than his full compensation, he will be deemed to be in service only if he is contributing to the Retirement System as provided in G.S. 135-8(b)(5). If he is so contributing, the annual rate of compensation paid to such employee immediately before the leave of absence began will be deemed to be the actual compensation rate of the employee during the leave of absence.

(i) Any person who became a member after June 30, 1947, and before July 1, 1955, and did not subsequently withdraw his contributions may, prior to his retirement, increase his creditable service to the extent of the period of time from the date he became a "teacher or employee" as the terms are defined in this Chapter to the date he became a member, but not exceeding three months immediately preceding membership, provided that he makes an additional contribution in one lump sum equal to five per centum (5%) of the compensation he received for the aforesaid period of time plus regular interest thereon from the date he became a member to the date of payment.

(j) Creditable service at retirement shall include any service rendered by a member while on leave of absence to serve as a member or officer of the General Assembly which is not creditable toward retirement under the Legislative Retirement Fund provided the allowance of such credit shall be contingent upon the cancellation of service credit in the Fund and the transfer of the member's contributions plus accumulated interest from the Fund to this System.

(j1) Any member may purchase creditable service for service as a member of the General Assembly not otherwise creditable under this section, provided the service is not credited in the Legislative Retirement Fund nor the Legislative Retirement System, and further provided the member pays a lump sum amount equal to the full cost of the additional service credits calculated on the basis of the assumptions used for the purposes of the actuarial valuation of the System's liabilities, taking into account the additional retirement allowance arising on account of the additional service credits commencing at the earliest age at which a member could retire on an unreduced retirement allowance as determined by the Board of Trustees upon the advice of the consulting actuary, plus an administrative fee to be set by the Board of Trustees. Notwithstanding the foregoing provisions of this subsection that provide for the purchase of service credits, the terms "full cost", "full liability", and "full actuarial cost" include assumed annual post-retirement allowance increases, as determined by the Board of Trustees, from the earliest age at which a member could retire on an unreduced service allowance.

(j2) The creditable service of a member who was a member of the Local Governmental Employees' Retirement System, the Consolidated Judicial Retirement System, or the Legislative Retirement System, and whose accumulated contributions and reserves are transferred from that System to this System, includes service that was creditable in the Local Governmental Employees' Retirement System, the Consolidated Judicial Retirement System, or the Legislative Retirement System, and membership service with those Retirement Systems is membership service with this Retirement System.

(k) Notwithstanding any other provision of this Chapter, any person who withdrew his contributions in accordance with the provisions of G.S. 128-27(f) or G.S. 135-5(f) or the rules and regulations of the Law-Enforcement Officers' Retirement System and who subsequently returns to service may, upon completion of five years of membership service, repay in a total lump sum any and all of the accumulated contributions previously withdrawn with interest compounded annually at the rate of six and one-half percent (6.5%) for each calendar year from the year of withdrawal to the year of repayment plus a fee to cover expense of handling which shall be determined by the Board of Trustees, and receive credit for the service forfeited at time of withdrawal. These provisions shall apply equally to retired members who had attained five years of membership service prior to retirement. The retirement allowance of a retired member who restores service under this subsection shall be increased the month following the month payment is received. The increase in the retirement allowance shall be the difference between the initial retirement allowance, under any optional allowance elected at the time of retirement, and the amount of the retirement allowance, under any optional allowance elected at the time of retirement, to which the retired member would have been entitled had the service not been previously forfeited, adjusted by any increases in the retirement accrual rate occurring between the member's date of retirement and the date of payment. The increase in the retirement allowance shall not include any adjustment for cost-of-living increases granted since the date of retirement.

Notwithstanding any provision to the contrary, a law enforcement officer who was transferred from the Law Enforcement Officers' Retirement System to this Retirement System pursuant to Article 12C of Chapter 143 of the General Statutes and withdrew his accumulated contributions prior to January 1, 1985, in accordance with G.S. 128-27(f) or G.S. 135-5(f) for non-law enforcement service and who has five years or more of membership service standing to his credit may repay in a total lump sum the accumulated contributions previously withdrawn with interest compounded annually at the rate of six and one-half percent (6.5%) for each calendar year from the year of withdrawal to the year of repayment plus a fee to cover expense of handling which shall be determined by the Board of Trustees, and receive credit for the service forfeited at time of withdrawal(s). The retirement allowance of a retired member who restores service under this subsection shall be increased the month following the month payment is received. The increase in the retirement allowance shall be the difference between the initial retirement allowance, under any optional allowance elected at the time of retirement, and the amount of the retirement allowance, under any optional allowance elected at the time of retirement, to which the retired member would have been entitled had the service not been previously forfeited, adjusted by any increases in the retirement accrual rate occurring between the member's date of retirement and the date of payment. The increase in the retirement allowance shall not include any adjustment for cost-of-living increases granted since the date of retirement.

(l)   Repealed by Session Laws 1981, c. 636, s. 1. For proviso as to inchoate or accrued rights, see Editor's Note below.

(l1)   Notwithstanding any other provision of this Chapter, any member and any retired member as herein described may purchase creditable service previously rendered to any state, territory, or other governmental subdivision of the United States other than this State by paying a total lump-sum payment determined as follows:

(1)   For members who completed 10 years of current membership service, and retired members who completed 10 years of current membership service prior to retirement, whose membership began on or before July 1, 1981, and who make such purchase within three years after first becoming eligible, the cost shall be an amount equal to the monthly compensation the member earned when he first entered membership service, times the employee contribution rate at that time, times the months of service to be purchased, times two, with sufficient interest added thereto so as to equal the full cost of allowing such service, plus an administrative fee to be set by the Board of Trustees.

(2)   For members who complete five years of current membership service, and retired members who complete five years of current membership service prior to retirement, and eligible members and retired members covered by subdivision (1) of this subsection, whose membership began on or before July 1, 1981, but who did not or do not make such purchase within three years after first becoming eligible, the cost shall be an amount equal to the full liability of the service credits calculated on the basis of the assumptions used for the purposes of the actuarial valuation of the System's liabilities and shall take into account the retirement allowance arising on account of the additional service credits commencing at the earliest age at which the member could retire on an unreduced allowance, as determined by the Board of Trustees upon the advice of the consulting actuary, plus an administrative fee to be set by the Board of Trustees. Notwithstanding the foregoing provisions of this subsection that provide for the purchase of service credits, the term "full liability" includes assumed postretirement allowance increases, as determined by the Board of Trustees, from the earliest age at which a member could retire on an unreduced service retirement allowance. Notwithstanding the requirement of five years of current membership service, a member whose membership began prior to the service the member desires to purchase shall be eligible to purchase creditable service under this subdivision upon returning to service as a teacher or employee upon completion of a total of five years of membership service and upon completion of one year of current membership service.

Current membership service shall mean membership service earned since the service previously rendered to any state, territory, or other governmental subdivision of the United States other than this State. Creditable service under this subsection shall be allowed only at the rate of one year of out-of-state service for each year of membership service in this State, with a maximum allowable of 10 years of out-of-state service. Such service is limited to full-time service which would be allowable under the laws governing this System. Credit will be allowed only if no benefit is allowable in another public retirement system as a result of the service.

(m) Notwithstanding any language to the contrary of any provision of this section, or of any repealed provision of this section that was repealed with the inchoate and accrued rights preserved, all repayments and purchases of service credits, allowed under the provisions of this section or of any repealed provision of this section that was repealed with inchoate and accrued rights preserved, must be made within three years after the member first becomes eligible to make such repayments and purchases. Any member who does not repay or purchase service credits within said three years after first eligibility to make such repayments and purchases may, under the same conditions as are otherwise required, repay or purchase service credits provided that the repayment or purchase equals the full cost of the service credits calculated on the basis of the assumptions used for purposes of the actuarial valuation of the system's liabilities and shall take into account the additional retirement allowance arising on account of such additional service credit commencing at the earliest age at which such member could retire on an unreduced retirement allowance as determined by the Board of Trustees upon the advice of the consulting actuary. Notwithstanding the foregoing provisions of this subsection that provide for the purchase of service credits, the terms "full cost", "full liability", and "full actuarial cost" include assumed annual post-retirement allowance increases, as determined by the Board of Trustees, from the earliest age at which a member could retire on an unreduced service allowance. Notwithstanding the foregoing, on and after July 1, 2001, the provisions of this subsection shall not apply to the repayment of contributions withdrawn pursuant to subsection (k) of this section.

(n) Repealed by Session Laws 1981, c. 636, s. 1. For proviso as to inchoate or accrued rights, see Editor's Note below.

(o) Repealed by Session Laws 1981, c. 636, s. 1. For proviso as to inchoate or accrued rights, see Editor's Note below.

(p) Credit for prior temporary State employment. - Notwithstanding any other provision of this Chapter, a member may purchase service credit for temporary State employment upon completion of 10 years of membership service and subject to the condition that the member had been classified as a temporary employee for more than three years. Each employer shall certify to the Board of Trustees that an employee is eligible to purchase this service credit prior to the member making payment. Payment for the service credit shall be in a single lump sum based upon the amount the member would have contributed if he had been properly classified as a permanent employee and been a member of this retirement system.

(p1)   Part-Time Service Credit. -

(1)   Notwithstanding any other provision of this Chapter, upon completion of five years of membership service, any member may purchase service previously rendered as a part-time teacher or employee of an employer as defined in G.S. 135-1(11) or G.S. 128-21(11), except for temporary or part-time service rendered while a full-time student in pursuit of a degree or diploma in a degree-granting program. Payment shall be made in a single lump sum in an amount equal to the full actuarial cost of providing credit for the service, together with interest and an administrative fee, as determined by the Board of Trustees on the advice of the Retirement System's actuary. Notwithstanding the provisions of G.S. 135-4(b), the Board of Trustees shall fix and determine by appropriate rules and regulations how much service in any year, as based on compensation, is equivalent to one year of service in proportion to "earnable compensation", but in no case shall more than one year of service be creditable for all service in one year. Service rendered for the regular school year in any district shall be equivalent to one year's service. Notwithstanding the foregoing provisions of this subdivision that provide for the purchase of service credits, the terms "full cost", "full liability", and "full actuarial cost" include assumed annual post-retirement allowance increases, as determined by the Board of Trustees, from the earliest age at which a member could retire on an unreduced service allowance.

(2)   Under all requirements and conditions set forth in the preceding subdivision of this subsection (p1), except for the requirement that the completion of five years of membership service be subsequent to service rendered as a part-time teacher or employee of the State, any member with five or more years of membership service standing to his credit may purchase additional membership service for service rendered as a part-time teacher or employee of the State if (i) the member terminates or has terminated employment in any capacity as a teacher or employee of the State, (ii) the purchase of the additional membership service causes the member to become eligible to commence an early or service retirement allowance, and (iii) the member immediately elects to commence retirement and become a beneficiary.

(3) Under all the requirements and conditions set forth in subdivision (1) of this subsection, except for the condition that part-time service rendered when a full-time student in pursuit of a degree or diploma in a degree-granting program is not eligible for purchase, any member with five or more years of membership service standing to the member's credit may purchase creditable service for service rendered as a part-time teacher or employee of the State if that service was rendered on a permanent part-time basis and required at least 20 hours of service per week.

(q) Notwithstanding any other provision of this Chapter, any member who entered service or was restored to service prior to July 1, 1982, and was excluded from membership service solely on account of having attained the age of 62 years, in accordance with former G.S. 135-3(6), may purchase membership service credits of such excluded service by making a lump-sum payment equal to the contributions that would have been deducted pursuant to G.S. 135-8(b) had he been a member of the Retirement System, increased by interest calculated at a rate of seven percent (7%) per annum.

(r) Notwithstanding any other provision of this Chapter, any member may purchase creditable service for periods of employer approved leaves of absence when in receipt of benefits under the North Carolina Workers' Compensation Act. This service shall be purchased by paying a cost calculated in the following manner:

(1) Leaves of Absence Terminated Prior to July 1, 1983. - The cost to a member whose employer approved leave of absence, when in receipt of benefits under the North Carolina Workers' Compensation Act, terminated upon return to service prior to July 1, 1983, shall be a lump sum amount payable to the Annuity Savings Fund equal to the full liability of the service credits calculated on the basis of the assumptions used for purposes of the actuarial valuation of the system's liabilities, and shall take into account the retirement allowance arising on account of the additional service credit commencing at the earliest age at which the member could retire on an unreduced retirement allowance, as determined by the board of trustees upon the advice of the consulting actuary, plus an administrative fee to be set by the board of trustees. Notwithstanding the foregoing provisions of this subdivision that provide for the purchase of service credits, the terms "full cost", "full liability", and "full actuarial cost" include assumed annual post-retirement allowance increases, as determined by the Board of Trustees, from the earliest age at which a member could retire on an unreduced service allowance.

(2) Leaves of Absence Terminating On and After July 1, 1983, but before January 1, 1988. - The cost to a member whose employer approved leave of absence, when in receipt of benefits under the North Carolina Workers' Compensation Act, terminates upon return to service on and after July 1, 1983, but before January 1, 1988, shall be a lump sum amount due and payable to the Annuity Savings Fund within six months from return to service equal to the total employee and employer percentage rates of contribution in effect at the time of purchase and based on the annual rate of compensation of the member immediately prior to the leave of absence; Provided, however, the cost to a member whose amount due is not paid within six months from return to service shall be the amount due plus one percent (1%) per month penalty for each month or fraction thereof the payment is made beyond the six-month period.

(3) Leaves of Absence Terminating On and After January 1, 1988. - The cost to a member whose employer approved leave of absence, when in receipt of benefits under the North Carolina Workers' Compensation Act, terminates upon or before a return to service on and after January 1, 1988, shall be due and payable to the Annuity Savings Fund within six months from return to service and shall be a lump sum amount equal to the employee percentage rate of contribution in effect at the time of purchase applied to the annual rate of compensation of the member immediately prior to the leave of absence. For members electing to make this payment, the member's employer which granted the leave of absence, or the member's employer upon a return to service, or both, shall make a matching lump sum payment to the Pension Accumulation Fund within six months from return to service equal to the employer percentage rate of contribution in effect at the time of purchase applied to the annual rate of compensation of the member immediately prior to the leave of absence. Such purchases of creditable service are applicable only when members have membership service credits within 30 days prior to the leave of absence and within 12 months following the leave of absence and such membership service is creditable service at the time of purchase. Notwithstanding any other provision of this subdivision, the cost to a member and to a member's employer or former employer or both employers whose amount due is not paid within six months from return to service shall be the amount due plus one percent (1%) per month penalty for each month or fraction thereof that the payment is made after the six-month period.

Notwithstanding the requirement of this provision that a member return to service, a member who is in receipt of Workers' Compensation during the period for which he or she would have otherwise been eligible to receive short-term benefits as provided in G.S. 135-105 and who subsequently becomes a beneficiary in receipt of a benefit as provided in G.S. 135-106 may purchase creditable service for any period of employer approved leave of absence when in receipt of benefits under the North Carolina Workers' Compensation Act. The cost to purchase such creditable service shall be as determined above provided the amount due if not paid within six months from the beginning of the long-term disability period as determined in G.S. 135-106 shall be the amount due plus one percent (1%) per month penalty for each month or fraction thereof that the payment is made after the six-month period.

Whenever the creditable service purchased pursuant to this subsection is for a period that occurs during the four consecutive calendar years that would have produced the highest average annual compensation pursuant to G.S. 135-1(5) had the member not been on leave of absence without pay, then the compensation that the member would have received during the purchased period shall be included in calculating the member's average final compensation. In such cases, the compensation that the member would have received during the purchased period shall be based on the annual rate of compensation of the member immediately prior to the leave of absence.

(s) Credit at Full Cost for Temporary Employment. - In addition to the provisions of subsection (p) above, any member may purchase creditable service for State employment when classified as a temporary teacher or employee subject to the conditions that the:

(1) Member was employed by an employer as defined in G.S. 135-1(11) or G.S. 128-21(11);

(2) Member's temporary employment met all other requirements of G.S. 135-1(10) or (25), or G.S. 128-21(10);

(3) Member has completed five years or more of membership service;

(4) Member acquires from the employer such certifications of temporary employment as are required by the Board of Trustees; and

(5) Member makes a lump sum payment into the Annuity Savings Fund equal to the full liability of the service credits calculated on the basis of the assumptions used for purposes of the actuarial valuation of the Retirement System's liabilities and shall take into account the retirement allowance arising on account of the additional service credit commencing at the earliest age at which the member could retire on an unreduced retirement allowance, as

determined by the Board of Trustees upon the advice of the actuary, plus an administrative expense fee to be determined by the Board of Trustees. Notwithstanding the foregoing provisions of this subdivision that provide for the purchase of service credits, the terms "full cost", "full liability", and "full actuarial cost" include assumed annual post-retirement allowance increases, as determined by the Board of Trustees, from the earliest age at which a member could retire on an unreduced service allowance.

The provisions of this subsection shall also apply to the purchase of creditable service for State employment when classified as a permanent hourly employee in accordance with G.S. 126-5(c4).

(t)   Credit at Full Cost for Local Government Employment. - Any member may purchase creditable service for any employment as an employee, as defined in G.S. 128-21(10), of a local government employer not creditable in the North Carolina Local Governmental Employees' Retirement System upon completion of five years of membership service by making a lump-sum payment into the Annuity Savings Fund. The payment by the member shall be equal to the full liability of the service credits calculated on the basis of the assumptions used for purposes of the actuarial valuation of the Retirement System's liabilities, taking into account the additional retirement allowance arising on account of the additional service credits commencing at the earliest age at which the member could retire with an unreduced retirement allowance, as determined by the Board of Trustees upon the advice of the actuary plus an administrative expense fee to be determined by the Board of Trustees. Notwithstanding the foregoing provisions of this subsection that provide for the purchase of service credits, the terms "full cost", "full liability", and "full actuarial cost" include assumed annual post-retirement allowance increases, as determined by the Board of Trustees, from the earliest age at which a member could retire on an unreduced service allowance.

(u)   Any member who was a wildlife protector who elected to become a member of the Law Enforcement Officers' Retirement System pursuant to Chapter 837 of the 1971 Session Laws by the transfer of accumulated contributions from this Retirement System to the Law Enforcement Officers' Retirement System and who has not subsequently applied for and received a return of accumulated contributions shall be entitled to creditable service for the service as a non-law enforcement officer forfeited as a result of the transfer pursuant to Chapter 837 of the 1971 Session Laws.

(v) Omitted Membership Service. - A member who had service as an employee as defined in G.S. 135-1(10) and G.S. 128-21(10) or as a teacher as defined in G.S. 135-1(25) and who was omitted from contributing membership through error may be allowed membership service, after submitting clear and convincing evidence of the error, as follows:

(1) Within 90 days of the omission, by the payment of employee and employer contributions that would have been paid; or

(2) After 90 days and prior to three years of the omission, by the payment of the employee and employer contributions that would have been paid plus interest compounded annually at a rate equal to the greater of the average yield on the pension accumulation fund for the preceding calendar year or the actuarial investment rate-of-return assumption, as adopted by the Board of Trustees; or

(3) After three years of the omission, by the payment of an amount equal to the full cost of the service credits calculated on the basis of the assumptions used for the purposes of the actuarial valuation of the system's liabilities, and shall take into account the additional retirement allowance arising on account of such additional service credit commencing at the earliest age at which a member could retire on an unreduced retirement allowance, as determined by the Board of Trustees upon the advice of the consulting actuary, plus an administrative fee to be set by the Board of Trustees. Notwithstanding the foregoing provisions of this subdivision that provide for the purchase of service credits, the terms "full cost", "full liability", and "full actuarial cost" include assumed annual post-retirement allowance increases, as determined by the Board of Trustees, from the earliest age at which a member could retire on an unreduced service allowance.

Nothing contained in this subsection shall prevent an employer or member from paying all or a part of the cost of the omitted membership service; and to the extent paid by the employer, the cost paid by the employer shall be credited to the pension accumulation fund; and to the extent paid by the member, the cost paid by the members shall be credited to the member's annuity savings account; provided, however, an employer does not discriminate against any member or group of members in his employ in paying all or any part of the cost of the omitted membership service.

(w) Credit at Full Cost for Federal Employment. - Notwithstanding any other provisions of this Chapter, a member, upon the completion of five years of membership service, may purchase creditable service for periods of federal employment, provided that the member is not receiving any retirement benefits resulting from this federal employment, and provided that the member is not vested in the particular federal retirement system to which the member may have belonged while a federal employee. The member shall purchase this service by making a lump sum amount payable to the Annuity Savings Fund equal to the full liability of the service credits calculated on the basis of the assumptions used for purposes of the actuarial valuation of the system's liabilities, and shall take into account the retirement allowance arising on account of the additional service credit commencing at the earliest age at which the member could retire on an unreduced retirement allowance, as determined by the Board of Trustees upon the advice of the consulting actuary, plus an administrative fee to be set by the Board of Trustees. Notwithstanding the foregoing provisions of this subsection that provide for the purchase of service credits, the terms "full cost", "full liability", and "full actuarial cost" include assumed annual post-retirement allowance increases, as determined by the Board of Trustees, from the earliest age at which a member could retire on an unreduced service allowance.

Members may also purchase creditable service for periods of employment with public community service entities within the State funded entirely with federal funds, other than the federal government, that are not covered by the provisions of G.S. 128-21(11) or G.S. 135-1(11), under the same terms and conditions that are applicable to the purchase of creditable service for periods of federal employment in accordance with this subsection. "Public community service entities" as used in this subsection shall mean community action, human relations, manpower development, and community development programs as defined in Articles 19 and 21 of Chapter 160A and Article 18 of Chapter 153A of the General Statutes and any other similar programs that the Board of Trustees may adopt.

(x)   Repealed by Session Laws 2001-424, s. 32.32(c), effective July 1, 2001.

(y)   A member who is a beneficiary of the Disability Income Plan provided for in Article 6 of this Chapter shall be granted creditable service for each month that the member is eligible for and for which a benefit is paid under the provisions of G.S. 135-105 and G.S. 135-106; provided, however, that in no instance shall a member be granted creditable service under this subsection if creditable service is earned or credited for the same month in this retirement system or any other retirement system administered by the State.

(z) Credit at Full Cost for Leave Due to Extended Illness. - Any member in service with five or more years of membership service standing to his credit may purchase creditable service for periods of interrupted service while on leave without pay status due to the member's illness or injury, excluding leave due to maternity, provided that any single such interrupted service shall have included such period of time during which the member failed to earn at least two months membership service, by making a lump sum amount payable to the Annuity Savings Fund equal to the full liability of the service credits calculated on the basis of the assumptions used for purposes of the actuarial valuation of the system's liabilities; and the calculation of the amount payable shall take into account the retirement allowance arising on account of the additional service credit commencing at the earliest age at which the member could retire on an unreduced retirement allowance, as determined by the Board of Trustees upon the advice of the consulting actuary, plus an administrative fee to be set by the Board of Trustees. Notwithstanding the foregoing provisions of this subsection that provide for the purchase of service credits, the terms "full cost", "full liability", and "full actuarial cost" include assumed annual post-retirement allowance increases, as determined by the Board of Trustees, from the earliest age at which a member could retire on an unreduced service allowance.

(aa) Credit at Full Cost for Maternity Leave. - Notwithstanding other provisions of this Chapter, any member in service with five or more years of credited membership service may purchase creditable service for periods of service which were interrupted due to parental leave, pregnancy or childbirth, or involuntary administrative furlough due to a lack of funds to support the position by making a lump sum amount payable to the Annuity Savings Fund equal to the full liability of the service credits calculated on the basis of the assumptions used for purposes of the actuarial valuation of the system's liabilities; and the calculation of the amount payable shall take into account the retirement allowance arising on account of the additional service credit commencing at the earliest age at which the member could retire on an unreduced retirement allowance, as determined by the Board of Trustees upon the advice of the consulting actuary, plus an administrative fee to be set by the Board of Trustees. Creditable service purchased under this subsection may not exceed six months per parental leave, pregnancy or childbirth, or involuntary administrative furlough due to a lack of funds to support the position. Notwithstanding the foregoing provisions of this subsection that provide for the purchase of service credits, the term "full liability" includes assumed annual postretirement allowance increases, as determined by the Board of Trustees, from the earliest age at which a member could retire on an unreduced service allowance.

(bb) Credit at Full Cost for Probationary Local Government Employment. - Notwithstanding any other provision of this Chapter, a member may purchase creditable service, prior to retirement, for employment with any local employer as defined in G.S. 128-21(11) when considered to be in a probationary or employer-imposed waiting period status, between the date of employment and the date of membership service with the Local Governmental Employees' Retirement System, provided that the former employer of such a member has revoked this probationary employment or waiting period policy.

The member shall purchase this service by making a lump-sum amount payable to the Annuity Savings Fund equal to the full liability of the service credits calculated on the basis of the assumptions used for purposes of the actuarial valuation of the liabilities of the retirement system, and the calculation of the amount payable shall take into account the retirement allowance arising on account of the additional service credit commencing at the earliest age at which the member could retire on an unreduced retirement allowance, as determined by the Board of Trustees upon the advice of the consulting actuary, plus an administrative fee to be set by the Board of Trustees. Notwithstanding the provisions of this subsection that provide for the purchase of service credits, the term "full liability" includes assumed annual postretirement allowance increases, as determined by the Board of Trustees, from the earliest age at which a member could retire on an unreduced service allowance.

(cc) Credit for Employment in Charter School Operated by a Private Nonprofit Corporation. - Any member may purchase creditable service for any employment as an employee of a charter school operated by a private nonprofit corporation whose board of directors did not elect to participate in the Retirement System under G.S. 135-5.3 upon completion of five years of membership service after that charter school employment by making a lump-sum payment into the Annuity Savings Fund. The payment by the member shall be equal to the full liability of the service credits calculated on the basis of the assumptions used for purposes of the actuarial valuation of the Retirement System's liabilities, taking into account the additional retirement allowance arising on account of the additional service credits commencing at the earliest age at which the member could retire with an unreduced retirement allowance, as determined by the Board of Trustees upon the advice of the actuary plus an administrative expense fee to be determined by the Board of Trustees. Notwithstanding the foregoing provisions of this subsection that provide for the purchase of service credits, the terms "full cost", "full liability", and "full actuarial cost" include assumed annual postretirement allowance increases, as determined by the Board of Trustees, from the earliest age at which a member could retire on an unreduced service allowance.

(dd)   Purchase of Service Credits Through Rollover Contributions From Certain Other Plans. - Notwithstanding any other provision of this Article, and without regard to any limitations on contributions otherwise set forth in this Article, a member, who is eligible to restore or purchase membership or creditable service pursuant to the provisions of G.S. 135-4, may, subject to such rules and regulations established by the Board of Trustees, purchase such service credits through rollover contributions to the Annuity Savings Fund from (i) an annuity contract described in Section 403(b) of the Internal Revenue Code, (ii) an eligible plan under Section 457(b) of the Internal Revenue Code which is maintained by a state, political subdivision of a state, or any agency or instrumentality of a state or political subdivision of a state, (iii) an individual retirement account or annuity described in Section 408(a) or 408(b) of the Internal Revenue Code that is eligible to be rolled over and would otherwise be includible in gross income, or (iv) a qualified plan described in Section 401(a) or 403(a) of the Internal Revenue Code. Notwithstanding the foregoing, the Retirement System shall not accept any amount as a rollover contribution unless such amount is eligible to be rolled over to a qualified trust in accordance with applicable law and the member provides evidence satisfactory to the Retirement System that such amount qualifies for rollover treatment. Unless received by the Retirement System in the form of a direct rollover, the rollover contribution must be paid to the Retirement System on or before the 60th day after the date it was received by the member.

Purchase of Service Credits Through Plan-to-Plan Transfers. - Notwithstanding any other provision of this Article, and without regard to any limitations on contributions otherwise set forth in this Article, a member, who is eligible to restore or purchase membership or creditable service pursuant to the provisions of G.S. 135-4, may, subject to such rules and regulations established by the Board of Trustees, purchase such service credits through a direct transfer to the Annuity Savings Fund of funds from (i) an annuity contract described in Section 403(b) of the Internal Revenue Code or (ii) an eligible plan under Section 457(b) of the Code which is maintained by a state, political subdivision of a state, or any agency or instrumentality of a state or political subdivision of a state.

(ee)   Purchase of Service Credits Through Plan-to-Plan Transfers. - Notwithstanding any other provision of this Article, and without regard to any limitations on contributions otherwise set forth in this Article, a member, who is eligible to restore or purchase membership or creditable service pursuant to the provisions of G.S. 135-4, may, subject to such rules and regulations established by the Board of Trustees, purchase such service credits through a direct transfer to the Annuity Savings Fund of funds from (i) the Supplemental Retirement Income Plans A, B, or C of North Carolina or (ii) any other defined contribution plan qualified under Section 401(a) of the Internal Revenue Code which is maintained by the State of North Carolina, a political subdivision of a state, or any agency or instrumentality of a state or political subdivision of a state.

(ff)   Retroactive Membership Service. - A member who is reinstated to service as an employee as defined in G.S. 135-1(10) or as a teacher as defined in G.S. 135-1(25) retroactively to the date of prior involuntary termination with back pay, as defined by the State Human Resources Commission, and associated benefits may be allowed membership service, after submitting clear and convincing evidence of the reinstatement, payment of back pay, and restoration of associated benefits, as follows:

(1)   When the reinstatement to service is by court order, final decision of an Administrative Law Judge, or decision of the State Human Resources Commission, and is:

a.   Within 90 days of the involuntary termination, by the payment of employee and employer contributions that would have been paid; or

b.   After 90 days of the involuntary termination, by the payment of the employee and employer contributions that would have been paid plus interest compounded annually at a rate equal to the greater of the average yield on the pension accumulation fund for the preceding calendar year or the actuarial investment rate-of-return assumption, as adopted by the Board of Trustees.

(2)   When the reinstatement to service is by settlement agreement voluntarily entered into by the affected parties, by the payment of a lump-sum amount equal to the full liability of the service credits calculated on the basis of the assumptions used for purposes of the actuarial valuation of the system's liabilities, taking into account the retirement allowance arising on account of the additional service credit commencing at the earliest age at which the member could retire on an unreduced retirement allowance, as determined by the Board of Trustees upon the advice of the consulting actuary, plus an administrative fee to be set by the Board of Trustees. Notwithstanding the foregoing provisions of this subsection that provide for the purchase of service credits, the terms "full cost," "full liability," and "full actuarial cost" include assumed annual

postretirement allowance increases, as determined by the Board of Trustees, from the earliest age at which a member could retire on an unreduced service allowance.

Nothing contained in this subsection shall prevent an employer or member from paying all or a part of the cost of the retroactive membership service; and to the extent paid by the employer, the cost paid by the employer shall be credited to the pension accumulation fund; and to the extent paid by the member, the cost paid by the member shall be credited to the member's annuity savings account; provided, however, an employer does not discriminate against any member or group of members in his employ in paying all or any part of the cost of the retroactive membership service.

In the event a member received a return of accumulated contributions subsequent to an involuntary termination as provided in G.S. 135-5(f), the member may redeposit, within 90 days of reinstatement retroactive to the date of prior involuntary termination, in the annuity savings fund by single payment an amount equal to the total amount he previously withdrew plus regular interest and restore the creditable service forfeited upon receiving his return of accumulated contributions.

(gg)   If a member who is an elected government official and has not vested in this System on July 1, 2007, is convicted of an offense listed in G.S. 135-18.10 for acts committed after July 1, 2007, then that member shall forfeit all benefits under this System, except for a return of member contributions plus interest. If a member who is an elected government official and has vested in this System on July 1, 2007, is convicted of an offense listed in G.S. 135-18.10 for acts committed after July 1, 2007, then that member is not entitled to any creditable service that accrued after July 1, 2007. No member shall forfeit any benefit or creditable service earned from a position not as an elected government official.

(hh)   Credit at Full Cost for Service With The University of North Carolina During Which a Member Participated in the Optional Retirement Program. – Notwithstanding any other provisions of this Chapter, a member upon the completion of five years of membership service may purchase creditable service for periods of employment with The University of North Carolina during which the member participated in the Optional Retirement Program as provided for in G.S. 135-5.1, provided that the member is not receiving, and is not entitled to receive, any retirement benefits resulting from this employment. The member shall purchase this service by making a lump-sum amount payable to the Annuity Savings Fund equal to the full liability of the service credits calculated on the basis of the assumptions used for purposes of the actuarial valuation of the system's liabilities and shall take into account the retirement allowance arising on account of the additional service credit commencing at the earliest age at which the member could retire on an unreduced retirement allowance, as determined by the Board of Trustees upon the advice of the consulting actuary, plus an administrative fee to be set by the Board of Trustees. Notwithstanding the foregoing provisions of this subsection that provide for the purchase of service credits, the terms "full cost," "full liability," and "full actuarial cost" include assumed annual postretirement allowance increases, as determined by the Board of Trustees, from the earliest age at which a member could retire on an unreduced service allowance.

(ii) If a member who is in service and has not vested in this System on December 1, 2012, is convicted of an offense listed in G.S. 135-18.10A for acts committed after December 1, 2012, then that member shall forfeit all benefits under this System, except for a return of member contributions plus interest. If a member who is in service and has vested in this System on December 1, 2012, is convicted of an offense listed in G.S. 135-18.10A for acts committed after December 1, 2012, then that member is not entitled to any creditable service that accrued after December 1, 2012. (1941, c. 25, s. 4; 1943, cc. 200, 783; 1945, c. 797; 1947, c. 575; 1949, c. 1056, ss. 2, 4; 1953, c. 1050, s. 3; 1959, c. 513, s. 11/2; 1961, c. 516, s. 3; c. 779, s. 2; 1963, c. 1262; 1965, c. 780, s. 1; c. 924; 1967, c. 720, s. 3; 1969, c. 1223, ss. 3, 4; 1971, c. 117, ss. 9, 10; c. 993; 1973, c. 241, s. 2; c. 242, s. 1; c. 667, s. 2; c. 737, s. 1; c. 816, s. 1; c. 1063; c. 1311, ss. 1-5; 1975, c. 205, s. 2; c. 875, s. 47; 1977, cc. 317, 790; 1979, c. 826; c. 866, s. 2; c. 867; c. 972, s. 3; 1981, c. 557, s. 3; c. 636, s. 1; c. 1116, s. 1; 1981 (Reg. Sess., 1982), c. 1396, s. 4; 1983, c. 533, s. 1; c. 725; 1983 (Reg. Sess., 1984), c. 1030; c. 1034, ss. 230, 231; c. 1045, ss. 1, 2; 1985, c. 401, ss. 1, 2; c. 407, s. 1; c. 479, s. 193; c. 512; c. 530; c. 649, ss. 1, 4; c. 749, s. 1; 1987, c. 533, s. 1; c. 717, s. 2; c. 738, s. 29(b); c. 809, s. 2; c. 821; c. 825; 1987 (Reg. Sess., 1988), c. 1088, ss. 1-4; c. 1103; c. 1110, s. 9; 1989, c. 255, ss. 11-20; c. 762, s. 3; 1991 (Reg. Sess., 1992), c. 1017, s. 2; c. 1029, s. 1; 1995, c. 507, s. 7.23D(b); 1998-71, ss. 3, 4; 1998-190, s. 1; 1998-212, s. 9.14A(c); 1998-214, s. 2; 1999-71, s. 1; 1999-158, s. 2; 2001-424, ss. 32.28(a), 32.32(a), 32.32(b), 32.32(c); 2002-71, s. 5; 2002-153, s. 4; 2002-174, s. 3; 2003-284, s. 30.18(b); 2003-358, s. 3; 2003-359, ss. 7, 8, 9, 12; 2005-91, s. 1; 2007-179, s. 3(b); 2007-233, s. 1; 2007-431, ss. 8, 11; 2009-281, s. 1; 2010-72, s. 5(a); 2011-183, s. 101; 2011-294, s. 5(a); 2012-130, s. 3(b), (c); 2012-193, s. 2; 2013-382, s. 9.1(c); 2013-405, s. 6(a).)

§ 135-4.1. Reciprocity of creditable service with other State-administered retirement systems.

(a) Only for the purpose of determining eligibility for benefits accruing under this Article, creditable service standing to the credit of a member of the Legislative Retirement System, Consolidated Judicial Retirement System, or the Local Governmental Employees' Retirement System or service standing to the credit of a member of the Optional Retirement Program shall be added to the creditable service standing to the credit of a member of this System; provided, that in the event a person is a retired member of any of the foregoing retirement systems or the Optional Retirement Program, such creditable service standing or service standing to the credit of the retired member prior to retirement shall be likewise counted. In no instance shall service credits maintained in the aforementioned retirement systems or the Optional Retirement Program be added to the creditable service in this System for application of this System's benefit accrual rate in computing a service retirement benefit unless specifically authorized by this Article.

(b) A person who was a former member of this System and who has forfeited his creditable service in this System by receiving a return of contributions and who has creditable service in the Legislative Retirement System, Consolidated Judicial Retirement System, or the Local Governmental Employees' Retirement System may count such creditable service for the purpose of restoring the creditable service forfeited in this System under the terms and conditions as set forth in this Article and reestablish membership in this System.

(c) Creditable service under this section shall not be counted twice for the same period of time whether earned as a member, purchased, or granted as prior service credits. (1989 (Reg. Sess., 1990), c. 1066, s. 35(c); 2006-264, s. 14; 2010-38, s. 1.)

§ 135-4A: Recodified.

§ 135-5. Benefits.

(a) Service Retirement Benefits.

(1) Any member who became a member prior to August 1, 2011, may retire upon electronic submission or written application to the Board of Trustees setting forth at what time, as of the first day of a calendar month, not less than one day nor more than 120 days subsequent to the execution of and filing thereof, he desires to be retired: Provided, that the said member at the time so specified for his retirement shall have attained the age of 60 years and have at least five years of membership service or shall have completed 30 years of creditable service.

(1a) Any member who became a member on or after August 1, 2011, may retire upon electronic submission or written application to the Board of Trustees setting forth at what time, as of the first day of a calendar month, not less than one day nor more than 120 days subsequent to the execution of and filing thereof, the member desires to be retired: Provided, that the said member at the time so specified for the member's retirement shall have attained the age of 60 years and have at least 10 years of membership service or shall have completed 30 years of creditable service.

(2) Repealed by Session Laws 1983 (Regular Session, 1984), c. 1019, s. 1.

(3) Any member who was in service October 8, 1981, who had attained 60 years of age, may retire upon electronic submission or written application to the Board of Trustees setting forth at what time, as of the first day of a calendar month, not less than one day nor more than 120 days subsequent to the execution and filing thereof, he desires to be retired.

(4) Any member who is a law-enforcement officer, who became a member prior to August 1, 2011, and who attains age 50 and completes 15 or more years of creditable service in this capacity or who attains age 55 and completes five or more years of creditable service in this capacity, may retire upon electronic submission or written application to the Board of Trustees setting forth at what time, as of the first day of a calendar month, not less than one day nor more than 120 days subsequent to the execution and filing thereof, he desires to be retired; Provided, also, any member who has met the conditions herein required but does not retire, and later becomes a teacher or an employee other than as a law-enforcement officer shall continue to have the right to commence retirement.

(4a) Any member who is a law-enforcement officer, who became a member on or after August 1, 2011, and who attains age 50 and completes 15 or more years of creditable service in this capacity or who attains age 55 and completes

10 or more years of creditable service in this capacity, may retire upon electronic submission or written application to the Board of Trustees setting forth at what time, as of the first day of a calendar month, not less than one day nor more than 120 days subsequent to the execution and filing thereof, the member desires to be retired; Provided, also, any member who has met the conditions herein required but does not retire, and later becomes a teacher or an employee other than as a law-enforcement officer shall continue to have the right to commence retirement.

(5)   Any member who is eligible for and is being paid a benefit under the Disability Income Plan as provided in G.S. 135-105 or G.S. 135-106 shall be deemed a member in service and may not retire under the provisions of this section. Any member who has made electronic submission or written application for long-term or extended short-term benefits under the Disability Income Plan as provided in G.S. 135-105 or G.S. 135-106, and who has been rejected by the Plan's Medical Board for a long-term or extended short-term benefit shall have 90 days from the date of notification of the rejection to convert his application to an early or service retirement application, provided that the member meets the eligibility requirements, effective the first day of the month following the month in which short-term disability benefits ended or the first day of the month following the month in which any salary continuation as may be provided in G.S. 135-104 ended, whichever is later.

(a1)   Early Service Retirement Benefits. - Any member may retire and receive a reduced retirement allowance upon electronic submission or written application to the Board of Trustees setting forth at what time, as of the first day of a calendar month, not less than one day nor more than 120 days subsequent to the execution of and filing thereof, he desires to be retired: Provided, that the said member at the time so specified for his retirement shall have attained the age of 50 years and have at least 20 years of creditable service.

(a2)   Early Service Retirement Benefits. - Any member who became a member on or after August 1, 2011, who is a law enforcement officer may retire and receive a reduced retirement allowance upon electronic submission or written application to the Board of Trustees setting forth at what time, as of the first day of a calendar month, not less than one day nor more than 120 days subsequent to the execution of and filing thereof, the member desires to be retired; however, the member at the time so specified for the member's retirement shall have attained the age of 50 years and have at least 15 years of creditable service.

(b) Service Retirement Allowances of Persons Retiring on or after July 1, 1959, but prior to July 1, 1963. - Upon retirement from service on or after July 1, 1959, but prior to July 1, 1963, a member shall receive a service retirement allowance which shall consist of:

(1) An annuity which shall be the actuarial equivalent of his accumulated contributions at the time of his retirement; and

(2) A pension equal to the annuity allowable at the age of 65 years or at his retirement age, whichever is the earlier age, computed on the basis of contributions made prior to such earlier age; and

(3) If he has a prior service certificate in full force and effect, an additional pension which shall be equal to the sum of:

a. The annuity which would have been provided at his retirement age by the contributions which he would have made during such prior service had the System been in operation and had he contributed thereunder at the rate of six and twenty-five hundredths per centum (6.25%) of his compensation; and

b. The pension which would have been provided on account of such contributions at age 65, or at his retirement age, whichever is the earlier age.

If the member has not less than 20 years of creditable service, he shall be entitled to a total retirement allowance of not less than seventy dollars ($70.00) per month; provided that the computation shall be made prior to any reduction resulting from the selection of an optional allowance as provided by subsection (g) of this section.

(b1) Service Retirement Allowances of Members Retiring on or after July 1, 1963, but prior to July 1, 1967. - Upon retirement from service, in accordance with subsection (a) above, on or after July 1, 1963, but prior to July 1, 1967, a member shall receive a service retirement allowance computed as follows:

(1) If the member's service retirement date occurs on or after his sixty-fifth birthday, such allowance shall be equal to the sum of (i) one percent (1%) of the portion of his average final compensation not in excess of forty-eight hundred dollars ($4,800) plus one and one-half percent (1 1/2%) of the portion of such compensation in excess of forty-eight hundred dollars ($4,800), multiplied by the number of years of his creditable service rendered prior to January 1, 1966, and (ii) one percent (1%) of the portion of his average final compensation not in

excess of fifty-six hundred dollars ($5,600) plus one and one-half percent (1 1/2%) of the portion of such compensation in excess of fifty-six hundred dollars ($5,600), multiplied by the number of years of his creditable service rendered after January 1, 1966.

(2) If the member's service retirement date occurs before his sixty-fifth birthday, his service retirement allowance shall be computed as in (1) above, but shall be reduced by five twelfths of one percent (5/12 of 1%) thereof for each month by which his retirement date precedes the first day of the month coincident with or next following his sixty-fifth birthday.

(3) Notwithstanding the foregoing provisions, any member whose creditable service commenced prior to July 1, 1963, shall receive not less than the benefit provided by G.S. 135-5(b).

(b2) Service Retirement Allowance of Members Retiring on or after July 1, 1967, but prior to July 1, 1969. - Upon retirement from service in accordance with subsection (a) above, on or after July 1, 1967, but prior to July 1, 1969, a member shall receive a service retirement allowance computed as follows:

(1) If the member's service retirement date occurs on or after his sixty-fifth birthday, such allowance shall be equal to one and one-quarter percent (1 1/4%) of the portion of his average final compensation not in excess of fifty-six hundred dollars ($5,600) plus one and one-half percent (1 1/2%) of the portion of such compensation in excess of fifty-six hundred dollars ($5,600), multiplied by the number of years of his creditable service.

(2) If the member's service retirement date occurs before his sixty-fifth birthday, his service retirement allowance shall be computed as in (1) above, but shall be reduced by one third of one percent (1/3 of 1%) thereof for each month by which his retirement date precedes the first day of the month coincident with or next following his sixty-fifth birthday.

(3) Notwithstanding the foregoing provisions, any member whose creditable service commenced prior to July 1, 1963, shall receive not less than the benefit provided by G.S. 135-5(b).

(b3) Service Retirement Allowances of Members Retiring on or after July 1, 1969, but prior to July 1, 1973. - Upon retirement from service, in accordance with subsection (a) above, on or after July 1, 1969, but prior to July 1, 1973, a member shall receive a service retirement allowance computed as follows:

(1)   If the member's service retirement date occurs on or after his sixty-fifth birthday, regardless of his years of creditable service, or on or after his sixty-second birthday and the completion of 30 years of creditable service, such allowance shall be equal to one and one-quarter percent (1 1/4%) of the portion of his average final compensation not in excess of fifty-six hundred dollars ($5,600) plus one and one-half percent (1 1/2%) of the portion of such compensation in excess of fifty-six hundred dollars ($5,600), multiplied by the number of years of his creditable service.

(2)   If the member's service retirement date occurs before his sixty-fifth birthday and prior to his completion of 30 or more years of creditable service, his service retirement allowance shall be computed as in (1) above, but shall be reduced by one quarter of one percent (1/4 of 1%) thereof for each month by which his retirement date precedes the first day of the month coincident with or next following his sixty-fifth birthday.

(3)   If the member's service retirement date occurs before his sixty-second birthday but on or after his completion of 30 or more years of creditable service, his service retirement allowance shall be computed as in (1) above, but shall be reduced by one quarter of one percent (1/4 of 1%) thereof for each month by which his retirement date precedes the first day of the month coincident with or next following his sixty-second birthday.

(4)   Notwithstanding the foregoing provisions, any member whose creditable service commenced prior to July 1, 1963, shall receive not less than the benefit provided by G.S. 135-5(b).

(b4)   Service Retirement Allowances of Members Retiring on or after July 1, 1973, but prior to July 1, 1975. - Upon retirement from service, in accordance with subsection (a) above, on or after July 1, 1973, but prior to July 1, 1975, a member shall receive a service retirement allowance computed as follows:

(1)   If the member's service retirement date occurs on or after his sixty-fifth birthday, regardless of his years of creditable service, or after the completion of 30 years of creditable service, such allowance shall be equal to one and one-quarter percent (1 1/4%) of the portion of his average final compensation not in excess of five thousand six hundred dollars ($5,600) plus one and one-half percent (1 1/2%) of the portion of such compensation in excess of five thousand six hundred dollars ($5,600), multiplied by the number of years of his creditable service.

(2) If the member's service retirement date occurs before his sixty-fifth birthday and prior to his completion of 30 or more years of creditable service, his service retirement allowance shall be computed as in (1) above, but shall be reduced by one quarter of one percent (1/4 of 1%) thereof for each month by which his retirement date precedes the first day of the month coincident with or next following his sixty-fifth birthday.

(3) Notwithstanding the foregoing provisions, any member whose creditable service commenced prior to July 1, 1963, shall receive not less than the benefit provided by G.S. 135-5(b).

(b5) Service Retirement Allowance of Members Retiring on or after July 1, 1975, but prior to July 1, 1977. - Upon retirement from service, in accordance with subsection (a) above, on or after July 1, 1975, but prior to July 1, 1977, a member shall receive a service retirement allowance computed as follows:

(1) If the member's service retirement date occurs on or after his sixty-fifth birthday, regardless of his years of creditable service, or after the completion of 30 years of creditable service, such allowance shall be equal to one and one-half percent (1 1/2%) of his average final compensation, multiplied by the number of years of his creditable service.

(2) If the member's service retirement date occurs before his sixty-fifth birthday and prior to his completion of 30 or more years of creditable service, his retirement allowance shall be computed as in (1) above, but shall be reduced by one quarter of one percent (1/4 of 1%) thereof for each month by which his retirement date precedes the first day of the month coincident with or next following his sixty-fifth birthday.

(3) Notwithstanding the foregoing provisions, any member whose creditable service commenced prior to July 1, 1963, shall receive not less than the benefit provided by G.S. 135-5(b).

(b6) Service Retirement Allowance of Members Retiring on or after July 1, 1977, but prior to July 1, 1980. - Upon retirement from service, in accordance with subsection (a) above, on or after July 1, 1977, but prior to July 1, 1980, a member shall receive a service retirement allowance computed as follows:

(1) If the member's service retirement date occurs on or after his sixty-fifth birthday, regardless of his years of creditable service, or after the completion of 30 years of creditable service, such allowance shall be equal to one and fifty-

five one hundredths percent (1.55%) of his average final compensation, multiplied by the number of years of his creditable service.

(2a)   If the member's service retirement date occurs after his sixtieth and before his sixty-fifth birthday and prior to his completion of 30 or more years of creditable service, his retirement allowance shall be computed as in (1) above, but shall be reduced by one quarter of one percent (1/4 of 1%) thereof for each month by which his retirement date precedes the first day of the month coincident with or next following his sixty-fifth birthday.

(2b)   If the member's service retirement date occurs before his sixtieth birthday and prior to his completion of 30 or more years of creditable service, his service retirement allowance shall be the actuarial equivalent of the allowance payable at the age of 60 years as computed in (2a) above.

(3)   Notwithstanding the foregoing provisions, any member whose creditable service commenced prior to July 1, 1963, shall receive not less than the benefit provided by G.S. 135-5(b).

(b7)   Service Retirement Allowance of Members Retiring on or after July 1, 1980, but prior to July 1, 1985. - Upon retirement from service, in accordance with subsection (a) above, on or after July 1, 1980, but prior to July 1, 1985, a member shall receive a service retirement allowance computed as follows:

(1)   If the member's service retirement date occurs on or after his sixty-fifth birthday or after the completion of 30 years of creditable service, such allowance shall be equal to one and fifty-seven hundredths percent (1.57%) of his average final compensation, multiplied by the number of years of his creditable service.

(2)   If the member's service retirement date occurs after his sixtieth and before his sixty-fifth birthday and prior to his completion of 30 or more years of creditable service, his retirement allowance shall be computed as in (1) above but shall be reduced by one-quarter of one percent (1/4 of 1%) thereof for each month by which his retirement date precedes the first day of the month coincident with or next following his sixty-fifth birthday.

(3)   If the member's service retirement date occurs before his sixtieth birthday and prior to his completion of 30 or more years of creditable service, his service retirement allowance shall be the actuarial equivalent of the allowance payable at the age of 60 years as computed in (2) above.

(4) Notwithstanding the foregoing provisions, any member whose creditable service commenced prior to July 1, 1963, shall receive not less than the benefit provided by G.S. 135-5(b).

(b8) Service Retirement Allowance of Law-Enforcement Officers Retiring on or after January 1, 1985 [on or after January 1, 1985, but prior to July 1, 1985]. - Upon retirement from service, in accordance with subsection (a) of this section, on or after January 1, 1985 [on or after January 1, 1985, but prior to July 1, 1985], a member who is a law-enforcement officer or an eligible former law-enforcement officer shall receive a service retirement allowance computed as follows:

(1) If the member's service retirement date occurs on or after his 55th birthday, and completion of five years of creditable service as a law-enforcement officer, or after the completion of 30 years of creditable service, the allowance shall be equal to one and fifty-seven one hundredths percent (1.57%) of his average final compensation, multiplied by the number of years of his creditable service.

(2) If the member's service retirement date occurs after his 50th and before his 55th birthday with 15 or more years of creditable service as a law-enforcement officer and prior to his completion of 30 years of creditable service, his retirement allowance shall be computed as in (1) above, but shall be reduced by one-third of one percent (1/3 of 1%) thereof for each month by which his retirement date precedes the first day of the month coincident with or next following his 55th birthday.

(b9) Service Retirement Allowance of Members Retiring on or after July 1, 1985, but before July 1, 1988. - Upon retirement from service, in accordance with subsection (a) above, on or after July 1, 1985, but before July 1, 1988, a member shall receive the following service retirement allowance:

(1) A member who is a law-enforcement officer or an eligible former law-enforcement officer shall receive a service retirement allowance computed as follows:

a. If the member's service retirement date occurs on or after his 55th birthday, and completion of five years of creditable service as a law-enforcement officer, or after the completion of 30 years of creditable service, the allowance shall be equal to one and fifty-eight one hundredths percent (1.58%)

of his average final compensation, multiplied by the number of years of his creditable service.

b. If the member's service retirement date occurs after his 50th and before his 55th birthday with 15 or more years of creditable service as a law-enforcement officer and prior to his completion of 30 years of creditable service, his retirement allowance shall be computed as in a. above, but shall be reduced by one-third of one percent (1/3 of 1%) thereof for each month by which his retirement date precedes the first day of the month coincident with or next following his 55th birthday.

(2) A member who is not a law-enforcement officer or an eligible former law-enforcement officer shall receive a service retirement allowance computed as follows:

a. If the member's service retirement date occurs on or after his 65th birthday or after the completion of 30 years of creditable service or on or after his 60th birthday upon the completion of 25 years of creditable service, such allowance shall be equal to one and fifty-eight hundredths percent (1.58%) of his average final compensation, multiplied by the number of years of his creditable service.

b. If the member's service retirement date occurs after his 60th and before his 65th birthday and prior to his completion of 25 or more years of creditable service, his retirement allowance shall be computed as in a. above but shall be reduced by one-quarter of one percent (1/4 of 1%) thereof for each month by which his retirement date precedes the first day of the month coincident with or next following his 65th birthday.

c. If the member's service retirement date occurs before his 60th birthday and prior to his completion of 30 or more years of creditable service, his service retirement allowance shall be the actuarial equivalent of the allowance payable at the age of 60 years as computed in b. above.

d. Notwithstanding the foregoing provisions, any member whose creditable service commenced prior to July 1, 1963, shall receive not less than the benefit provided by G.S. 135-5(b).

(b10) Service Retirement Allowance of Members Retiring on or after July 1, 1988, but before July 1, 1989. - Upon retirement from service in accordance with subsection (a) above, on or after July 1, 1988, but before July 1, 1989, a member shall receive the following service retirement allowance:

(1) A member who is a law enforcement officer or an eligible former law enforcement officer shall receive a service retirement allowance computed as follows:

a. If the member's service retirement date occurs on or after his 55th birthday, and completion of five years of creditable service as a law enforcement officer, or after the completion of 30 years of creditable service, the allowance shall be equal to one and sixty hundredths percent (1.60%) of his average final compensation, multiplied by the number of years of his creditable service.

b. This allowance shall also be governed by the provisions of G.S. 135-5(b9)(1)b.

(2) A member who is not a law enforcement officer or an eligible former law enforcement officer shall receive a service retirement allowance computed as follows:

a. If the member's service retirement date occurs on or after his 65th birthday upon the completion of five years of creditable service or after the completion of 30 years of creditable service or on or after his 60th birthday upon the completion of 25 years of creditable service, such allowance shall be equal to one and sixty hundredths percent (1.60%) of his average final compensation, multiplied by the number of years of his creditable service.

b. This allowance shall also be governed by the provisions of G.S. 135-5(b9)(2)b, c and d.

(b11) Service Retirement Allowance of Members Retiring on or after July 1, 1989, but before July 1, 1990. - Upon retirement from service in accordance with subsection (a) above, on or after July 1, 1989, but before July 1, 1990, a member shall receive the following service retirement allowance:

(1) A member who is a law enforcement officer or an eligible former law enforcement officer shall receive a service retirement allowance computed as follows:

a. If the member's service retirement date occurs on or after his 55th birthday, and completion of five years of creditable service as a law enforcement officer, or after the completion of 30 years of creditable service, the allowance shall be equal to one and sixty-three hundredths percent (1.63%) of his average final compensation, multiplied by the number of years of his creditable service.

b.   This allowance shall also be governed by the provisions of G.S. 135-5(b9)(1)b.

(2)   A member who is not a law enforcement officer or an eligible former law enforcement officer shall receive a service retirement allowance computed as follows:

a.   If the member's service retirement date occurs on or after his 65th birthday upon the completion of five years of creditable service or after the completion of 30 years of creditable service or on or after his 60th birthday upon the completion of 25 years of creditable service, the allowance shall be equal to one and sixty-three hundredths percent (1.63%) of his average final compensation, multiplied by the number of years of creditable service.

b.   This allowance shall also be governed by the provisions of G.S. 135-5(b9)(2)b, c and d.

(b12)   Service Retirement Allowance of Members Retiring on or after July 1, 1990, but before July 1, 1992. - Upon retirement from service in accordance with subsection (a) above, on or after July 1, 1990, but before July 1, 1992, a member shall receive the following service retirement allowance:

(1)   A member who is a law enforcement officer or an eligible former law enforcement officer shall receive a service retirement allowance computed as follows:

a.   If the member's service retirement date occurs on or after his 55th birthday, and completion of five years of creditable service as a law enforcement officer, or after the completion of 30 years of creditable service, the allowance shall be equal to one and sixty-four hundredths percent (1.64%) of his average final compensation, multiplied by the number of years of his creditable service.

b.   This allowance shall also be governed by the provisions of G.S. 135-5(b9)(1)b.

(2) A member who is not a law enforcement officer or an eligible former law enforcement officer shall receive a service retirement allowance computed as follows:

a. If the member's service retirement date occurs on or after his 65th birthday upon the completion of five years of creditable service or after the completion of 30 years of creditable service or on or after his 60th birthday upon the completion of 25 years of creditable service, the allowance shall be equal to one and sixty-four hundredths percent (1.64%) of his average final compensation, multiplied by the number of years of creditable service.

b. This allowance shall also be governed by the provisions of G.S. 135-5(b9)(2)b, c and d.

(b13) Service Retirement Allowance of Members Retiring on or after July 1, 1992, but before July 1, 1993. - Upon retirement from service in accordance with subsection (a) above, on or after July 1, 1992, but before July 1, 1993, a member shall receive the following service retirement allowance:

(1) A member who is a law enforcement officer or an eligible former law enforcement officer shall receive a service retirement allowance computed as follows:

a. If the member's service retirement date occurs on or after his 55th birthday, and completion of five years of creditable service as a law enforcement officer, or after the completion of 30 years of creditable service, the allowance shall be equal to one and seventy hundredths percent (1.70%) of his average final compensation, multiplied by the number of years of his creditable service.

b. This allowance shall also be governed by the provisions of G.S. 135-5(b9)(1)b.

(2) A member who is not a law enforcement officer or an eligible former law enforcement officer shall receive a service retirement allowance computed as follows:

a. If the member's service retirement date occurs on or after his 65th birthday upon the completion of five years of creditable service or after the completion of 30 years of creditable service or on or after his 60th birthday upon the completion of 25 years of creditable service, the allowance shall be equal to one and seventy hundredths percent (1.70%) of his average final compensation, multiplied by the number of years of creditable service.

b. This allowance shall also be governed by the provisions of G.S. 135-5(b9)(2)b., c., and d.

(b14) Service Retirement Allowance of Members Retiring on or after July 1, 1993, but before July 1, 1994. - Upon retirement from service in accordance with subsection (a) above, on or after July 1, 1993, but before July 1, 1994, a member shall receive the following service retirement allowance:

(1) A member who is a law enforcement officer or an eligible former law enforcement officer shall receive a service retirement allowance computed as follows:

a. If the member's service retirement date occurs on or after his 55th birthday, and completion of five years of creditable service as a law enforcement officer, or after the completion of 30 years of creditable service, the allowance shall be equal to one and seventy-one hundredths percent (1.71%) of his average final compensation, multiplied by the number of years of his creditable service.

b. If the member's service retirement date occurs after his 50th and before his 55th birthday with 15 or more years of creditable service as a law enforcement officer and prior to the completion of 30 years of creditable service, the allowance shall be computed as in G.S. 135-5(b14)(1)a., but shall be reduced by one-third of one percent (1/3 of 1%) thereof for each month by which the retirement date precedes the first day of the month coincident with or next following his 55th birthday.

(2) A member who is not a law enforcement officer or an eligible former law enforcement officer shall receive a service retirement allowance computed as follows:

a. If the member's service retirement date occurs on or after his 65th birthday upon the completion of five years of creditable service or after the completion of 30 years of creditable service or on or after his 60th birthday upon the completion of 25 years of creditable service, the allowance shall be equal to one and seventy-one hundredths percent (1.71%) of his average final compensation, multiplied by the number of years of creditable service.

b. If the member's service retirement date occurs after his 60th birthday and before his 65th birthday and prior to the completion of 25 years or more of creditable service, the retirement allowance shall be computed as in G.S. 135-5(b14)(2)a. but shall be reduced by one-quarter of one percent (1/4 of 1%) thereof for each month by which his retirement date precedes the first day of the month coincident with or next following his 65th birthday.

c. If the member's service retirement date occurs before his 60th birthday and prior to the completion of 30 or more years of creditable service, the service retirement allowance shall be the actuarial equivalent of the allowance payable at the age of 60 years as computed in G.S. 135-5(b14)(2)b.

d. Notwithstanding the foregoing provisions, any member whose creditable service commenced prior to July 1, 1963, shall receive not less than the benefit provided by G.S. 135-5(b).

(b15) Service Retirement Allowance of Members Retiring on or after July 1, 1994, but before July 1, 1995. - Upon retirement from service in accordance with subsection (a) or (a1) above, on or after July 1, 1994, but before July 1, 1995, a member shall receive the following service retirement allowance:

(1) A member who is a law enforcement officer or an eligible former law enforcement officer shall receive a service retirement allowance computed as follows:

a. If the member's service retirement date occurs on or after his 55th birthday, and completion of five years of creditable service as a law enforcement officer, or after the completion of 30 years of creditable service, the allowance shall be equal to one and seventy-three hundredths percent (1.73%) of his average final compensation, multiplied by the number of years of his creditable service.

b. If the member's service retirement date occurs on or after his 50th birthday and before his 55th birthday with 15 or more years of creditable service as a law enforcement officer and prior to the completion of 30 years of creditable service, his retirement allowance shall be equal to the greater of:

1. The service retirement allowance payable under G.S. 135-5(b15)(1)a. reduced by one-third of one percent (1/3 of 1%) thereof for each month by which his retirement date precedes the first day of the month coincident with or next following the month the member would have attained his 55th birthday; or

2. The service retirement allowance as computed under G.S. 135-5(b15)(1)a. reduced by five percent (5%) times the difference between 30 years and his creditable service at retirement.

(2) A member who is not a law enforcement officer or an eligible former law enforcement officer shall receive a service retirement allowance computed as follows:

a. If the member's service retirement date occurs on or after his 65th birthday upon the completion of five years of creditable service or after the completion of 30 years of creditable service or on or after his 60th birthday upon the completion of 25 years of creditable service, the allowance shall be equal to one and seventy-three hundredths percent (1.73%) of his average final compensation, multiplied by the number of years of creditable service.

b. If the member's service retirement date occurs after his 60th and before his 65th birthday and prior to his completion of 25 years or more of creditable service, his retirement allowance shall be computed as in G.S. 135-5(b15)(2)a. but shall be reduced by one-quarter of one percent (1/4 of 1%) thereof for each month by which his retirement date precedes the first day of the month coincident with or next following his 65th birthday.

c. If the member's early service retirement date occurs on or after his 50th birthday and before his 60th birthday and after completion of 20 years of creditable service but prior to the completion of 30 years of creditable service, his early service retirement allowance shall be equal to the greater of:

1. The service retirement allowance as computed under G.S. 135-5(b15)(2)a. but reduced by the sum of five-twelfths of one percent (5/12 of 1%) thereof for each month by which his retirement date precedes the first day of the month coincident with or next following the month the member would have attained his 60th birthday, plus one-quarter of one percent (1/4 of 1%) thereof for each month by which his 60th birthday precedes the first day of the month coincident with or next following his 65th birthday; or

2. The service retirement allowance as computed under G.S. 135-5(b15)(2)a. reduced by five percent (5%) times the difference between 30 years and his creditable service at retirement; or

3. If the member's creditable service commenced prior to July 1, 1994, the service retirement allowance provided by G.S. 135-5(b14)(2)c.

d. Notwithstanding the foregoing provisions, any member whose creditable service commenced prior to July 1, 1963, shall not receive less than the benefit provided by G.S. 135-5(b).

(b16) Service Retirement Allowance of Members Retiring on or After July 1, 1995, but Before July 1, 1997. - Upon retirement from service in accordance with subsection (a) or (a1) above, on or after July 1, 1995, but before July 1, 1997, a member shall receive the following service retirement allowance:

(1) A member who is a law enforcement officer or an eligible former law enforcement officer shall receive a service retirement allowance computed as follows:

a. If the member's service retirement date occurs on or after his 55th birthday, and completion of five years of creditable service as a law enforcement officer, or after the completion of 30 years of creditable service, the allowance shall be equal to one and seventy-five hundredths percent (1.75%) of his average final compensation, multiplied by the number of years of his creditable service.

b. If the member's service retirement date occurs on or after his 50th birthday and before his 55th birthday with 15 or more years of creditable service as a law enforcement officer and prior to the completion of 30 years of creditable service, his retirement allowance shall be equal to the greater of:

1. The service retirement allowance payable under G.S. 135-5(b16)(1)a. reduced by one-third of one percent (1/3 of 1%) thereof for each month by which his retirement date precedes the first day of the month coincident with or next following the month the member would have attained his 55th birthday; or

2. The service retirement allowance as computed under G.S. 135-5(b16)(1)a. reduced by five percent (5%) times the difference between 30 years and his creditable service at retirement.

(2) A member who is not a law enforcement officer or an eligible former law enforcement officer shall receive a service retirement allowance computed as follows:

a. If the member's service retirement date occurs on or after his 65th birthday upon the completion of five years of creditable service or after the completion of 30 years of creditable service or on or after his 60th birthday upon the completion of 25 years of creditable service, the allowance shall be equal to one and seventy-five hundredths percent (1.75%) of his average final compensation, multiplied by the number of years of creditable service.

b. If the member's service retirement date occurs after his 60th and before his 65th birthday and prior to his completion of 25 years or more of creditable service, his retirement allowance shall be computed as in G.S. 135-5(b16)(2)a. but shall be reduced by one-quarter of one percent (¼ of 1%) thereof for each month by which his retirement date precedes the first day of the month coincident with or next following his 65th birthday.

c. If the member's early service retirement date occurs on or after his 50th birthday and before his 60th birthday and after completion of 20 years of creditable service but prior to the completion of 30 years of creditable service, his early service retirement allowance shall be equal to the greater of:

1. The service retirement allowance as computed under G.S. 135-5(b16)(2)a. but reduced by the sum of five-twelfths of one percent (5/12 of 1%) thereof for each month by which his retirement date precedes the first day of the month coincident with or next following the month the member would have attained his 60th birthday, plus one-quarter of one percent (1/4 of 1%) thereof for each month by which his 60th birthday precedes the first day of the month coincident with or next following his 65th birthday; or

2. The service retirement allowance as computed under G.S. 135-5(b16)(2)a. reduced by five percent (5%) times the difference between 30 years and his creditable service at retirement; or

3. If the member's creditable service commenced prior to July 1, 1994, the service retirement allowance equal to the actuarial equivalent of the allowance payable at the age of 60 years as computed in G.S. 135-5(b16)(2)b.

d. Notwithstanding the foregoing provisions, any member whose creditable service commenced prior to July 1, 1963, shall not receive less than the benefit provided by G.S. 135-5(b).

(b17) Service Retirement Allowance of Members Retiring on or After July 1, 1997, but Before July 1, 2000. - Upon retirement from service in accordance with subsection (a) or (a1) above, on or after July 1, 1997, but before July 1, 2000, a member shall receive the following service retirement allowance.

(1) A member who is a law enforcement officer or an eligible former law enforcement officer shall receive a service retirement allowance computed as follows:

a. If the member's service retirement date occurs on or after his 55th birthday, and completion of five years of creditable service as a law enforcement officer, or after the completion of 30 years of creditable service, the allowance shall be equal to one and eighty hundredths percent (1.80%) of his average final compensation, multiplied by the number of years of his creditable service.

b. If the member's service retirement date occurs on or after his 50th birthday and before his 55th birthday with 15 or more years of creditable service as a law enforcement officer and prior to the completion of 30 years of creditable service, his retirement allowance shall be equal to the greater of:

1. The service retirement allowance payable under G.S. 135-5(b17)(1)a, reduced by one-third of one percent (1/3 of 1%) thereof for each month by which his retirement date precedes the first day of the month coincident with or next following the month the member would have attained his 55th birthday; or

2. The service retirement allowance as computed under G.S. 135-5(b17)(1)a. reduced by five percent (5%) times the difference between 30 years and his creditable service at retirement.

(2) A member who is not a law enforcement officer or an eligible former law enforcement officer shall receive a service retirement allowance computed as follows:

a. If the member's service retirement date occurs on or after his 65th birthday upon the completion of five years of membership service or after the completion of 30 years of creditable service or on or after his 60th birthday upon the completion of 25 years of creditable service, the allowance shall be equal to one and eighty hundredths percent (1.80%) of his average final compensation, multiplied by the number of years of creditable service.

b. If the member's service retirement date occurs after his 60th birthday and before his 65th birthday and prior to his completion of 25 years or more of creditable service, his retirement allowance shall be computed as in G.S. 135-5(b17)(2)a. but shall be reduced by one-quarter of one percent (1/4 of 1%) thereof for each month by which his retirement date precedes the first day of the month coincident with or next following his 65th birthday.

c. If the member's early service retirement date occurs on or after his 50th birthday and before his 60th birthday and after completion of 20 years of creditable service but prior to the completion of 30 years of creditable service, his early service retirement allowance shall be equal to the greater of:

1. The service retirement allowance as computed under G.S. 135-5(b17)(2)a. but reduced by the sum of five-twelfths of one percent (5/12 of 1%) thereof for each month by which his retirement date precedes the first day of the month coincident with or next following the month the member would have attained his 60th birthday, plus one-quarter of one percent (1/4 of 1%) thereof for each month by which his 60th birthday precedes the first day of the month coincident with or next following his 65th birthday; or

2. The service retirement allowance as computed under G.S. 135-5(b17)(2)a. reduced by five percent (5%) times the difference between 30 years and his creditable service at retirement; or

3. If the member's creditable service commenced prior to July 1, 1994, the service retirement allowance equal to the actuarial equivalent of the allowance payable at the age of 60 years as computed in G.S. 135-5(b17)(2)b.

d. Notwithstanding the foregoing provisions, any member whose creditable service commenced prior to July 1, 1963, shall not receive less than the benefit provided by G.S. 135-5(b).

(b18) Service Retirement Allowance of Members Retiring on or After July 1, 2000, but Before July 1, 2002. - Upon retirement from service in accordance with subsection (a) or (a1) above, on or after July 1, 2000, but before July 1, 2002, a member shall receive the following service retirement allowance.

(1) A member who is a law enforcement officer or an eligible former law enforcement officer shall receive a service retirement allowance computed as follows:

a. If the member's service retirement date occurs on or after his 55th birthday, and completion of five years of creditable service as a law enforcement officer, or after the completion of 30 years of creditable service, the allowance shall be equal to one and eighty-one hundredths percent (1.81%) of his average final compensation, multiplied by the number of years of his creditable service.

b. If the member's service retirement date occurs on or after his 50th birthday and before his 55th birthday with 15 or more years of creditable service as a law enforcement officer and prior to the completion of 30 years of creditable service, his retirement allowance shall be equal to the greater of:

1. The service retirement allowance payable under G.S. 135-5(b18)(1)a. reduced by one-third of one percent (1/3 of 1%) thereof for each month by which his retirement date precedes the first day of the month coincident with or next following the month the member would have attained his 55th birthday; or

2. The service retirement allowance as computed under G.S. 135-5(b18)(1)a. reduced by five percent (5%) times the difference between 30 years and his creditable service at retirement.

(2) A member who is not a law enforcement officer or an eligible former law enforcement officer shall receive a service retirement allowance computed as follows:

a. If the member's service retirement date occurs on or after his 65th birthday upon the completion of five years of membership service or after the completion of 30 years of creditable service or on or after his 60th birthday upon the completion of 25 years of creditable service, the allowance shall be equal to one and eighty-one hundredths percent (1.81%) of his average final compensation, multiplied by the number of years of creditable service.

b. If the member's service retirement date occurs after his 60th birthday and before his 65th birthday and prior to his completion of 25 years or more of creditable service, his retirement allowance shall be computed as in G.S. 135-5(b18)(2)a. but shall be reduced by one-quarter of one percent (1/4 of 1%) thereof for each month by which his retirement date precedes the first day of the month coincident with or next following his 65th birthday.

c. If the member's early service retirement date occurs on or after his 50th birthday and before his 60th birthday and after completion of 20 years of creditable service but prior to the completion of 30 years of creditable service, his early service retirement allowance shall be equal to the greater of:

1. The service retirement allowance as computed under G.S. 135-5(b18)(2)a. but reduced by the sum of five-twelfths of one percent (5/12 of 1%) thereof for each month by which his retirement date precedes the first day of the month coincident with or next following the month the member would have

attained his 60th birthday, plus one-quarter of one percent (1/4 of 1%) thereof for each month by which his 60th birthday precedes the first day of the month coincident with or next following his 65th birthday; or

2. The service retirement allowance as computed under G.S. 135-5(b18)(2)a. reduced by five percent (5%) times the difference between 30 years and his creditable service at retirement; or

3. If the member's creditable service commenced prior to July 1, 1994, the service retirement allowance equal to the actuarial equivalent of the allowance payable at the age of 60 years as computed in G.S. 135-5(b18)(2)b.

d. Notwithstanding the foregoing provisions, any member whose creditable service commenced prior to July 1, 1963, shall not receive less than the benefit provided by G.S. 135-5(b).

(b19) Service Retirement Allowance of Members Who Became a Member Prior to August 1, 2011, Retiring on or After July 1, 2002. - Upon retirement from service in accordance with subdivision (a)(1), (a)(4), or subsection (a1) of this section, on or after July 1, 2002, a member shall receive the following service retirement allowance:

(1) A member who is a law enforcement officer or an eligible former law enforcement officer shall receive a service retirement allowance computed as follows:

a. If the member's service retirement date occurs on or after his 55th birthday, and completion of five years of creditable service as a law enforcement officer, or after the completion of 30 years of creditable service, the allowance shall be equal to one and eighty-two hundredths percent (1.82%) of his average final compensation, multiplied by the number of years of his creditable service.

b. If the member's service retirement date occurs on or after his 50th birthday and before his 55th birthday with 15 or more years of creditable service as a law enforcement officer and prior to the completion of 30 years of creditable service, his retirement allowance shall be equal to the greater of:

1. The service retirement allowance payable under G.S. 135-5(b19)(1)a. reduced by one-third of one percent (1/3 of 1%) thereof for each month by which his retirement date precedes the first day of the month coincident with or next following the month the member would have attained his 55th birthday; or

2. The service retirement allowance as computed under G.S. 135-5(b19)(1)a. reduced by five percent (5%) times the difference between 30 years and his creditable service at retirement.

(2) A member who is not a law enforcement officer or an eligible former law enforcement officer shall receive a service retirement allowance computed as follows:

a. If the member's service retirement date occurs on or after his 65th birthday upon the completion of five years of membership service or after the completion of 30 years of creditable service or on or after his 60th birthday upon the completion of 25 years of creditable service, the allowance shall be equal to one and eighty-two hundredths percent (1.82%) of his average final compensation, multiplied by the number of years of creditable service.

b. If the member's service retirement date occurs after his 60th birthday and before his 65th birthday and prior to his completion of 25 years or more of creditable service, his retirement allowance shall be computed as in G.S. 135-5(b19)(2)a. but shall be reduced by one-quarter of one percent (1/4 of 1%) thereof for each month by which his retirement date precedes the first day of the month coincident with or next following his 65th birthday.

c. If the member's early service retirement date occurs on or after his 50th birthday and before his 60th birthday and after completion of 20 years of creditable service but prior to the completion of 30 years of creditable service, his early service retirement allowance shall be equal to the greater of:

1. The service retirement allowance as computed under G.S. 135-5(b19)(2)a. but reduced by the sum of five-twelfths of one percent (5/12 of 1%) thereof for each month by which his retirement date precedes the first day of the month coincident with or next following the month the member would have attained his 60th birthday, plus one-quarter of one percent (1/4 of 1%) thereof for each month by which his 60th birthday precedes the first day of the month coincident with or next following his 65th birthday; or

2. The service retirement allowance as computed under G.S. 135-5(b19)(2)a. reduced by five percent (5%) times the difference between 30 years and his creditable service at retirement; or

3. If the member's creditable service commenced prior to July 1, 1994, the service retirement allowance equal to the actuarial equivalent of the allowance payable at the age of 60 years as computed in G.S. 135-5(b19)(2)b.

d. Notwithstanding the foregoing provisions, any member whose creditable service commenced prior to July 1, 1963, shall not receive less than the benefit provided by G.S. 135-5(b).

(b20) Service Retirement Allowance of Members Who Became a Member On or After August 1, 2011. - Upon retirement from service in accordance with subdivision (a)(1a) or (a)(4a) or subsection (a1) or (a2) of this section, a member shall receive the following service retirement allowance:

(1) A member who is a law enforcement officer or an eligible former law enforcement officer shall receive a service retirement allowance computed as follows:

a. If the member's service retirement date occurs on or after the member's 55th birthday, and completion of 10 years of creditable service as a law enforcement officer, or after the completion of 30 years of creditable service, the allowance shall be equal to one and eighty-two hundredths percent (1.82%) of the member's average final compensation, multiplied by the number of years of his creditable service.

b. If the member's service retirement date occurs on or after the member's 50th birthday and before the member's 55th birthday with 15 or more years of creditable service as a law enforcement officer and prior to the completion of 30 years of creditable service, the member's retirement allowance shall be equal to the greater of:

1. The service retirement allowance payable under G.S. 135-5(b20)(1)a. reduced by one-third of one percent (1/3 of 1%) thereof for each month by which the member's retirement date precedes the first day of the month coincident with or next following the month the member would have attained the member's 55th birthday; or

2. The service retirement allowance as computed under G.S. 135-5(b20)(1)a. reduced by five percent (5%) times the difference between 30 years and the member's creditable service at retirement.

(2) A member who is not a law enforcement officer or an eligible former law enforcement officer shall receive a service retirement allowance computed as follows:

a. If the member's service retirement date occurs on or after his 65th birthday upon the completion of 10 years of membership service or after the completion of 30 years of creditable service or on or after the member's 60th birthday upon the completion of 25 years of creditable service, the allowance shall be equal to one and eighty-two hundredths percent (1.82%) of the member's average final compensation, multiplied by the number of years of creditable service.

b. If the member's service retirement date occurs after the member's 60th birthday and before the member's 65th birthday and prior to the member's completion of 25 years or more of creditable service, the member's retirement allowance shall be computed as in G.S. 135-5(b20)(2)a. but shall be reduced by one-fourth of one percent (1/4 of 1%) thereof for each month by which the member's retirement date precedes the first day of the month coincident with or next following the member's 65th birthday.

c. If the member's early service retirement date occurs on or after the member's 50th birthday and before the member's 60th birthday and after completion of 20 years of creditable service but prior to the completion of 30 years of creditable service, the member's early service retirement allowance shall be equal to the greater of:

1. The service retirement allowance as computed under G.S. 135-5(b20)(2)a. but reduced by the sum of five-twelfths of one percent (5/12 of 1%) thereof for each month by which the member's retirement date precedes the first day of the month coincident with or next following the month the member would have attained his 60th birthday, plus one-fourth of one percent (1/4 of 1%) thereof for each month by which his 60th birthday precedes the first day of the month coincident with or next following the member's 65th birthday; or

2. The service retirement allowance as computed under G.S. 135-5(b20)(2)a. reduced by five percent (5%) times the difference between 30 years and the member's creditable service at retirement.

(c) Disability Retirement Benefits of Members Leaving Service Prior to January 1, 1988. - The provisions of this subsection shall not be applicable to members in service on or after January 1, 1988. Upon the application of a member or of his employer, any member who has had five or more years of creditable service may be retired by the Board of Trustees, on the first day of any calendar month, not less than one day nor more than 120 days next following the date of filing such application, on a disability retirement allowance: Provided, that the medical board, after a medical examination of such member, shall certify that such member is mentally or physically incapacitated for the further performance of duty, that such incapacity was incurred at the time of active employment and has been continuous thereafter, that such incapacity is likely to be permanent, and that such member should be retired; Provided further the medical board shall determine if the member is able to engage in gainful employment and, if so, the member may still be retired and the disability retirement allowance as a result thereof shall be reduced as in subsection (e) below. Provided further, that the medical board shall not certify any member as disabled who:

(1)   Applies for disability retirement based upon a mental or physical incapacity which existed when the member first established membership in the system; or

(2)   Is in receipt of any payments on account of the same disability which existed when the member first established membership in the system.

The Board of Trustees shall require each employee upon enrolling in the retirement system to provide information on the membership application concerning any mental or physical incapacities existing at the time the member enrolls.

Supplemental disability benefits heretofore provided are hereby made a permanent part of disability benefits after age 65, and shall not be discontinued at age 65.

Notwithstanding the requirement of five or more years of creditable service to the contrary, a member who is a law-enforcement officer and who has had one year or more of creditable service and becomes incapacitated for duty as the natural and proximate result of an accident occurring while in the actual performance of duty, and meets all other requirements for disability retirement benefits, may be retired by the Board of Trustees on a disability retirement allowance.

Notwithstanding the foregoing to the contrary, any beneficiary who commenced retirement with an early or service retirement benefit has the right, within three years of his retirement, to convert to an allowance with disability retirement benefits without modification of any election of optional allowance previously made; provided, the beneficiary presents clear and convincing evidence that the beneficiary would have met all applicable requirements for disability retirement benefits while still in service as a member. The allowance on account of disability retirement benefits to the beneficiary shall be retroactive to the effective date of early or service retirement.

Notwithstanding the foregoing, the surviving designated beneficiary of a deceased member who met all other requirements for disability retirement benefits, except whose death occurred before the first day of the calendar month in which the member's disability retirement allowance was to be due and payable, may elect to receive the reduced retirement allowance provided by a one hundred percent (100%) joint and survivor payment option in lieu of a return of accumulated contributions, provided the following conditions apply:

(1) At the time of the member's death, one and only one beneficiary is eligible to receive a return of accumulated contributions, and

(2) The member had not instructed the Board of Trustees in writing that he did not wish the provision of this subsection to apply.

(d) Allowance on Disability Retirement of Persons Retiring on or after July 1, 1959, but prior to July 1, 1963. - Upon retirement for disability, in accordance with subsection (c) above, on or after July 1, 1959, but prior to July 1, 1963, a member shall receive a service retirement allowance if he has attained the age of 60 years, otherwise he shall receive a disability retirement allowance which shall consist of:

(1) An annuity which shall be the actuarial equivalent of his accumulated contributions at the time of retirement;

(2) A pension equal to seventy-five per centum (75%) of the pension that would have been payable upon service retirement at the age of 65 years had the member continued in service to the age of 65 years without further change in compensation.

If the member has not less than 20 years of creditable service, he shall be entitled to a total retirement allowance of not less than seventy dollars ($70.00) per month; provided, that the computation shall be made prior to any reduction resulting from an optional allowance as provided by subsection (g) of this section.

(d1) Allowance on Disability Retirement of Persons Retiring on or after July 1, 1963, but prior to July 1, 1969. - Upon retirement for disability, in accordance with subsection (c) above, on or after July 1, 1963, but prior to July 1, 1969, a member shall receive a service retirement allowance if he has attained the age of 60 years, otherwise he shall receive a disability retirement allowance which shall be computed as follows:

(1) Such allowance shall be equal to the service retirement allowance which would have been payable had he continued in service without further change in compensation, to the age of 60 years, minus the actuarial equivalent to the contributions he would have made during such continued service.

(2) Notwithstanding the foregoing provisions, any member whose creditable service commenced prior to July 1, 1963, shall receive not less than the benefit provided by G.S. 135-5(d).

(d2) Allowance on Disability Retirement of Persons Retiring on or after July 1, 1969, but prior to July 1, 1971. - Upon retirement for disability, in accordance with subsection (c) above, on or after July 1, 1969, but prior to July 1, 1971, a member shall receive a service retirement allowance if he has attained the age of 60 years, otherwise he shall receive a disability retirement allowance which shall be computed as follows:

(1) Such allowance shall be equal to the service retirement allowance which would have been payable had he continued in service without further change in compensation to the age of 65 years, minus the actuarial equivalent of the contributions he would have made during such continued service.

(2) Notwithstanding the foregoing provisions, any member whose creditable service commenced prior to July 1, 1963, shall receive not less than the benefit provided by G.S. 135-5(d).

(d3) Allowance on Disability Retirement of Persons Retiring on or after July 1, 1971, but prior to July 1, 1982. - Upon retirement for disability, in accordance with subsection (c) of this section on or after July 1, 1971, but prior to July 1, 1982, a member shall receive a service retirement allowance if he has attained the age of 65 years; otherwise he shall receive a disability retirement allowance which shall be computed as follows:

(1) Such allowance shall be equal to a service retirement allowance calculated on the basis of the member's average final compensation prior to his disability retirement and the creditable service he would have had at the age of 65 years if he had continued in service.

(2) Notwithstanding the foregoing provisions,

a. Any member whose creditable service commenced prior to July 1, 1971, shall receive not less than the benefit provided by G.S. 135-5(d2);

b. The amount of disability allowance payable from the reserve funds of the Retirement System to any member retiring on or after July 1, 1974, who is eligible for and in receipt of a disability benefit under the Social Security Act shall be seventy percent (70%) of the amount calculated under a above, and the balance shall be provided by the employer from time to time during each year in such amounts as may be required to cover such payments as current disbursements; and

c. The amount of disability allowance payable to any member retiring on or after July 1, 1974, who is not eligible for and in receipt of a disability benefit under the Social Security Act shall not be payable from the reserve funds of the Retirement System but shall be provided by the employer from time to time during each year in such amounts as may be required to cover such payments as current disbursements.

(d4) Allowance on Disability Retirement of Persons Retiring on or after July 1, 1982, Who Left Service prior to January 1, 1988. - Upon retirement for disability, in accordance with subsection (c) of this section on or after July 1, 1982, a member who left service prior to January 1, 1988 shall receive a service retirement allowance if he has qualified for an unreduced service retirement allowance; otherwise the allowance shall be equal to a service retirement allowance calculated on the member's average final compensation prior to his disability retirement and the creditable service he would have had had he continued in service until the earliest date on which he would have qualified for an unreduced service retirement allowance.

(e) Reexamination of Beneficiaries Retired for Disability. - The provisions of this subsection shall be applicable to members retired on a disability retirement allowance and shall not be applicable to members in service on or after January 1, 1988. Once each year during the first five years following retirement of a member on a disability retirement allowance, and once in every three-year period thereafter, the Board of Trustees may, and upon his application shall, require any disability beneficiary who has not yet attained the age of 60 years to undergo a medical examination, such examination to be made at the place of residence of said beneficiary or other place mutually agreed upon, by a physician or physicians designated by the Board of Trustees. Should any disability beneficiary who has not yet attained the age of 60 years refuse to submit to at least one medical examination in any such year by a physician or physicians designated by the Board of Trustees, his allowance may be discontinued until his withdrawal of such refusal, and should his refusal continue for one year all his rights in and to his pension may be revoked by the Board of Trustees.

(1) The Board of Trustees shall determine whether a disability beneficiary is engaged in or is able to engage in a gainful occupation paying more than the difference, as hereinafter indexed, between his disability retirement allowance and the gross compensation earned as an employee during the 12 consecutive months of service in the final 48 months prior to retirement producing the highest gross compensation excluding any compensation received on account of termination. If the disability beneficiary is earning or is able to earn more than the difference, the portion of his disability retirement allowance not provided by his contributions shall be reduced to an amount which, together with the portion of the disability retirement allowance provided by his contributions and the amount earnable by him shall equal the amount of his gross compensation prior to retirement. This difference shall be increased on January 1 each year by the ratio of the Consumer Price Index to the Index one year earlier, calculated to the nearest tenth of one percent (1/10th of 1%). Should the earning capacity of the disability beneficiary later change, the portion of his disability retirement allowance not provided by his contributions may be further modified. In lieu of the reductions on account of a disability beneficiary earning more than the aforesaid difference, he may elect to convert his disability retirement allowance to a service retirement allowance calculated on the basis of his average final compensation and creditable service at the time of disability and his age at the time of conversion to service retirement. This election is irrevocable. Provided, the provisions of this subdivision shall not apply to beneficiaries of the Law-Enforcement Officers' Retirement System transferred to this Retirement System who commenced retirement on and before July 1, 1981.

(2) Should a disability beneficiary under the age of 60 years be restored to active service at a compensation not less than his average final compensation, his retirement allowance shall cease, he shall again become a member of the Retirement System, and he shall contribute thereafter at the same rate he paid

prior to disability; provided that, on and after July 1, 1971, if a disability beneficiary under the age of 62 years is restored to active service at a compensation not less than his average final compensation, his retirement allowance shall cease, he shall again become a member of the Retirement System, and he shall contribute thereafter at the uniform contribution rate payable by all members. Any such prior service certificate on the basis of which his service was computed at the time of his retirement shall be restored to full force and effect, and, in addition, upon his subsequent retirement he shall be credited with all his service as a member, but should he be restored to active service on or after the attainment of the age of 50 years his pension upon subsequent retirement shall not exceed the sum of the pension which he was receiving immediately prior to his last restoration and the pension that he would have received on account of his service since his last restoration had he entered service at the time as a new entrant.

(3)   Notwithstanding the foregoing, a member retired on a disability retirement allowance who is restored to service and subsequently retires on or after July 1, 1971, shall be entitled to an allowance not less than the allowance described in a. below reduced by the amount in b. below:

a.   The allowance to which he would have been entitled if he were retiring for the first time, calculated on the basis of his total creditable service represented by the sum of his creditable service at the time of his first retirement and his creditable service after he was restored to service.

b.   The actuarial equivalent of the retirement benefits he previously received.

(3a)   Notwithstanding the foregoing, should a beneficiary who retired on a disability retirement allowance be restored to service as an employee or teacher, then the retirement allowance shall cease as of the first day of the month following the month in which the beneficiary is restored to service and the beneficiary shall become a member of the Retirement System and shall contribute thereafter as allowed by law at the uniform contribution payable by all members. Upon the subsequent retirement of the beneficiary, he shall be entitled to an allowance to which he would have been entitled if he were retiring for the first time, calculated on the basis of his total creditable service represented by the sum of his creditable service at the time of his first retirement and his creditable service after he was restored to service. Provided, however, any election of an optional allowance cannot be changed unless the member subsequently completes three years of membership service after being restored to service.

(4)   As a condition to the receipt of the disability retirement allowance provided for in G.S. 135-5(d), (d1),(d2) and (d3) each member retired on a disability retirement allowance shall, on or before April 15 of each calendar year, provide the Board of Trustees with a statement of his or her income received as compensation for services, including fees, commissions or similar items, and income received from business, for the previous calendar year. Such statement shall be filed on a form as required by the Board of Trustees. The benefit payable to a beneficiary who does not or refuses to provide the information requested within 60 days after such request shall not be paid a benefit until the information so requested is provided, and should such refusal or failure to provide such information continue for 240 days after such request, the right of a beneficiary to a benefit under the Article may be terminated.

The Director of the State Retirement System shall contact any State or federal agency which can provide information to substantiate the statement required to be submitted by this subdivision and may enter into agreements for the exchange of information.

(5)   Notwithstanding any other provisions of this Article to the contrary, a beneficiary who was a beneficiary retired on a disability retirement with the Law-Enforcement Officers' Retirement System at the time of the transfer of law-enforcement officers employed by a participating employer and beneficiaries last employed by a participating employer to this Retirement System and who also was a contributing member of this Retirement System at that time, shall continue to be paid his retirement allowance without restriction and may continue as a member of this Retirement System with all the rights and privileges appendant to membership. Any beneficiary who retired on a disability retirement allowance as an employee of any participating employer under the Law-Enforcement Officers' Retirement System and becomes employed as an employee other than as a law-enforcement officer by an employer participating in the Retirement System after the aforementioned transfer shall continue to be paid his retirement allowance without restriction and may continue as a member of this Retirement System with all the rights and privileges appendant to membership until January 1, 1989, at which time his retirement allowance shall cease and his subsequent retirement shall be determined in accordance with the preceding subdivision (3a) of this subsection. Any beneficiary as hereinbefore described who becomes employed as a law-enforcement officer by an employer participating in the Retirement System shall cease to be a

beneficiary and shall immediately commence membership and his subsequent retirement shall be determined in accordance with subdivision (3a) of this subsection.

(6) Notwithstanding any other provision to the contrary, a beneficiary in receipt of a disability retirement allowance until the earliest date on which he would have qualified for an unreduced service retirement allowance shall thereafter (i) not be subject to further reexaminations as to disability, (ii) not be subject to any reduction in allowance on account of being engaged in a gainful occupation other than with an employer participating in the Retirement System, and (iii) be considered a beneficiary in receipt of a service retirement allowance. Provided, however, a beneficiary in receipt of a disability retirement allowance whose allowance is reduced on account of reexamination as to disability or to ability to engage in a gainful occupation prior to the date on which he would have qualified for an unreduced service retirement allowance shall have only the right to elect to convert to an early or service retirement allowance as permitted under subdivision (1) above.

(f) Return of Accumulated Contributions. - Should a member cease to be a teacher or State employee except by death or retirement under the provisions of this Chapter, he shall upon submission of an application be paid, not earlier than 60 days from the date of termination of service, his contributions, and if he has attained at least five years of membership service or if termination of his membership service is involuntary as certified by the employer, the accumulated regular interest thereon, provided that he has not in the meantime returned to service. Upon payment of such sum his membership in the System shall cease and, if he thereafter again becomes a member, no credit shall be allowed for any service previously rendered except as provided in G.S. 135-4, and such payment shall be in full and complete discharge of any rights in or to any benefits otherwise payable hereunder. Upon receipt of proof satisfactory to the Board of Trustees of the death, prior to retirement, of a member or former member there shall be paid to such person or persons as he shall have nominated by electronic submission prior to completing 10 years of service in a form approved by the Board of Trustees or by written designation duly acknowledged and filed with the Board of Trustees, if such person or persons are living at the time of the member's death, otherwise to the member's legal representatives, the amount of his accumulated contributions at the time of his death, unless the beneficiary elects to receive the alternate benefit under the provisions of (m) below. An extension service employee who made contributions to the Local Governmental Employees' Retirement System and the Teachers' and State Employees' Retirement System as a result of dual employment may not be paid his accumulated contributions unless he is eligible to be paid his accumulated contributions in both systems for the same period of service.

Pursuant to the provisions of G.S. 135-56.2, a member who is also a member of the Consolidated Judicial Retirement System may irrevocably elect to transfer any accumulated contributions to the Consolidated Judicial Retirement System or to the Supplemental Retirement Income Plan and forfeit any rights in or to any benefits otherwise payable hereunder.

A member who is a participant or beneficiary of the Disability Income Plan of North Carolina as is provided in Article 6 of this Chapter shall not be paid a return of accumulated contributions, notwithstanding the member's status as an employee or teacher. Notwithstanding any other provision of law to the contrary, a member who is a beneficiary of the Disability Income Plan of North Carolina as provided in Article 6 of this Chapter and who is receiving disability benefits under the transition provisions as provided in G.S. 135-112, shall not be prohibited from receiving a return of accumulated contributions as provided in this subsection.

(f1)   Expired.

(g)   (See Editor's note) Election of Optional Allowance. - With the provision that until the first payment on account of any benefit becomes normally due, or his first retirement check has been cashed, any member may elect to receive his benefits in a retirement allowance payable throughout life, or he may elect to receive the actuarial equivalent of such retirement allowance, including any special retirement allowance, in a reduced allowance payable throughout life under the provisions of one of the options set forth below. The election of Option 2, 3, or 6 or nomination of the person thereunder shall be revoked if such person nominated dies prior to the date the first payment becomes normally due or until the first retirement check has been cashed. Such election may be revoked by the member prior to the date the first payment becomes normally due or until his first retirement check has been cashed. Provided, however, in the event a member has elected Option 2, 3, or 5 and nominated his or her spouse to receive a retirement allowance upon the member's death, and the spouse predeceases the member after the first payment becomes normally due or the first retirement check has been cashed, if the member remarries he or she may request to nominate a new spouse to receive the retirement allowance under the previously elected option, within 90 days of the remarriage, and may nominate a new spouse to receive the retirement allowance under the previously elected option by written designation duly acknowledged and filed with the Board of Trustees within 120 days of the remarriage. The new nomination shall be effective on the first day of the month in which it is made and shall provide for a retirement allowance computed to be the actuarial equivalent of the retirement allowance in effect immediately prior to the effective date of the new nomination. Any member having elected Option 2, 3, 5, or 6 and nominated his or her spouse to receive a retirement allowance upon the member's death may, after divorce from his or her spouse, revoke the nomination and elect a new option, effective on the first day of the month in which the new option is elected, providing for a retirement allowance computed to be the actuarial equivalent of the retirement allowance in effect immediately prior to the effective date of the new option. Except as provided in this section, the member may not change the member's retirement benefit option or the member's designated beneficiary for survivor benefits, if any, after the member has cashed the first retirement check or after the 25th day of the month following the month in which the first check is mailed, whichever comes first.

Option 1.(a) In the Case of a Member Who Retires prior to July 1, 1963. - If he dies before he has received in annuity payments the present value of his annuity as it was at the time of his retirement, the balance shall be paid to his legal representatives or to such person as he shall nominate by written designation duly acknowledged and filed with the Board of Trustees.

(b) In the Case of a Member Who Retires on or after July 1, 1963, but prior to July 1, 1993. - If he dies within 10 years from his retirement date, an amount equal to his accumulated contributions at retirement, less 1/120 thereof for each month for which he has received a retirement allowance payment, shall be paid to his legal representatives or to such person as he shall nominate by written designation duly acknowledged and filed with the Board of Trustees; or

Option 2. Upon his death his reduced retirement allowance shall be continued throughout the life of and paid to such person as he shall nominate by written designation duly acknowledged and filed with the Board of Trustees at the time of his retirement, provided that if the person selected is other than his spouse the reduced retirement allowance payable to the member shall not be less than one half of the retirement allowance without optional modification which would otherwise be payable to him; or

Option 3. Upon his death, one half of his reduced retirement allowance shall be continued throughout the life of, and paid to such person as he shall nominate by written designation duly acknowledged and filed with the Board of Trustees at the time of his retirement; or

Option 4. Adjustment of Retirement Allowance for Social Security Benefits. - Until the first payment on account of any benefit becomes normally due, any member may elect to convert his benefit otherwise payable on his account after retirement into a retirement allowance of equivalent actuarial value of such amount that with his benefit under Title II of the Federal Social Security Act, he will receive, so far as possible, approximately the same amount per year before and after the earliest age at which he becomes eligible, upon application therefor, to receive a social security benefit.

Option 5. For Members Retiring Prior to July 1, 1993. - The member may elect to receive a reduced retirement allowance under the conditions of Option 2 or Option 3, as provided for above, with the modification that if both he and the person nominated die within 10 years from his retirement date, an amount equal to his accumulated contributions at retirement, less 1/120 thereof for each month for which a retirement allowance has been paid, shall be paid to his legal representatives or to such person as he shall nominate by written designation duly acknowledged and filed with the Board of Trustees.

Option 6. A member may elect either Option 2 or Option 3 with the added provision that in the event the designated beneficiary predeceases the member, the retirement allowance payable to the member after the designated beneficiary's death shall be equal to the retirement allowance which would have been payable had the member not elected the option.

Upon the death of a member after the effective date of a retirement for which the member has been approved and following receipt by the Board of Trustees of an election of benefits (Form 6-E or Form 7-E) but prior to the cashing of the first benefit check, the retirement benefit shall be payable as provided by the member's election of benefits under this subsection.

Upon the death of a member after the effective date of a retirement for which the member has been approved but prior to the receipt by the Board of Trustees of an election of benefits (Form 6-E or Form 7-E), properly acknowledged and filed by the member, the member's designated beneficiary for a return of accumulated contributions may elect to receive the benefit, if only one beneficiary is eligible to receive the return of accumulated contributions. If more than one beneficiary is eligible to receive the return of accumulated contributions, the administrator or executor of the member's estate will select an option and name the beneficiary or beneficiaries. (See editor's note.)

(g1) In the event of the death of a retired member while in receipt of a retirement allowance under the provisions of this Article, there shall be paid to such person or persons as the retiree shall have nominated by electronic submission in a form approved by the Board of Trustees or by written designation duly acknowledged and filed with the Board of Trustees, if such person or persons are living at the time of the retiree's death, otherwise to the retiree's legal representatives, a death benefit equal to the excess, if any, of the accumulated contributions of the retiree at the date of retirement over the total of the retirement allowances paid prior to the death of the retiree. In the event that a retiree is receiving a Special Retirement Allowance under subsection (m1) of this section, there shall be paid to such person or persons as the retiree shall have nominated by electronic submission in a form approved by the Board of Trustees or by written designation duly acknowledged and filed with the Board of Trustees, if such person or persons are living at the time of the retiree's death, otherwise to the retiree's legal representatives, an additional death benefit equal to the excess, if any, of the employee's voluntary contributions that were transferred from the Supplemental Retirement Income Plan of North Carolina or the North Carolina Public Employee Deferred Compensation Plan to this Retirement System over the total of the Special Retirement Allowances paid prior to the death of the retiree. For purposes of this paragraph, the term "accumulated contributions" excludes any amount transferred under subsection (m2) of this section.

In the event that a retirement allowance becomes payable to the designated survivor of a retired member under the provisions above and such retirement allowance to the survivor shall terminate upon the death of the survivor before the total of the retirement allowances paid to the retiree and the designated survivor combined equals the amount of the accumulated contributions of the retiree at the date of retirement, the excess, if any, of such accumulated contributions over the total of the retirement allowances paid to the retiree and the survivor combined shall be paid in a lump sum to such person or persons as the retiree shall have nominated by electronic submission in a form approved by the Board of Trustees or by written designation duly acknowledged and filed with the Board of Trustees, if such person or persons are living at the time such payment falls due, otherwise to the retiree's legal representative. For purposes of this paragraph, the term "accumulated contributions" includes amounts of employee voluntary contributions that were transferred from the Supplemental Retirement Income Plan of North Carolina to this Retirement System at retirement by eligible law enforcement officers.

In the event that a retirement allowance becomes payable to the principal beneficiary designated to receive a return of accumulated contributions pursuant to subsection (m) of this section and that beneficiary dies before the total of the retirement allowances paid equals the amount of the accumulated contributions of the member at the date of the member's death, the excess of those accumulated contributions over the total of the retirement allowances paid to the beneficiary shall be paid in a lump sum to the person or persons the member has designated as the contingent beneficiary for return of accumulated contributions, if the person or persons are living at the time the payment falls due, otherwise to the principal beneficiary's legal representative. For purposes of this paragraph, the term "accumulated contributions" includes amounts of employee voluntary contributions that were transferred from the Supplemental Retirement Income Plan of North Carolina to this Retirement System at retirement by eligible law enforcement officers.

In the event a retiree purchases creditable service as provided in G.S. 135-4, there shall be paid to such person or persons as the retiree shall have nominated by electronic submission in a form approved by the Board of Trustees or by written designation duly acknowledged and filed with the Board of Trustees, if such person or persons are living at the time of the retiree's death, otherwise to the retiree's legal representatives, an additional death benefit equal to the excess, if any, of the cost of the creditable service purchased less the administrative fee, if any, over the total of the increase in the retirement allowance attributable to the additional creditable service, paid from the month following the month in which payment was received to the death of the retiree.

In the event that a retirement allowance becomes payable to the designated survivor of a retired member under the provisions above and such retirement allowance to the survivor shall terminate upon the death of the survivor before the total of the increase in the retirement allowance attributable to the additional creditable service paid to the retiree and the designated survivor combined equals the cost of the creditable service purchased less the administrative fee, the excess, if any, shall be paid in a lump sum to such person or persons as the retiree shall have nominated by electronic submission in a form approved by the Board of Trustees or by written designation duly acknowledged and filed with the Board of Trustees, if such person or persons are living at the time such payment falls due, otherwise to the retiree's legal representative.

In the event that a retiree dies without having designated a beneficiary to receive a benefit under the provisions of this subsection, any such benefit that becomes payable shall be paid to the member's estate.

(h) Computation of Benefits Payable Prior or Subsequent to July 1, 1947. - Prior to July 1, 1947, all benefits payable as of February 22, 1945, shall be computed on the basis of the provisions of Chapter 135 as they existed at the time of the retirement of such beneficiaries. On and after July 1, 1947, all benefits payable to, or on account of, such beneficiaries shall be adjusted to take into account, under such rule as the Board of Trustees may adopt, the provisions of this Article as if they had been in effect at the date of retirement, and no further contributions on account of such adjustment shall be required of such beneficiaries. The Board of Trustees may authorize such transfers of reserve between the funds of the Retirement System as may be required by the provisions of this subsection.

(i) Restoration to Service of Certain Former Members. - If a former member who ceased to be a member prior to July 1, 1949, for any reason other than retirement, again becomes a member and prior to July 1, 1951, redeposits in the annuity savings fund by a single payment the amount, if any, he previously withdrew therefrom, he shall, anything in this Chapter to the contrary, be entitled to any membership service credits he had when his membership ceased, and any prior service certificate which became void at the time his membership ceased shall be restored to full force and effect: Provided, that, for the purpose of computing the amount of any retirement allowance which may become payable to or on account of such member under the Retirement System, any amount redeposited as provided herein shall be deemed to represent contributions made by the member after July 1, 1947.

(j) Notwithstanding anything herein to the contrary, effective July 1, 1959, the following provisions shall apply with respect to any retirement allowance payments due after such date to any retired member who was retired prior to July 1, 1959, on a service or disability retirement allowance:

(1) If such retired member has not made an election of an optional allowance in accordance with G.S. 135-5(g), the monthly retirement allowance payable to him from and after July 1, 1959, shall be equal to the allowance previously payable, increased by fifteen percent (15%) thereof, or by fifteen dollars ($15.00), whichever is the lesser; provided that, if such member had rendered not less than 20 years of creditable service, the retirement allowance

payable to him from and after July 1, 1959, shall be not less than seventy dollars ($70.00) per month.

(2) If such retired member has made an effective election of an optional allowance, the allowance payable to him from and after July 1, 1959, shall be equal to the allowance previously payable under such election plus an increase which shall be computed in accordance with (1) above as if he had not made such an election; provided that such increase shall be payable only during the retired member's remaining life and no portion of such increase shall become payable to the beneficiary designated under the election.

(k) Increase in Benefits to Those Persons Who Were in Receipt of Benefits prior to July 1, 1967. - From and after July 1, 1967, the monthly benefits to or on account of persons who commenced receiving benefits from the System prior to July 1, 1967, shall be increased by a percentage thereof. Such percentage shall be determined in accordance with the following schedule:

Period in Which Benefits Commenced	Percentage
January 1, 1966, to June 30, 1967	5%
Year 1965	6%
Year 1964	7%
Year 1963	8%

and so on concluding with

Year 1942	29%

The minimum increase pursuant to this subsection (k) shall be ten dollars ($10.00) per month; provided that, if an optional benefit has been elected, said minimum shall be reduced actuarially as determined by the Board and shall be applicable to the retired member, if surviving, otherwise to his designated beneficiary under the option elected.

(l) Death Benefit Plan. - There is hereby created a Group Life Insurance Plan (hereinafter called the "Plan") which is established as an employee welfare benefit plan that is separate and apart from the Retirement System and under which the members of the Retirement System shall participate and be eligible for group life insurance benefits. Upon receipt of proof, satisfactory to the Board of Trustees in their capacity as trustees under the Group Life Insurance Plan, of the death, in service, of a member who had completed at least one full calendar year of membership in the Retirement System, there shall be paid to such person as he shall have nominated by electronic submission prior to completing 10 years of service in a form approved by the Board of Trustees or by written designation duly acknowledged and filed with the Board of Trustees, if such person is living at the time of the member's death, otherwise to the member's legal representatives, a death benefit. Such death benefit shall be equal to the greater of:

(1) The compensation on which contributions were made by the member during the calendar year preceding the year in which his death occurs, or

(2) The greatest compensation on which contributions were made by the member during a 12-month period of service within the 24-month period of service ending on the last day of the month preceding the month in which his last day of actual service occurs;

(3), (4) Repealed by Session Laws 1983 (Regular Session, 1984), c. 1049, s. 2.

subject to a minimum of twenty-five thousand dollars ($25,000) and to a maximum of fifty thousand dollars ($50,000). Such death benefit shall be payable apart and separate from the payment of the member's accumulated contributions under the System on his death pursuant to the provisions of subsection (f) of this section. For the purpose of the Plan, a member shall be deemed to be in service at the date of his death if his death occurs within 180 days from the last day of his actual service.

The death benefit provided in this subsection (l) shall not be payable, notwithstanding the member's compliance with all the conditions set forth in the preceding paragraph, if his death occurs

(1) After December 31, 1968 and after he has attained age 70; or

(2) After December 31, 1969 and after he has attained age 69; or

(3) After December 31, 1970 and after he has attained age 68; or

(4) After December 31, 1971 and after he has attained age 67; or

(5) After December 31, 1972 and after he has attained age 66; or

(6) After December 31, 1973 and after he has attained age 65; or

(7) After December 31, 1978, but before January 1, 1987, and after he has attained age 70.

Notwithstanding the above provisions, the death benefit shall be payable on account of the death of any member who died or dies on or after January 1, 1974, but before January 1, 1979, after attaining age 65, if he or she had not yet attained age 65, if he or she had not yet attained age 66, was at the time of death completing the work year for those individuals under specific contract, or during the fiscal year for those individuals not under specific contract, in which he or she attained 65, and otherwise met all conditions for payment of the death benefit.

Notwithstanding the above provisions, the Board of Trustees may and is specifically authorized to provide the death benefit according to the terms and conditions otherwise appearing in this Plan in the form of group life insurance, either (i) by purchasing a contract or contracts of group life insurance with any life insurance company or companies licensed and authorized to transact business in this State for the purpose of insuring the lives of members in service, or (ii) by establishing a separate trust fund qualified under Section 501(c)(9) of the Internal Revenue Code of 1954, as amended, for such purpose. To that end the Board of Trustees is authorized, empowered and directed to investigate the desirability of utilizing group life insurance by either of the foregoing methods for the purpose of providing the death benefit. If a separate trust fund is established, it shall be operated in accordance with rules and regulations adopted by the Board of Trustees and all investment earnings on the trust fund shall be credited to such fund.

In administration of the death benefit the following shall apply:

(1) For the purpose of determining eligibility only, in this subsection "calendar year" shall mean any period of 12 consecutive months or, if less, the period covered by an annual contract of employment. For all other purposes in this subsection "calendar year" shall mean the 12 months beginning January 1 and ending December 31.

(2) Last day of actual service shall be:

a. When employment has been terminated, the last day the member actually worked.

b. When employment has not been terminated, the date on which an absent member's sick and annual leave expire, unless he is on approved leave of absence and is in service under the provisions of G.S. 135-4(h).

c. When a participant's employment is interrupted by reason of service in the Uniformed Services, as that term is defined in section 4303(16) of the Uniformed Services Employment and Reemployment Rights Act, Public Law 103-353, and the participant does not return immediately after that service to employment with a covered employer in this System, the date on which the participant was first eligible to be separated or released from his or her involuntary military service.

(3) For a period when a member is on leave of absence, his status with respect to the death benefit will be determined by the provisions of G.S. 135-4(h).

(4) A member on leave of absence from his position as a teacher or State employee for the purpose of serving as a member or officer of the General Assembly shall be deemed to be in service during sessions of the General Assembly and thereby covered by the provisions of the death benefit. The amount of the death benefit for such member shall be the equivalent of the salary to which the member would have been entitled as a teacher or State employee during the 12-month period immediately prior to the month in which death occurred, not to be less than twenty-five thousand dollars ($25,000) nor to exceed fifty thousand dollars ($50,000).

The provisions of the Retirement System pertaining to Administration, G.S. 135-6, and management of funds, G.S. 135-7, are hereby made applicable to the Plan.

A member who is a beneficiary of the Disability Income Plan provided for in Article 6 of this Chapter, or a member who is in receipt of Workers' Compensation during the period for which he or she would have otherwise been eligible to receive short-term benefits or extended short-term benefits as provided in G.S. 135-105 and dies on or after 181 days from the last day of his or her actual service but prior to the date the benefits as provided in G.S. 135-105 would have ended, shall be eligible for group life insurance benefits as provided in this subsection, notwithstanding that the member is no longer an employee or teacher or that the member's death occurs after the eligibility period after active service. The basis of the death benefit payable hereunder shall be the higher of the death benefit computed as above or a death benefit based on compensation used in computing the benefit payable under G.S. 135-105 and G.S. 135-106, as may be adjusted for percentage post-disability increases, all subject to the maximum dollar limitation as provided above. A member in receipt of benefits from the Disability Income Plan under the provisions of G.S. 135-112 whose right to a benefit accrued under the former Disability Salary Continuation Plan shall not be covered under the provisions of this paragraph.

Upon receipt of proof, satisfactory to the Board of Trustees in its capacity under this subsection, of the death of a retired member of the Retirement System on or after July 1, 1988, but before January 1, 1999, there shall be paid a death benefit to the surviving spouse of the deceased retired member or to the deceased retired member's legal representative if not survived by a spouse; provided the retired member has elected, when first eligible, to make, and has continuously made, in advance of his death required contributions as determined by the Board of Trustees on a fully contributory basis, through retirement allowance deductions or other methods adopted by the Board of Trustees, to a group death benefit trust fund administered by the Board of Trustees separate and apart from the Retirement System's Annuity Savings Fund and Pension Accumulation Fund. This death benefit shall be a lump-sum payment in the amount of five thousand dollars ($5,000) upon the completion of twenty-four months of contributions required under this subsection. Should death occur before the completion of twenty-four months of contributions required under this subsection, the deceased retired member's surviving spouse or legal representative if not survived by a spouse shall be paid the sum of the retired member's contributions required by this subsection plus interest to be determined by the Board of Trustees.

Upon receipt of proof, satisfactory to the Board of Trustees in its capacity under this subsection, of the death of a retired member of the Retirement System on or after January 1, 1999, but before July 1, 2004, there shall be paid a death benefit to the surviving spouse of the deceased retired member or to the deceased retired member's legal representative if not survived by a spouse; provided the retired member has elected, when first eligible, to make, and has continuously made, in advance of his death required contributions as determined by the Board of Trustees on a fully contributory basis, through retirement allowance deductions or other methods adopted by the Board of Trustees, to a group death benefit trust fund administered by the Board of

Trustees separate and apart from the Retirement System's Annuity Savings Fund and Pension Accumulation Fund. This death benefit shall be a lump-sum payment in the amount of six thousand dollars ($6,000) upon the completion of 24 months of contributions required under this subsection. Should death occur before the completion of 24 months of contributions required under this subsection, the deceased retired member's surviving spouse or legal representative if not survived by a spouse shall be paid the sum of the retired member's contributions required by this subsection plus interest to be determined by the Board of Trustees.

Upon receipt of proof, satisfactory to the Board of Trustees in its capacity under this subsection, of the death of a retired member of the Retirement System on or after July 1, 2004, but before July 1, 2007, there shall be paid a death benefit to the surviving spouse of the deceased retired member or to the deceased retired member's legal representative if not survived by a spouse; provided the retired member has elected, when first eligible, to make, and has continuously made, in advance of his death required contributions as determined by the Board of Trustees on a fully contributory basis, through retirement allowance deductions or other methods adopted by the Board of Trustees, to a group death benefit trust fund administered by the Board of Trustees Fund and Pension Accumulation Fund. This death benefit shall be a lump-sum payment in the amount of nine thousand dollars ($9,000) upon the completion of 24 months of contributions required under this subsection. Should death occur before the completion of 24 months of contributions required under this subsection, the deceased retired member's surviving spouse or legal representative if not survived by a spouse shall be paid the sum of the retired member's contributions required by this subsection plus interest to be determined by the Board of Trustees.

Upon receipt of proof, satisfactory to the Board of Trustees in its capacity under this subsection, of the death of a retired member of the Retirement System on or after July 1, 2007, there shall be paid a death benefit to the surviving spouse of the deceased retired member or to the deceased retired member's legal representative if not survived by a spouse; provided the retired member has elected, when first eligible, to make, and has continuously made, in advance of his death required contributions as determined by the Board of Trustees on a fully contributory basis, through retirement allowance deductions or other methods adopted by the Board of Trustees, to a group death benefit trust fund administered by the Board of Trustees Fund and Pension Accumulation Fund. This death benefit shall be a lump-sum payment in the amount of ten thousand dollars ($10,000) upon the completion of 24 months of contributions required under this subsection. Should death occur before the completion of 24 months of contributions required under this subsection, the deceased retired member's surviving spouse or legal representative if not survived by a spouse shall be paid the sum of the retired member's contributions required by this subsection plus interest to be determined by the Board of Trustees.

(l1)   Reciprocity of Death Benefit Plan. - Only for the purpose of determining eligibility for the death benefit provided for in subsection (l) of this section, membership service standing to the credit of a member of the Legislative Retirement System or the Consolidated Judicial Retirement System shall be added to the membership service standing to the credit of a member of the Teachers' and State Employees' Retirement System. However, in the event that a participant or beneficiary is a retired member of the Legislative Retirement System or the Consolidated Judicial Retirement System whose retirement benefit was suspended upon entrance into membership in the Teachers' and State Employees' Retirement System, such membership service standing to the credit of the retired member prior to retirement shall be likewise counted. Membership service under this section shall not be counted twice for the same period of time. In no event shall a death benefit provided for in G.S. 135-5(l) be paid if a death benefit is paid under G.S. 135-63.

(m)   Survivor's Alternate Benefit. - Upon the death of a member in service, who became a member prior to August 1, 2011, the beneficiary designated to receive a return of accumulated contributions shall have the right to elect to receive in lieu thereof the reduced retirement allowance provided by Option 2 of subsection (g) above computed by assuming that the member had retired on the first day of the month following the date of his death, provided that all four of the following conditions apply:

(1)   a.   The member had attained such age and/or creditable service to be eligible to commence retirement with an early or service retirement allowance, or

b.   The member had obtained 20 years of creditable service in which case the retirement allowance shall be computed in accordance with G.S. 135-5(b19)(1)b. or G.S. 135-5(b19)(2)c., notwithstanding the requirement of obtaining age 50, or

b1.   The member was a law enforcement officer who had obtained 15 years of service as a law enforcement officer and was killed in the line of duty, in which case the retirement allowance shall be computed in accordance with G.S. 135-5(b19)(1)b., notwithstanding the requirement of obtaining age 50.

c. Repealed by Session Laws 2010-72, s. 2(a), effective July 1, 2010.

(2) At the time of the member's death, one and only one beneficiary is eligible to receive a return of his accumulated contributions.

(3) The member had not instructed the Board of Trustees in writing that he did not wish the provisions of this subsection to apply.

(4) The member had not commenced to receive a retirement allowance as provided under this Chapter.

For the purpose of this benefit, a member is considered to be in service at the date of his death if his death occurs within 180 days from the last day of his actual service. The last day of actual service shall be determined as provided in subsection (l) of this section. Upon the death of a member in service, the surviving spouse may make all purchases for creditable service as provided for under this Chapter for which the member had made application in writing prior to the date of death, provided that the date of death occurred prior to or within 60 days after notification of the cost to make the purchase. The term "in service" as used in this subsection includes a member in receipt of a benefit under the Disability Income Plan as provided in Article 6 of this Chapter.

Notwithstanding the foregoing, a member who is in receipt of Workers' Compensation during the period for which the member would have otherwise been eligible to receive short-term benefits, as provided in G.S. 135-105, and who dies on or after 181 days from the last day of the member's actual service but on or before the date the benefits as provided in G.S. 135-105 would have ended, shall be considered in service at the time of the member's death for the purpose of this benefit.

For the purpose of calculating this benefit any terminal payouts made after the date of death that meet the definition of compensation shall be credited to the month prior to the month of death. These terminal payouts do not include salary or wages paid for work performed during the month of death.

(m1) Special Retirement Allowance for Law Enforcement Officers. - Upon retirement, a member who is a law enforcement officer vested as of June 30, 2010, may elect to transfer any portion of his eligible accumulated contributions, not including any Roth after-tax contributions and the earnings thereon, from the Supplemental Retirement Income Plan of North Carolina to this Retirement System and receive, in addition to his basic service, early or disability retirement allowance, a special retirement allowance which shall be based upon his eligible accumulated account balance at the date of the transfer of the assets to this System. For the purpose of determining the special retirement allowance, the Board of Trustees shall adopt straight life annuity factors on the basis of mortality tables, such other tables as may be necessary and the interest assumption rate recommended by the actuary based upon actual experience including an assumed annual post-retirement allowance increase of four percent (4%). The Board of Trustees shall modify such factors every five years, as shall be deemed necessary, based upon the five year experience study as required by G.S. 135-6(n). Provided, however, a member, who transfers his eligible accumulated contributions from the Supplemental Retirement Income Plan of North Carolina, shall be taxed for North Carolina State Income tax purposes on the special retirement allowance the same as if that special retirement allowance had been paid directly by the Supplemental Retirement Income Plan of North Carolina. The Teachers' and State Employees' Retirement System shall be responsible to determine the taxable amount, if any, and report accordingly.

(m2) Special Retirement Allowance. - At any time coincident with or following retirement, a member may make a one-time election to transfer any portion of the member's eligible accumulated contributions, not including any Roth after-tax contributions and the earnings thereon, from the Supplemental Retirement Income Plan of North Carolina or the North Carolina Public Employee Deferred Compensation Plan to this Retirement System and receive, in addition to the member's basic service, early or disability retirement allowance, a special retirement allowance which shall be based upon the member's transferred balance.

A member who became a member of the Supplemental Retirement Income Plan prior to retirement and who remains a member of the Supplemental Retirement Income Plan may make a one-time election to transfer eligible balances, not including any Roth after-tax contributions and the earnings thereon, from any of the following plans to the Supplemental Retirement Income Plan, subject to the applicable requirements of the Supplemental Retirement Income Plan, and then through the Supplemental Retirement Income Plan to this Retirement System:

(1) A plan participating in the North Carolina Public School Teachers' and Professional Educators' Investment Plan.

(2) A plan described in section 403(b) of the Internal Revenue Code.

(3) A plan described in section 457(b) of the Internal Revenue Code that is maintained by a state, political subdivision of a state, or any agency or instrumentality of a state or political subdivision of a state.

(4) An individual retirement account or annuity described in Section 408(a) or 408(b) of the Internal Revenue Code that is eligible to be rolled over and would otherwise be includible in gross income.

(5) A tax-qualified plan described in section 401(a) or 403(a) of the Internal Revenue Code.

Notwithstanding anything to the contrary, a member may not transfer such amounts as will cause the member's retirement allowance under the System to exceed the amount allowable under G.S. 135-18.7(b). The Board of Trustees may establish a minimum amount that must be transferred if a transfer is elected. The member may elect a special retirement allowance with no postretirement increases or a special retirement allowance with annual postretirement increases equal to the annual increase in the U.S. Consumer Price Index. Postretirement increases on any other allowance will not apply to the special retirement allowance. The Board of Trustees shall provide educational materials to the members who apply for the transfer authorized by this section. Those materials shall describe the special retirement allowance and shall explain (i) the relationship between the transferred balance and the monthly benefit; and (ii) how the member's heirs may be impacted by the election to make this transfer and any costs and fees involved.

For the purpose of determining the special retirement allowance, the Board of Trustees shall adopt straight life annuity factors on the basis of yields on U.S. Treasury Bonds and mortality and such other tables as may be necessary based upon actual experience. A single set of mortality and such other tables will be used for all members, with factors differing only based on the age of the member and the election of postretirement increases. The Board of Trustees shall modify the mortality and such other tables every five years, as shall be deemed necessary, based upon the five-year experience study as required by G.S. 135-6(n). Provided, however, a member who transfers the member's eligible accumulated contributions from an eligible retirement plan pursuant to this subsection to this Retirement System shall be taxed for North Carolina State Income Tax purposes on the special retirement allowance the same as if that special retirement allowance had been paid directly by the eligible plan or the plan through which the transfer was made, whichever is most favorable to the member. The Teachers' and State Employees' Retirement System shall be responsible to determine the taxable amount, if any, and report accordingly.

The Supplemental Retirement Board of Trustees established under G.S. 135-96 may assess a one-time flat administrative fee not to exceed the actual cost of the administrative expenses relating to these transfers. An eligible plan shall not assess a fee specifically relating to a transfer of accumulated contributions authorized under this subsection. This provision shall not prohibit other fees that may be assessable under the plan. Each plan, contract, account, or annuity shall fully disclose to any member participating in a transfer under this subsection any surrender charges or other fees, and such disclosure shall be made contemporaneous with the initiation of the transfer by the member.

The special retirement allowance shall continue for the life of the member and the beneficiary designated to receive a monthly survivorship benefit under Option 2, 3 or 6 as provided in G.S. 135-5(g), if any. The Board of Trustees, however, shall establish two payment options that guarantee payments as follows:

(1)   A member may elect to receive the special retirement allowance for life but with payments guaranteed for a number of months to be specified by the Board of Trustees. Under this plan, if the member dies before the expiration of the specified number of months, the special retirement allowance will continue to be paid to the member's designated beneficiary for the life of the beneficiary, if Option 2, 3 or 6 is selected. If Option 2, 3 or 6 is not selected, the member's designated beneficiary will receive the benefit only for the remainder of the specified number of months. If the member's designated beneficiary dies before receiving payments for the specified number of months, any remaining payments will be paid to the member's estate.

(2)   A member may elect to receive the special retirement allowance for life but is guaranteed that the sum of the special allowance payments will equal the total of the transferred amount. Under this payment option, if the member dies before receiving the total transferred amount, the special retirement allowance will continue to be paid to the member's designated beneficiary for the life of the beneficiary, if Option 2, 3 or 6 is selected. If Option 2, 3 or 6 is not selected, the member's designated beneficiary or the member's estate shall be paid any remaining balance of the transferred amount.

The Board of Trustees shall report annually to the Joint Legislative Commission on Governmental Operations on the number of persons who made an election in the previous calendar year, with any recommendations it might make on amendment or repeal based on any identified problems.

The General Assembly reserves the right to repeal or amend this subsection, but such repeal or amendment shall not affect any person who has already made the one-time election provided in this subsection.

(m3)   Survivor's Alternate Benefit. - Upon the death of a member in service who became a member on or after August 1, 2011, the principal beneficiary designated to receive a return of accumulated contributions shall have the right to elect to receive in lieu thereof the reduced retirement allowance provided by Option 2 of subsection (g) of this section computed by assuming that the member had retired on the first day of the month following the date of the member's death, provided that the following conditions apply:

(1)   The member had attained such age and/or creditable service to be eligible to commence retirement with an early or service retirement allowance.

b.   The member had obtained 20 years of creditable service in which case the retirement allowance shall be computed in accordance with G.S. 135-5(b20)(1)b. or G.S. 135-5(b20)(2)c., notwithstanding the requirement of obtaining age 50,

b1.   The member was a law enforcement officer who had attained 15 years of service as a law enforcement officer and was killed in the line of duty, in which case the retirement allowance shall be computed in accordance with G.S. 135-5(b20)(1)b., notwithstanding the requirement of attaining age 50.

c.   The member had not commenced to receive a retirement allowance as provided under this Chapter.

(2)   At the time of the member's death, one and only one person is eligible to receive a return of the member's contributions.

(3)   The member had not instructed the Board of Trustees in writing that the member did not wish the provisions of this subsection to apply.

For the purpose of this benefit, a member is considered to be in service at the date of the member's death if the member's death occurs within 180 days from the last day of the member's actual service. The last day of actual service shall be determined as provided in subdivision (1) of this subsection. Upon the death of a member in service, the surviving spouse may make all purchases for creditable service as provided for under this Chapter for which the member had made application in writing prior to the date of death, provided that the date of death occurred prior to or within 60 days after notification of the cost to make the purchase. The term, "in service" as used in this subsection, includes a member in receipt of a benefit under the Disability Income Plan as provided in Article 6 of this Chapter.

Notwithstanding the foregoing, a member who is in receipt of Workers' Compensation during the period for which the member would have otherwise been eligible to receive short-term benefits, as provided in G.S. 135-105, and who dies on or after 181 days from the last day of the member's actual service but on or before the date the benefits as provided in G.S. 135-105 would have ended, shall be considered in service at the time of the member's death for the purpose of this benefit.

For the purpose of calculating this benefit, any terminal payouts made after the date of death that meet the definition of compensation shall be credited to the month prior to the month of death. These terminal payouts do not include salary or wages paid for work performed during the month of death.

(n) No action shall be commenced against the State or the Retirement System by any retired member or beneficiary respecting any deficiency in the payment of benefits more than three years after such deficient payment was made, and no action shall be commenced by the State or the Retirement System against any retired member or former member or beneficiary respecting any overpayment of benefits or contributions more than three years after such overpayment was made.

(o) Post-Retirement Increases in Allowances. - As of December 31, 1969, the ratio of the Consumer Price Index to such index one year earlier shall be determined. If such ratio indicates an increase that equals or exceeds three per centum (3%), each beneficiary receiving a retirement allowance as of December 31, 1968, shall be entitled to have his allowance increased three per centum (3%) effective July 1, 1970.

As of December 31, 1970, the ratio of the Consumer Price Index to such index one year earlier shall be determined. If such ratio indicates an increase of at least one per centum (1%), each beneficiary on the retirement rolls as of July 1,

1970, shall be entitled to have his allowance increased effective July 1, 1971 as follows:

Increase In Index	Increase In Allowance
1.00 to 1.49%	1%
1.50 to 2.49%	2%
2.50 to 3.49%	3%
3.50% or more	4%

As of December 31, 1971, an increase in retirement allowances shall be calculated and made effective July 1, 1972, in the manner described in the preceding paragraph. As of December 31 of each year after 1971, the ratio (R) of the Consumer Price Index to such index one year earlier shall be determined, and each beneficiary on the retirement rolls as of July 1 of the year of determination shall be entitled to have his allowance increased effective on July 1 of the year following the year of determination by the same percentage of increase indicated by the ratio (R) calculated to the nearest tenth of one per centum, but not more than four per centum (4%); provided that any such increase in allowances shall become effective only if the additional liabilities on account of such increase do not require an increase in the total employer rate of contributions.

The allowance of a surviving annuitant of a beneficiary whose allowance is increased under this subsection shall, when and if payable, be increased by the same per centum.

Any increase in allowance granted hereunder shall be permanent, irrespective of any subsequent decrease in the Consumer Price Index, and shall be included in determining any subsequent increase.

For purposes of this subsection, Consumer Price Index shall mean the Consumer Price Index (all items - United States city average), as published by the United States Department of Labor, Bureau of Labor Statistics.

Notwithstanding the above paragraphs, retired members and beneficiaries may receive cost-of-living increases in retirement allowances if active members of the system receive across-the-board cost-of-living salary increases. Such increases in post-retirement allowances shall be comparable to cost-of-living salary increases for active members in light of the differences between the statutory payroll deductions for State retirement contributions, Social Security taxes, State income withholding taxes, and federal income withholding taxes required of each group. The increases for retired members shall include the cost-of-living increases provided in this section. The cost-of-living increases allowed retired and active members of the system shall be comparable when each group receives an increase that has the same relative impact upon the net disposable income of each group.

(p) Increases in Benefits Paid in Respect to Members Retired prior to July 1, 1967. - From and after July 1, 1971, the monthly benefits to or on account of persons who commenced receiving benefits prior to July 1, 1963, shall be increased by twenty percent (20%) thereof; the monthly benefits to or on account of persons who commenced receiving benefits after June 30, 1963 and before July 1, 1967, shall be increased by five percent (5%) thereof. These increases shall be calculated after monthly retirement allowances as of July 1, 1971, have been increased to the extent provided for in the preceding subsection (o).

(q) Increases in Benefits to Those Persons Who Were Retired prior to January 1, 1970. - From and after July 1, 1973, the monthly benefits to or on account of persons who commenced receiving benefits from the System prior to January 1, 1970, shall be increased by a percentage thereof. Such percentage shall be determined in accordance with the following schedule:

Year(s) in Which Benefits Commenced	Percentage
1969	1
1968	4
1967	6
1965 through 1966	9

1964	12
1963	14
1959 through 1962	17
1942 through 1958	22

These increases shall be calculated after monthly retirement allowances as of July 1, 1973, have been increased to the extent provided for in the preceding subsection (o).

(r) Notwithstanding anything herein to the contrary, effective July 1, 1973, any member who retired after attaining the age of 60 with 15 or more years of creditable service shall receive a monthly benefit of no less than seventy-five dollars ($75.00) prior to the application of any optional benefit.

(s) Increases in Benefits to Those Persons on Disability Retirement Who Were Retired prior to July 1, 1971. - From and after July 1, 1974, the monthly benefits to members who commenced receiving disability benefits prior to July 1, 1963, shall be increased by one percent (1%) thereof for each year by which the member retired prior to the age of 65 years; the monthly benefits to members who commenced receiving disability benefits after June 30, 1963, and before July 1, 1971, shall be increased by five percent (5%) thereof. These increases shall be calculated before monthly retirement allowances as of June 30, 1974, have been increased to the extent provided for in the preceding subsection (o).

(t) Notwithstanding any of the foregoing provisions, the increase in allowance to each beneficiary on the retirement rolls as of July 1, 1973, which shall become effective on July 1, 1974, as otherwise provided in G.S. 135-5(o), shall be the current maximum four percent (4%) plus an additional two percent (2%) to a total of six percent (6%) for the year 1974 only. The provisions of this subsection shall apply also to the allowance of a surviving annuitant of a beneficiary.

(u) Repealed by Session Laws 1975, c. 875, s. 47.

(v) Notwithstanding any of the foregoing provisions, the increase in allowance to each beneficiary on the retirement rolls as of July 1, 1974, which shall become payable on July 1, 1975, and to each beneficiary on the retirement rolls as of July 1, 1975, which shall become payable on July 1, 1976, as otherwise provided in G.S. 135-5(o), shall be the current maximum four percent (4%) plus an additional four percent (4%) to a total of eight percent (8%) for the years 1975 and 1976 only, provided that the increases do not exceed the actual percentage increase in the Consumer Price Index as determined in G.S. 135-5(o). The provisions of this subsection shall apply also to the allowance of a surviving annuitant of a beneficiary.

(w)   Notwithstanding any other provision of this section, the increase in the allowance to each beneficiary on the retirement rolls as otherwise provided in G.S. 135-5(o) shall be the current maximum of four per centum (4%) plus an additional four per centum (4%) to a total of eight per centum (8%) on July 1, 1975, and July 1, 1976, provided the increases do not exceed the actual percentage increase in the cost of living as determined in G.S. 135-5(o). The provisions of this subsection shall apply also to the allowance of a surviving annuitant of a beneficiary. The cost of these increases shall be borne from the funds of the Retirement System unless the 1975 Session of the General Assembly provides an appropriation to fund this provision.

(x)   Increases in Benefits to Those Persons on Disability Retirement Who Were Retired prior to July 1, 1971. - From and after July 1, 1975, the monthly benefits to members who commenced receiving disability benefits prior to July 1, 1963, shall be increased one percent (1%) thereof for each year by which the member retired prior to age 65 years; the monthly benefits to members who commenced receiving disability benefits after June 30, 1963, and before July 1, 1971, shall be increased by five percent (5%) thereof. These increases shall be calculated before monthly retirement allowances as of June 30, 1975, have been increased to the extent provided in the preceding provisions of this Chapter.

(y)   Notwithstanding the foregoing provisions, the increase in allowance to each beneficiary on the retirement rolls as of July 1, 1976, which shall become payable on July 1, 1977, and to each beneficiary on the retirement rolls as of July 1, 1977, which shall become payable on July 1, 1978, as otherwise provided in G.S. 135-5(o), shall be the current maximum four percent (4%) plus an additional two and one-half percent (2½%) for the years beginning July 1, 1977, and July 1, 1978. The provisions of this subsection shall apply also to the allowance of a surviving annuitant of a beneficiary.

(z)   Increases in Benefits Paid in Respect to Members Retired prior to July 1, 1975. - From and after July 1, 1977, the monthly benefits to or on account of persons who commenced receiving benefits prior to July 1, 1975, shall be increased by seven percent (7%) thereof. This increase shall be calculated before monthly retirement allowances as of July 1, 1977, have been increased to the extent provided for in the preceding subsection (o). The provisions of this subsection shall apply also to the allowance of a surviving annuitant of a beneficiary.

(aa) Notwithstanding the foregoing provisions, the increase in allowance to each beneficiary on the retirement rolls as of July 1, 1978, which shall become payable on July 1, 1979, as otherwise provided in G.S. 135-5(o), shall be the current maximum four percent (4%) plus an additional one percent (1%) for the year beginning July 1, 1979. Provisions of this subsection shall apply also to the allowance of a surviving annuitant of a beneficiary.

(bb) Notwithstanding the foregoing provisions, the increase in allowance to each beneficiary on the retirement rolls as of July 1, 1979, which shall become payable on July 1, 1980, as otherwise provided in G.S. 135-5(o), shall be the current maximum four percent (4%) plus an additional three percent (3%) computed on the retirement allowance prior to any increase authorized by paragraph (cc) of this section. Provisions of this subsection shall apply also to the allowance of a surviving annuitant of a beneficiary.

(cc) Increases in Benefits to Those Persons Who Were Retired Prior to July 1, 1977. - From and after July 1, 1980, the monthly benefits to or on account of persons who commenced receiving benefits from the system prior to July 1, 1977, shall be increased by a percentage in accordance with the following schedule:

Period in Which Benefits Commenced	Percentage
On or before June 30, 1963	10%
July 1, 1963, to June 30, 1968	7%
July 1, 1968, to June 30, 1977	2%

This increase shall be calculated before monthly retirement allowances, as of July 1, 1980, have been increased for all cost-of-living increases allowed for the same period.

(dd)   From and after July 1, 1981, the retirement allowance to or on account of the beneficiaries whose retirement commenced prior to July 1, 1980, shall be increased by three percent (3%). These increases shall be calculated on the basis of the allowance payable and in effect on June 30, 1980, so as not to compound on the increases otherwise payable under paragraphs (bb), (cc) and (ee) of this section.

(ee)   Adjustment in Allowances Paid Beneficiaries Whose Retirement Commenced Prior to July 1, 1980. - From and after July 1, 1981, the retirement allowance to or on account of beneficiaries whose retirement commenced prior to July 1, 1980, shall be adjusted by an increase of one and three-tenths percent (1.3%). This adjustment shall be calculated on the basis of the allowance payable and in effect on June 30, 1980, so as not to compound on the increases otherwise payable under paragraphs (bb), (cc) and (dd) of this section.

(ff)   From and after July 1, 1982, the retirement allowance to or on account of beneficiaries on the retirement rolls as of July 1, 1981, shall be increased by one-tenth of one percent (0.1%) of the allowance payable on July 1, 1981.

(gg)   From and after July 1, 1983, the retirement allowance to or on account of beneficiaries on the retirement rolls as of July 1, 1982, shall be increased by two and one-half percent (2.5%) of the allowance payable on July 1, 1982, provided the increase in retirement allowances shall be payable in accordance with all requirements, stipulations and conditions set forth in subsection (o) of this section, plus an additional one and one-half percent (1.5%) of the allowance payable on July 1, 1982, in order to supplement the increase payable in accordance with subsection (o) of this section.

(hh)   Notwithstanding any other provision of this Chapter, from and after July 1, 1983, the retirement allowance payable to each teacher and State employee, who retired prior to July 1, 1973, and who is in receipt of a reduced retirement allowance based upon 30 or more years of contributing membership service, shall be increased by the elimination of the reduction factors applicable at the time of their retirement under G.S. 135-3(8) or G.S. 135-5(b3). The provisions of this subsection shall apply equally to the allowance of a surviving annuitant of a beneficiary.

(ii)   From and after July 1, 1984, the retirement allowance to or on account of beneficiaries whose retirement commenced on or before July 1, 1983, shall be increased by three and eight-tenths percent (3.8%) of the allowance payable on July 1, 1983, in accordance with G.S. 135-5(o), plus an additional four and two-tenths percent (4.2%) of the allowance payable on July 1, 1983.

(jj) Increase in Allowance Where Retirement Commenced on or before July 1, 1984, or after that Date, but before June 30, 1985. - From and after July 1, 1985, the retirement allowance to or on account of beneficiaries whose retirement commenced on or before July 1, 1984, shall be increased by four percent (4%) of the allowance payable on July 1, 1984, in accordance with G.S. 135-5(o). Furthermore, from and after July 1, 1985, the retirement allowance to or on account of beneficiaries whose retirement commenced after July 1, 1984, but before June 30, 1985, shall be increased by a prorated amount of four percent (4%) of the allowance payable as determined by the Board of Trustees based upon the number of months that a retirement allowance was paid between July 1, 1984, and June 30, 1985.

(kk) Increase in Allowance as to Persons on Retirement Rolls as of June 1, 1985. - From and after July 1, 1985, the retirement allowance to or on account of beneficiaries on the retirement rolls as of June 1, 1985, shall be increased by six-tenths percent (0.6%) of the allowance payable on June 1, 1985. This allowance shall be calculated on the basis of the allowance payable and in effect on June 30, 1985, so as not to be compounded on any other increases payable under subsection (o) of this section or otherwise granted by act of the 1985 Session of the General Assembly.

(ll) From and after July 1, 1986, the retirement allowance to or on account of beneficiaries whose retirement commenced on or before July 1, 1985, shall be increased by three and eight-tenths percent (3.8%) of the allowance payable on July 1, 1985, in accordance with G.S. 135-5(o). Furthermore, from and after July 1, 1986, the retirement allowance to or on account of beneficiaries whose retirement commenced after July 1, 1985, but before June 30, 1986, shall be increased by a prorated amount of three and eight-tenths percent (3.8%) of the allowance payable as determined by the Board of Trustees based upon the number of months that a retirement allowance was paid between July 1, 1985, and June 30, 1986.

(mm) From and after July 1, 1987, the retirement allowance to or on account of beneficiaries whose retirement commenced on or before July 1, 1986, shall be increased by four percent (4.0%) of the allowance payable on July 1, 1986, in accordance with G.S. 135-5(o). Furthermore, from and after July 1, 1987, the retirement allowance to or on account of beneficiaries whose retirement commenced after July 1, 1986, but before June 30, 1987, shall be increased by a prorated amount of four percent (4.0%) of the allowance payable as determined by the Board of Trustees based upon the number of months that a retirement allowance was paid between July 1, 1986, and June 30, 1987.

(nn) From and after July 1, 1988, the retirement allowance to or on account of beneficiaries whose retirement commenced on or before July 1, 1987, shall be increased by three and six-tenths percent (3.6%) of the allowance payable on July 1, 1987, in accordance with G.S. 135-5(o). Furthermore, from and after July 1, 1988, the retirement allowance to or on account of beneficiaries whose retirement commenced after July 1, 1987, but before June 30, 1988, shall be increased by a prorated amount of three and six-tenths percent (3.6%) of the allowance payable as determined by the Board of Trustees based upon the number of months that a retirement allowance was paid between July 1, 1987, and June 30, 1988.

(oo) Increase in Allowance as to Persons on Retirement Rolls as of June 1, 1988. - From and after July 1, 1988, the retirement allowance to or on account of beneficiaries on the retirement rolls as of June 1, 1988, shall be increased by one and two-tenths percent (1.2%) of the allowance payable on June 1, 1988. This allowance shall be calculated on the basis of the allowance payable and in effect on June 30, 1988, so as not to be compounded on any other increase payable under subsection (o) of this section or otherwise granted by act of the 1987 Session of the General Assembly.

(pp) From and after July 1, 1989, the retirement allowance to or on account of beneficiaries whose retirement commenced on or before July 1, 1988, shall be increased by three and one-half percent (3.5%) of the allowance payable on July 1, 1988, in accordance with G.S. 135-5(o). Furthermore, from and after July 1, 1989, the retirement allowance to or on account of beneficiaries whose retirement commenced after July 1, 1988, but before June 30, 1989, shall be increased by a prorated amount of three and one-half percent (3.5%) of the allowance payable as determined by the Board of Trustees based upon the number of months that a retirement allowance was paid between July 1, 1988, and June 30, 1989.

(qq) Increase in Allowance as to Persons on Retirement Rolls as of June 1, 1989. - From and after July 1, 1989, the retirement allowance to or on account of beneficiaries on the retirement rolls as of June 1, 1989, shall be increased by one and nine-tenths percent (1.9%) of the allowance payable on June 1, 1989. This allowance shall be calculated on the basis of the allowance payable and in effect on June 30, 1989, so as not to be compounded on any other increase payable under subsection (o) of this section or otherwise granted by act of the 1989 Session of the General Assembly.

(rr) Increase in Allowance as to Persons on Retirement Rolls as of June 1, 1990. From and after July 1, 1990, the retirement allowance to or on account of beneficiaries on the retirement rolls as of June 1, 1990, shall be increased by six-tenths of one percent (0.6%) of the allowance payable on June 1, 1990. This allowance shall be calculated on the basis of the allowance payable and in effect on June 30, 1990, so as not to be compounded on any other increase granted by act of the 1989 Session of the General Assembly (1990 Regular Session).

(ss) From and after July 1, 1990, the retirement allowance to or on account of beneficiaries whose retirement commenced on or before July 1, 1989, shall be increased by six and one-tenth percent (6.1%) of the allowance payable on July 1, 1989, in accordance with G.S. 135-5(o). Furthermore, from and after July 1, 1990, the retirement allowance to or on account of beneficiaries whose retirement commenced after July 1, 1989, but before June 30, 1990, shall be increased by a prorated amount of six and one-tenth percent (6.1%) of the allowance payable as determined by the Board of Trustees based upon the number of months that a retirement allowance was paid between July 1, 1989, and June 30, 1990.

(tt) Increase in Allowance as to Persons on Retirement Rolls as of June 1, 1992. - From and after July 1, 1992, the retirement allowance to or on account of beneficiaries on the retirement rolls as of June 1, 1992, shall be increased by three and six-tenths percent (3.6%) of the allowance payable on June 1, 1992. This allowance shall be calculated on the allowance payable and in effect on June 30, 1992, so as not to be compounded on any other increase granted by act of the 1991 Session of the General Assembly, 1992 Regular Session.

(uu) From and after July 1, 1992, the retirement allowance to or on account of beneficiaries whose retirement commenced on or before July 1, 1991, shall be increased by one and six-tenths percent (1.6%) of the allowance payable on July 1, 1991, in accordance with G.S. 135-5(o). Furthermore, from and after July 1, 1992, the retirement allowance to or on account of beneficiaries whose retirement commenced after July 1, 1991, but before June 30, 1992, shall be increased by a prorated amount of one and six-tenths percent (1.6%) of the allowance payable as determined by the Board of Trustees based upon the number of months that a retirement allowance was paid between July 1, 1991 and June 30, 1992.

(vv) Increase in Allowance as to Persons on Retirement Rolls as of June 1, 1993. - From and after July 1, 1993, the retirement allowance to or on account of beneficiaries on the retirement rolls as of June 1, 1993, shall be increased by six-tenths of one percent (.6%) of the allowance payable on June 1, 1993. This allowance shall be calculated on the allowance payable and in effect on June 30, 1993, so as not to be compounded on any other increase granted by act of the 1993 General Assembly.

(ww) From and after July 1, 1993, the retirement allowance to or on account of beneficiaries whose retirement commenced on or before July 1, 1992, shall be increased by one and six-tenths percent (1.6%) of the allowance payable on July 1, 1992, in accordance with G.S. 135-5(o). Furthermore, from and after July 1, 1993, the retirement allowance to or on account of beneficiaries whose retirement commenced after July 1, 1992, but before June 30, 1993, shall be increased by a prorated amount of one and six-tenths percent (1.6%) of the allowance payable as determined by the Board of Trustees based upon the number of months that a retirement allowance was paid between July 1, 1992, and June 30, 1993.

(xx) Increase in Allowance as to Persons on Retirement Rolls as of June 1, 1994. - From and after July 1, 1994, the retirement allowance to or on account of beneficiaries on the retirement rolls as of June 1, 1994, shall be increased by one and two-tenths of one percent (1.2%) of the allowance payable on June 1, 1994. This allowance shall be calculated on the allowance payable and in effect on June 30, 1994, so as not to be compounded on any other increase granted by act of the 1993 General Assembly, 1994 Regular Session.

(yy) From and after July 1, 1994, the retirement allowance to or on account of beneficiaries whose retirement commenced on or before July 1, 1993, shall be increased by three and one-half percent (3.5%) of the allowance payable on July 1, 1993, in accordance with G.S. 135-5(o). Furthermore, from and after July 1, 1994, the retirement allowance to or on account of beneficiaries whose retirement commenced after July 1, 1993, but before June 30, 1994, shall be increased by a prorated amount of three and one-half percent (3.5%) of the allowance payable as determined by the Board of Trustees based upon the number of months that a retirement allowance was paid between July 1, 1993, and June 30, 1994.

(zz) From and after July 1, 1995, the retirement allowance to or on account of beneficiaries whose retirement commenced on or before July 1, 1994, shall be increased by two percent (2%) of the allowance payable on July 1, 1994, in accordance with G.S. 135-5(o). Furthermore, from and after July 1, 1995, the retirement allowance to or on account of beneficiaries whose retirement commenced after July 1, 1994, but before June 30, 1995, shall be increased by a prorated amount of two percent (2%) of the allowance payable as determined by the Board of Trustees based upon the number of months that a retirement allowance was paid between July 1, 1994, and June 30, 1995.

(aaa)   Increase in Allowance as to Persons on Retirement Rolls as of June 1, 1995. - From and after July 1, 1995, the retirement allowance to or on account of beneficiaries on the retirement rolls as of June 1, 1995, shall be increased by one and two-tenths of one percent (1.2%) of the allowance payable on June 1, 1995. This allowance shall be calculated on the allowance payable and in effect on June 30, 1995, so as not to be compounded on any other increase granted by act of the 1995 General Assembly.

(bbb)   From and after September 1, 1996, the retirement allowance to or on account of beneficiaries whose retirement commenced on or before July 1, 1995, shall be increased by four and four-tenths percent (4.4%) of the allowance payable on July 1, 1995, in accordance with G.S. 135-5(o). Furthermore, from and after September 1, 1996, the retirement allowance to or on account of beneficiaries whose retirement commenced after July 1, 1995, but before June 30, 1996, shall be increased by a prorated amount of four and four-tenths percent (4.4%) of the allowance payable as determined by the Board of Trustees based upon the number of months that a retirement allowance was paid between July 1, 1995, and June 30, 1996.

(ccc)   From and after July 1, 1997, the retirement allowance to or on account of beneficiaries whose retirement commenced on or before July 1, 1996, shall be increased by four percent (4%) of the allowance payable on June 1, 1997, in accordance with G.S. 135-5(o). Furthermore, from and after July 1, 1997, the retirement allowance to or on account of beneficiaries whose retirement commenced after July 1, 1996, but before June 30, 1997, shall be increased by a prorated amount of four percent (4%) of the allowance payable as determined by the Board of Trustees based upon the number of months that a retirement allowance was paid between July 1, 1996, and June 30, 1997.

(ddd)   Increase in Allowance as to Persons on Retirement Rolls as of June 1, 1997. - From and after July 1, 1997, the retirement allowance to or on account of beneficiaries on the retirement rolls as of June 1, 1997, shall be increased by two and two-tenths percent (2.2%) of the allowance payable on June 1, 1997. This allowance shall be calculated on the allowance payable and in effect on

June 30, 1997, so as not to be compounded on any other increase granted by act of the 1997 General Assembly.

(eee) From and after July 1, 1998, the retirement allowance to or on account of beneficiaries whose retirement commenced on or before July 1, 1997, shall be increased by two and one-half percent (2.5%) of the allowance payable on June 1, 1998, in accordance with G.S. 135-5(o). Furthermore, from and after July 1, 1998, the retirement allowance to or on account of beneficiaries whose retirement commenced after July 1, 1997, but before June 30, 1998, shall be increased by a prorated amount of two and one-half percent (2.5%) of the allowance payable as determined by the Board of Trustees based upon the number of months that a retirement allowance was paid between July 1, 1997, and June 30, 1998.

(fff) From and after July 1, 1999, the retirement allowance to or on account of beneficiaries whose retirement commenced on or before July 1, 1998, shall be increased by two and three-tenths percent (2.3%) of the allowance payable on June 1, 1999, in accordance with G.S. 135-5(o). Furthermore, from and after July 1, 1999, the retirement allowance to or on account of beneficiaries whose retirement commenced after July 1, 1998, but before June 30, 1999, shall be increased by a prorated amount of two and three-tenths percent (2.3%) of the allowance payable as determined by the Board of Trustees based upon the number of months that a retirement allowance was paid between July 1, 1998, and June 30, 1999.

(ggg) Increase in Allowance as to Persons on Retirement Rolls as of June 1, 2000. - From and after July 1, 2000, the retirement allowance to or on account of beneficiaries on the retirement rolls as of June 1, 2000, shall be increased by six-tenths percent (0.6%) of the allowance payable on June 1, 2000. This allowance shall be calculated on the allowance payable and in effect on June 30, 2000, so as not to be compounded on any other increase granted by act of the 1999 General Assembly, 2000 Regular Session.

(hhh) From and after July 1, 2000, the retirement allowance to or on account of beneficiaries whose retirement commenced on or before July 1, 1999, shall be increased by three and six-tenths percent (3.6%) of the allowance payable on June 1, 2000, in accordance with G.S. 135-5(o). Furthermore, from and after July 1, 2000, the retirement allowance to or on account of beneficiaries whose retirement commenced after July 1, 1999, but before June 30, 2000, shall be increased by a prorated amount of three and six-tenths percent (3.6%) of the allowance payable as determined by the Board of Trustees based upon the number of months that a retirement allowance was paid between July 1, 1999, and June 30, 2000.

(iii) From and after July 1, 2001, the retirement allowance to or on account of beneficiaries whose retirement commenced on or before July 1, 2000, shall be increased by two percent (2%) of the allowance payable on June 1, 2001, in accordance with G.S. 135-5(o). Furthermore, from and after July 1, 2001, the retirement allowance to or on account of beneficiaries whose retirement commenced after July 1, 2000, but before June 30, 2001, shall be increased by a prorated amount of two percent (2%) of the allowance payable as determined by the Board of Trustees based upon the number of months that a retirement allowance was paid between July 1, 2000, and June 30, 2001.

(jjj) From and after July 1, 2002, the retirement allowance to or on account of beneficiaries whose retirement commenced on or before July 1, 2001, shall be increased by one and four-tenths percent (1.4%) of the allowance payable on June 1, 2002, in accordance with G.S. 135-5(o). Furthermore, from and after July 1, 2002, the retirement allowance to or on account of beneficiaries whose retirement commenced after July 1, 2001, but before June 30, 2002, shall be increased by a prorated amount of one and four-tenths percent (1.4%) of the allowance payable as determined by the Board of Trustees based upon the number of months that a retirement allowance was paid between July 1, 2001, and June 30, 2002.

(kkk) Increase in Allowance as to Persons on Retirement Rolls as of June 1, 2002. - From and after July 1, 2002, the retirement allowance to or on account of beneficiaries on the retirement rolls as of June 1, 2002, shall be increased by six-tenths of one percent (0.6%) of the allowance payable on June 1, 2002. This allowance shall be calculated on the allowance payable and in effect on June 30, 2002, so as not to be compounded on any other increase granted by act of the 2002 Regular Session of the 2001 General Assembly.

(lll) From and after July 1, 2003, the retirement allowance to or on account of beneficiaries whose retirement commenced on or before July 1, 2002, shall be increased by one and twenty-eight hundredths percent (1.28%) of the allowance payable on June 1, 2003, in accordance with G.S. 135-5(o). Furthermore, from and after July 1, 2003, the retirement allowance to or on account of beneficiaries whose retirement commenced after July 1, 2002, but before June 30, 2003, shall be increased by a prorated amount of one and twenty-eight hundredths percent (1.28%) of the allowance payable as determined by the Board of

Trustees based upon the number of months that a retirement allowance was paid between July 1, 2002, and June 30, 2003.

(mmm) From and after July 1, 2004, the retirement allowance to or on account of beneficiaries whose retirement commenced on or before July 1, 2003, shall be increased by one and seven-tenths percent (1.7%) of the allowance payable on June 1, 2004, in accordance with G.S. 135-5(o). Furthermore, from and after July 1, 2004, the retirement allowance to or on account of beneficiaries whose retirement commenced after July 1, 2003, but before June 30, 2004, shall be increased by a prorated amount of one and seven-tenths percent (1.7%) of the allowance payable as determined by the Board of Trustees based upon the number of months that a retirement allowance was paid between July 1, 2003, and June 30, 2004.

(nnn) From and after July 1, 2005, the retirement allowance to or on account of beneficiaries whose retirement commenced on or before July 1, 2004, shall be increased by two percent (2%) of the allowance payable on June 1, 2005, in accordance with G.S. 135-5(o). Furthermore, from and after July 1, 2005, the retirement allowance to or on account of beneficiaries whose retirement commenced after July 1, 2004, but before June 30, 2005, shall be increased by a prorated amount of two percent (2%) of the allowance payable as determined by the Board of Trustees based upon the number of months that a retirement allowance was paid between July 1, 2004, and June 30, 2005.

(ooo) From and after July 1, 2006, the retirement allowance to or on account of beneficiaries whose retirement commenced on or before July 1, 2005, shall be increased by three percent (3%) of the allowance payable on June 1, 2006, in accordance with G.S. 135-5(o). Furthermore, from and after July 1, 2006, the retirement allowance to or on account of beneficiaries whose retirement commenced after July 1, 2005, but before June 30, 2006, shall be increased by a prorated amount of three percent (3%) of the allowance payable as determined by the Board of Trustees based upon the number of months that a retirement allowance was paid between July 1, 2005, and June 30, 2006.

(ppp) Repealed by Session Laws 2007-431, s. 7, effective July 1, 2007.

(qqq) From and after July 1, 2007, the retirement allowance to or on account of beneficiaries whose retirement commenced on or before July 1, 2006, shall be increased by two and two-tenths percent (2.2%) of the allowance payable on June 1, 2007, in accordance with G.S. 135-5(o). Furthermore, from and after July 1, 2007, the retirement allowance to or on account of beneficiaries whose retirement commenced after July 1, 2006, but before June 30, 2007, shall be increased by a prorated amount of two and two-tenths percent (2.2%) of the allowance payable as determined by the Board of Trustees based upon the number of months that a retirement allowance was paid between July 1, 2006, and June 30, 2007.

(rrr)   From and after July 1, 2008, the retirement allowance to or on account of beneficiaries whose retirement commenced on or before July 1, 2007, shall be increased by two and two-tenths percent (2.2%) of the allowance payable on June 1, 2008, in accordance with G.S. 135-5(o). Furthermore, from and after July 1, 2008, the retirement allowance to or on account of beneficiaries whose retirement commenced after July 1, 2007, but before June 30, 2008, shall be increased by a prorated amount of two and two-tenths percent (2.2%) of the allowance payable as determined by the Board of Trustees based upon the number of months that a retirement allowance was paid between July 1, 2007, and June 30, 2008.

(sss)   From and after July 1, 2012, the retirement allowance to or on account of beneficiaries whose retirement commenced on or before July 1, 2011, shall be increased by one percent (1%) of the allowance payable on June 1, 2012, in accordance with G.S. 135-5(o). Furthermore, from and after July 1, 2012, the retirement allowance to or on account of beneficiaries whose retirement commenced after July 1, 2011, but before June 30, 2012, shall be increased by a prorated amount of one percent (1%) of the allowance payable as determined by the Board of Trustees based upon the number of months that a retirement allowance was paid between July 1, 2011, and June 30, 2012. (1941, c. 25, s. 5; 1945, c. 218; 1947, c. 458, ss. 3, 4, 7, 8a; 1949, c. 1056, ss. 3, 5; 1955, c. 1155, ss. 1, 2; 1957, c. 855, ss. 5-8; 1959, c. 490; c. 513, ss. 2, 3; c. 620, ss. 1-3; c. 624; 1961, c. 516, s. 4; c. 779, s. 1; 1963, c. 687, s. 3; 1965, c. 780, s. 1; 1967, c. 720, ss. 4-10; c. 1223; 1969, c. 1223, ss. 2, 5-12; 1971, c. 117, ss. 11-15; c. 118, ss. 3-7; 1973, c. 241, ss. 3-7; c. 242, ss. 2-4; c. 737, s. 2; c. 816, s. 2; c. 994, ss. 1, 3; c. 1312, ss. 1-3; 1975, c. 457, ss. 2-4; c. 511, ss. 1, 2; c. 634, ss. 1, 2; c. 875, s. 47; 1977, c. 561; c. 802, ss. 50.65-50.70; 1979, c. 838, s. 99; c. 862, ss. 1, 4, 5; c. 972, s. 4; c. 975, s. 1; 1979, 2nd Sess., c. 1137, ss. 63, 64, 66; c. 1196, s. 1; c. 1216; 1981, c. 672, s. 1; c. 689, s. 2; c. 859, ss. 42, 42.1, 44; c. 940, s. 1; c. 975, s. 3; c. 978, ss. 1, 2; c. 980, ss. 3, 4; 1981 (Reg. Sess., 1982), c. 1282, s. 11; 1983, c. 467; c. 761, ss. 218, 219, 228, 229; c. 902, s. 1; 1983 (Reg. Sess., 1984), c. 1019, s. 1; c. 1034, ss. 222, 232-235, 237; c. 1049, ss. 1-3; 1985, c. 348, s. 2; c. 479, ss. 189(a), 190, 191, 192(a), 194; c. 520, s. 2; c. 649, ss. 8, 10; 1985 (Reg. Sess., 1986), c. 1014, s. 49(a); 1987, c. 181, s. 1; c. 513, s. 1; c. 738, ss. 27(a), 29(c)-(j), 37(a); c. 824, s. 3; 1987 (Reg. Sess.,

1988), c. 1061, s. 1; c. 1086, s. 22(a); c. 1108, s. 1; c. 1110, ss. 1-3; 1989, c. 717, ss. 1-6; c. 731, s. 1; c. 752, s. 41(a); c. 770, s. 31; c. 792, ss. 3.1-3.3; 1989 (Reg. Sess., 1990), c. 1077, ss. 2-5; 1991 (Reg. Sess., 1992), c. 766, s. 2; c. 900, ss. 52(a)-(c), 53(b); 1993, c. 321, ss. 74(c)-(e), 74.1(e), (f), 74.2(a); c. 531, s. 5; 1993 (Reg. Sess., 1994), c. 769, ss. 7.30(g)-(j), (m), (r); 1995, c. 507, ss. 7.22(a), 7.23(a), (b), 7.23A(a), (b); c. 509, ss. 74, 75; 1996, 2nd Ex. Sess., c. 18, s. 28.21(a); 1997-443, s. 33.22(a)-(d); 1998-153, s. 21(a); 1998-212, ss. 28.26(c), 28.27(a); 1999-237, s. 28.23(a); 2000-67, ss. 26.20(a)-(d); 2001-424, s. 32.22(a); 2002-126, ss. 28.8(a), 28.9(a)-(d); 2003-284, s. 30.17(a); 2003-359, ss. 3-6, 11; 2004-124, s. 31.17(a); 2004-147, s. 1; 2005-91, ss. 2, 3; 2005-276, s. 29.25(a); 2006-66, s. 22.18(a); 2006-172, s. 1; 2007-323, s. 28.20(a); 2007-384, ss. 10.3, 10.4; 2007-431, ss. 1, 5, 7, 12, 13; 2007-496, s. 1; 2008-107, s. 26.23(a); 2009-66, ss. 3(a)-(d), 5(a)-(c), 6(a), 9, 11(e)-(g), 12(c), (d); 2009-109, s. 1; 2010-72, ss. 1(a), 2(a), 3(b), 9(a), 10(a); 2010-96, s. 40.7; 2010-124, ss. 1, 2, 3, 6.1; 2011-232, ss. 2-7; 2011-294, s. 3(a); 2012-142, s. 25.13(a); 2013-405, s. 1.)

§ 135-5.1. Optional retirement program for The University of North Carolina.

(a) An Optional Retirement Program provided for in this section is authorized and established and shall be implemented by the Board of Governors of The University of North Carolina. The Optional Retirement Program shall be underwritten by the purchase of annuity contracts, which may be both fixed and variable contracts or a combination thereof, or financed through the establishment of a trust, for the benefit of participants in the Program. Participation in the Optional Retirement Program shall be limited to University personnel who are eligible for membership in the Teachers' and State Employees' Retirement Program and who are:

(1) Administrators and faculty of The University of North Carolina with the rank of instructor or above;

(2) The President and employees of The University of North Carolina who are appointed by the Board of Governors on recommendation of the President pursuant to G.S. 116-11(4), 116-11(5), and 116-14 or who are appointed by the Board of Trustees of a constituent institution of The University of North Carolina upon the recommendation of the Chancellor pursuant to G.S. 116-40.22(b);

(3) Nonfaculty instructional and research staff who are exempt from the North Carolina Human Resources Act, as defined by the provisions of G.S. 126-

5(c1)(8), and the faculty of the North Carolina School of Science and Mathematics; and

(4)   Field faculty of the Cooperative Agriculture Extension Service, and tenure track faculty in North Carolina State University agriculture research programs who are exempt from the North Carolina Human Resources Act and who are eligible for membership in the Teachers' and State Employees' Retirement System pursuant to G.S. 135-3(1), who in any of the cases described in this subsection (i) had been members of the Optional Retirement Program under the provisions of Chapter 338, Session Laws of 1971, immediately prior to July 1, 1985, or (ii) have sought membership as required in subsection (b), below. Under the Optional Retirement Program, the State and the participant shall contribute, to the extent authorized or required, toward the purchase of such contracts or deposited in such trust on the participant's behalf.

(5)   Employees of The University of North Carolina Health Care System, subject to rules for eligibility and participation as may be adopted by the Board of Governors in the Optional Retirement Program plan document.

(6)   Employees hired on or after January 1, 2013.

(b)   Participation in the Optional Retirement Program shall be governed as follows:

(1)   Those participating in the Optional Retirement Program immediately prior to July 1, 1985, under the provisions of Chapter 338, Session Laws of 1971, are deemed automatically enrolled in the Program as established by this section.

(2)   Eligible employees initially appointed on or after July 1, 1985, shall at the same time of entering upon eligible employment elect (i) to join the Retirement System in accordance with the provisions of law applicable thereto or (ii) to participate in the Optional Retirement Program. This election shall be in writing and filed with the Retirement System and with the employing institution and shall be effective as of the date of entry into eligible service. For purposes of this provision, the Optional Retirement Program shall be permitted to file individual election forms with the Retirement System using electronic transmission.

(3)   An election to participate in the Optional Retirement Program shall be irrevocable. An eligible employee failing to elect to participate in the Optional

Retirement Program at the time of entry into eligible service shall automatically be enrolled as a member of the Retirement System.

(4)   No election by an eligible employee of the Optional Retirement Program shall be effective unless it is accompanied by an appropriate application for the issuance of a contract or contracts or trust participation under the Program.

(5)   If any participant in the Optional Retirement Program having less than five years of total membership service under any combination of the Teachers' and State Employees' Retirement System, the Local Governmental Employees' Retirement System, the Consolidated Judicial Retirement System, or the Optional Retirement Program leaves the employ of The University of North Carolina and either retires or commences employment with an employer not having a retirement program with the same company underwriting the participant's annuity contract, regardless of whether the annuity contract is held by the participant, a trust, or the Retirement System, the participant's interest in the Optional Retirement Program attributable to contributions of The University of North Carolina shall be forfeited. Consistent with Section 401(a) of the Internal Revenue Code, no part of the corpus or income of the Optional Retirement Program, or any trust established under that Program, may be (within the taxable year or thereafter) used for purposes other than for the exclusive benefit of participants and their beneficiaries, except that contributions made under a good faith mistake of fact may be returned, consistent with the rules adopted by the University.

(c)   Each employing institution shall contribute on behalf of each participant in the Optional Retirement Program an amount equal to a percentage of the participant's compensation as established from time to time by the General Assembly. Each participant shall contribute the amount which he or she would be required to contribute if a member of the Retirement System. Contributions authorized or required by the provisions of this subsection on behalf of each participant shall be made, consistent with Section 414(h) of the Internal Revenue Code, by salary reduction according to rules and regulations established by The University of North Carolina. Additional personal contributions may also be made by a participant by payroll deduction or salary reduction to an annuity or retirement income plan established pursuant to G.S. 116-17. Payment of contributions shall be made by the employing institution to the designated company or companies underwriting the annuities or the trustees for the benefit of each participant, and this employer contribution shall not be subject to any State tax if made under the Optional Retirement Program or, otherwise, by salary reduction.

(d) The Board of Governors of The University of North Carolina shall designate the company or companies from which contracts are to be purchased or the trustee responsible for the investment of contributions under the Optional Retirement Program, and shall approve the form and contents of such contracts or trust agreement. In making this designation and giving such approval, the Board shall give due consideration to the following:

(1) The nature and extent of the rights and benefits to be provided by these contracts or trust agreement for participants and their beneficiaries;

(2) The relation of these rights and benefits to the amount of contributions to be made;

(3) The suitability of these rights and benefits to the needs of the participants and the interest of the institutions of The University of North Carolina in recruiting and retaining faculty in a national market; and

(4) The ability of the designated company or companies underwriting the annuity contracts or trust agreement to provide these suitable rights and benefits under such contracts or trust agreement for these purposes.

Notwithstanding the provisions of this subsection, no contractual relationship established under the Optional Retirement Program pursuant to the authority granted by Chapter 338, Session Laws of 1971, is deemed terminated by the provisions of this section.

(e) The Board of Governors of The University of North Carolina may provide for the administration of the Optional Retirement Program and may perform or authorize the performance of all functions necessary for its administration.

(f) Any eligible employee electing to participate in the Optional Retirement Program is ineligible for membership in the Retirement System so long as he or she remains employed in any eligible position within The University of North Carolina, and, in this event, he or she shall continue to participate in the Optional Retirement Program.

(g) No retirement benefit, death benefit, or other benefit under the Optional Retirement Program shall be paid by the State of North Carolina, or The University of North Carolina, or the Board of Trustees of the Teachers' and State Employees' Retirement System with respect to any employee selecting and participating in the Optional Retirement Program or with respect to any beneficiary of that employee. Benefits shall be payable to participants or their beneficiaries only by the designated company in accordance with the terms of the contracts or trust agreement.

(h) The Board of Governors of The University of North Carolina shall ensure that the Optional Retirement Program contains benefit forfeiture provisions equivalent to those contained in G.S. 135-18.10A for University personnel who are eligible for membership in the Teachers' and State Employees' Retirement System and have elected participation in the Optional Retirement Program. Any funds forfeited shall be deposited in the Optional Retirement Program trust fund(s). (1971, c. 338, s. 2; c. 916; 1973, c. 1425; 1977, c. 1070; 1985, c. 309; 1987 (Reg. Sess., 1988), c. 1086, s. 28; 2001-424, s. 32.27; 2003-356, s. 1; 2006-172, ss. 2, 3; 2011-145, ss. 29.26, 29.27; 2012-142, ss. 25.11, 25.12; 2012-193, s. 11; 2013-288, s. 5; 2013-382, s. 9.1(c).)

§ 135-5.2. Chapel Hill utilities and telephone employees.

Notwithstanding any other provision to the contrary, all persons employed by Chapel Hill Telephone Company or University Service Plants at the time the Chapel Hill telephone services and utilities services are sold to the Southern Bell Company and Duke Power Company respectively, shall be entitled to retire upon early retirement after 30 years of combined service with the Teachers' and State Employees' Retirement System and either Southern Bell or Duke Power Company. An employee must have had at least five years' service with the Teachers' and State Employees' Retirement System and at least five years with either Southern Bell or Duke Power Company in order to be eligible for benefits under this provision. This provision is in addition to any other retirement benefits or privileges the employee may have under the Teachers' and State Employees' Retirement System. (1977, c. 1007.)

§ 135-5.3. Optional participation for charter schools operated by private nonprofit corporations.

(a) The board of directors of each charter school operated by a private nonprofit corporation shall elect whether to become a participating employer in the Retirement System in accordance with this Article. This election shall be in writing, shall be made no later than 30 days after this section becomes law, and shall be filed with the Retirement System and with the State Board of Education. For each charter school employee who is employed on or before the date the board makes the election to participate, membership in the System is effective as of the date the board makes the election to participate. For each charter school employee who is employed after the date the board makes the election, membership in the System is effective as of the date of that employee's entry into eligible service. This subsection applies only to charter schools that received State Board of Education approval under G.S. 115C-238.29D in 1997 or 1998.

(b) No later than 30 days after both parties have signed the written charter under G.S. 115C-238.29E, the board of directors of a charter school operated by a private nonprofit corporation shall elect whether to become a participating employer in the Retirement System in accordance with this Article. This election shall be in writing and filed with the Retirement System and with the State Board of Education and is effective for each charter school employee as of the date of that employee's entry into eligible service. This subsection applies to charter schools that receive State Board of Education approval under G.S. 115C-238.29D after 1998.

(c) A board's election to become a participating employer in the Retirement System under this section is irrevocable and shall require all eligible employees of the charter school to participate.

(d) No retirement benefit, death benefit, or other benefit payable under the Retirement System shall be paid by the State of North Carolina or the Board of Trustees of the Teachers' and State Employees' Retirement System on account of employment with a charter school with respect to any employee, or with respect to any beneficiary of an employee, of a charter school whose board of directors does not elect to become a participating employer in the Retirement System under this section.

(e) The board of directors of each charter school shall notify each of its employees as to whether the board elected to become a participating employer in the Retirement System under this section. This notification shall be in writing and shall be provided within 30 days of the board's election or at the time an initial offer for employment is made, whichever occurs last. If the board did not elect to join the Retirement System, the notice shall include a statement that the employee shall have no legal recourse against the board or the State for any possible credit or reimbursement under the Retirement System. The employee shall provide written acknowledgment of the employee's receipt of the notification under this subsection. (1998-212, s. 9.14A(b).)

§ 135-5.4. Optional retirement program for State-funded community colleges.

(a) An Optional Retirement Program provided for in this section is authorized and established and shall be implemented by the North Carolina Community Colleges System, ("System"). The Optional Retirement Program shall be underwritten by the purchase of annuity contracts, which may be both fixed and variable contracts or a combination thereof, or financed through the establishment of a trust, for the benefit of the presidents of the community colleges all of whom are appointed after the implementation of the Program and who elect membership as required by subsection (b) of this section. Under the Optional Retirement Program, the State and the participant shall contribute, to the extent authorized or required, toward the purchase of such contracts or deposited in such trust on the participant's behalf.

(b) Participation in the Optional Retirement Program shall be governed as follows:

(1) Employees initially appointed on or after the implementation of the Optional Retirement Program shall at the same time of entering upon eligible employment elect (i) to join the Retirement System in accordance with the provisions of law applicable thereto or (ii) to participate in the Optional Retirement Program. This election shall be in writing and filed with the Retirement System and with the employing institution and shall be effective as of the date of entry into eligible service.

(2) An election to participate in the Optional Retirement Program shall be irrevocable. An eligible employee failing to elect to participate in the Optional Retirement Program at the time of entry into eligible service shall automatically be enrolled as a member of the Retirement System.

(3) No election by an eligible employee of the Optional Retirement Program shall be effective unless it is accompanied by an appropriate application for the issuance of a contract or contracts or trust participation under the Program.

(4) If any participant having less than five years coverage under the Optional Retirement Program leaves the employ of the System and either retires

or commences employment with an employer not having a retirement program with the same company underwriting the participant's annuity contract, regardless of whether the annuity contract is held by the participant, a trust, or the Retirement System, the participant's interest in the Optional Retirement Program attributable to contributions of the employing institution shall be forfeited and shall either (i) be refunded to the employing institution and forthwith paid by it to the Retirement System and credited to the pension accumulation fund or (ii) be paid directly to the Retirement System and credited to the pension accumulation fund.

(c) Each employing institution shall contribute on behalf of each participant in the Optional Retirement Program an amount equal to a percentage of the participant's compensation as established from time to time by the General Assembly. Each participant shall contribute the amount that he or she would be required to contribute if a member of the Retirement System. Contributions authorized or required by the provisions of this subsection on behalf of each participant shall be made, consistent with section 414(h) of the Internal Revenue Code, by salary reduction according to rules and regulations established by the employing institution. Additional personal contributions may also be made by a participant by payroll deduction or salary reduction to an annuity or retirement income plan established pursuant to G.S. 115D-25. Payment of contributions shall be made by the employing institution to the designated company or companies underwriting the annuities or the trustees for the benefit of each participant, and this employer contribution shall not be subject to any State tax if made under the Optional Retirement Program or, otherwise, by salary reduction.

(d) The System shall designate the company or companies from which contracts are to be purchased or the trustee responsible for the investment of contributions under the Optional Retirement Program and shall approve the form and contents of such contracts or trust agreement. In making this designation and giving such approval, the Board shall give due consideration to the following:

(1) The nature and extent of the rights and benefits to be provided by these contracts or trust agreement for participants and their beneficiaries;

(2) The relation of these rights and benefits to the amount of contributions to be made;

(3) The suitability of these rights and benefits to the needs of the participants and the interest of the institutions of the System in recruiting and retaining faculty in a national and market;

(4) The ability of the designated company or companies underwriting the annuity contracts or trust agreement to provide these suitable rights and benefits under such contracts or trust agreement for these purposes.

In lieu of such designation and in order to provide a more efficient, cost-effective, and flexible Program, the System may designate the company or companies designated for the Optional Retirement Program for State institutions of higher education as prescribed in G.S. 135-5.1(d).

Notwithstanding the provisions of this subsection, no contractual relationship established under the Optional Retirement Program pursuant to the authority granted by Chapter 338, Session Laws of 1971, is deemed terminated by the provisions of this section.

(e) The System or employing institution may provide for the administration of the Optional Retirement Program and may perform or authorize the performance of all functions necessary for its administration.

(f) Any eligible employee electing to participate in the Optional Retirement Program is ineligible for membership in the Retirement System so long as he or she remains employed in any eligible position within the System, and, in this event, he or she shall continue to participate in the Optional Retirement Program.

(g) No retirement benefit, death benefit, or other benefit under the Optional Retirement Program shall be paid by the State of North Carolina, or the System, or the Board of Trustees of the Teachers' and State Employees' Retirement System with respect to any employee selecting and participating in the Optional Retirement Program or with respect to any beneficiary of that employee. Benefits shall be payable to participants or their beneficiaries only by the designated company in accordance with the terms of the contracts or trust agreement.

(h) The North Carolina Community College System shall ensure that the Optional Retirement Program for State-funded community colleges contains benefit forfeiture provisions equivalent to those contained in G.S. 135-18.10A for community college personnel eligible for membership in the Teachers' and State

Employees' Retirement System and have elected participation in the Optional Retirement Program. Any funds forfeited shall be deposited in the Optional Retirement Program trust fund(s). (2001-424, s. 32.24(a); 2001-513, s. 24; 2012-193, s. 12.)

§ 135-6. Administration.

(a) Administration by Board of Trustees; Corporate Name; Rights and Powers; Tax Exemption. - The general administration and responsibility for the proper operation of the Retirement System and for making effective the provisions of the Chapter are hereby vested in a Board of Trustees which shall be organized immediately after a majority of the trustees provided for in this section shall have qualified and taken the oath of office.

The Board of Trustees shall be a body politic and corporate under the name "Board of Trustees Teachers' and State Employees' Retirement System"; and as a body politic and corporate shall have the right to sue and be sued, shall have perpetual succession and a common seal, and in said corporate name shall be able and capable in law to take, demand, receive and possess all kinds of real and personal property necessary and proper for its corporate purposes, and to bargain, sell, grant, alien, or dispose of all such real and personal property as it may lawfully acquire. All such property owned or acquired by said body politic and corporate shall be exempt from all taxes imposed by the State or any political subdivision thereof, and shall not be subject to income taxes.

(b) Membership of Board; Terms. - The Board shall consist of 13 members, as follows:

(1) The State Treasurer, ex officio;

(2) The Superintendent of Public Instruction, ex officio;

(3) Nine members to be appointed by the Governor and confirmed by the Senate of North Carolina. One of the appointive members shall be a member of the teaching profession of the State; one of the appointive members shall be a representative of higher education appointed by the Governor for a term of four years commencing July 1, 1969, and quadrennially thereafter; one of the appointive members shall be a retired teacher who is drawing a retirement allowance, appointed by the Governor for a term of four years commencing July

1, 1969, and quadrennially thereafter; one shall be a retired State employee who is drawing a retirement allowance, appointed by the Governor for a term of four years commencing July 1, 1977, and quadrennially thereafter; one to be a general State employee, and two who are not members of the teaching profession or State employees; two to be appointed for a term of two years, two for a term of three years and one for a term of four years; one appointive member shall be a law-enforcement officer employed by the State, appointed by the Governor, for a term of four years commencing April 1, 1985. One member shall be an active or retired member of the North Carolina National Guard appointed by the Governor for a term of four years commencing July 1, 2013. At the expiration of these terms of office the appointment shall be for a term of four years;

(4) Two members appointed by the General Assembly, one appointed upon the recommendation of the Speaker of the House of Representatives, and one appointed upon the recommendation of the President Pro Tempore of the Senate in accordance with G.S. 120-121. Neither of these members may be an active or retired teacher or State employee or an employee of a unit of local government. The initial members appointed by the General Assembly shall serve for terms expiring June 30, 1983. Thereafter, their successors shall serve for two-year terms beginning July 1 of odd-numbered years. Vacancies in appointments made by the General Assembly shall be filled in accordance with G.S. 120-122.

(c) Compensation of Trustees. - The trustees shall be paid during sessions of the Board at the prevailing rate established for members of State boards and commissions, and they shall be reimbursed for all necessary expenses that they incur through service on the Board.

(d) Oath. - Each trustee other than the ex officio members shall, within 10 days after his appointment, take an oath of office, that, so far as it devolves upon him, he will diligently and honestly administer the affairs of the said Board, and that he will not knowingly violate or willingly permit to be violated any of the provisions of law applicable to the Retirement System. Such oath shall be subscribed to by the member making it, and certified by the officer before whom it is taken, and immediately filed in the office of the Secretary of State.

(e) Voting Rights. - Each trustee shall be entitled to one vote in the Board. A majority of affirmative votes by trustees in attendance shall be necessary for a decision by the trustees at any meeting of the Board. A vote may only be taken if at least seven members of the Board are in attendance, in person or by telephone, for the meeting at which a vote on a decision is taken.

(f) Rules and Regulations. - Subject to the limitations of this Chapter, the Board of Trustees shall, from time to time, establish rules and regulations for the administration of the funds created by this Chapter and for the transaction of its business. The Board of Trustees shall also, from time to time, in its discretion, adopt rules and regulations to prevent injustices and inequalities which might otherwise arise in the administration of this Chapter.

(g) Officers and Other Employees; Salaries and Expenses. - The State Treasurer shall be ex officio chairman of the Board of Trustees. The Board of Trustees shall, by a majority vote of all the members, appoint a director, who may be, but need not be, one of its members. The salary of the director of the Retirement System is subject to the provisions of Chapter 126 of the General Statutes of North Carolina. The Board of Trustees shall engage such actuarial and other service as shall be required to transact the business of the Retirement System. The compensation of all persons, other than the director, engaged by the Board of Trustees, and all other expenses of the Board necessary for the operation of the Retirement System, shall be paid at such rates and in such amounts as the Board of Trustees shall approve, subject to the approval of the Director of the Budget.

(h) Actuarial Data. - The Board of Trustees shall keep in convenient form such data as shall be necessary for actuarial valuation of the various funds of the Retirement System, and for checking the experience of the System.

(i) Record of Proceedings; Annual Report. - The Board of Trustees shall keep a record of all of its proceedings which shall be open to public inspection. It shall publish annually a report showing the fiscal transactions of the Retirement System for the preceding year, the amount of the accumulated cash and securities of the System, and the last balance sheet showing the financial condition of the System by means of an actuarial valuation of the assets and liabilities of the Retirement System.

(j) Legal Adviser. - The Attorney General shall be the legal adviser of the Board of Trustees.

(k) Medical Board. - The Board of Trustees shall designate a medical board to be composed of not less than three nor more than five physicians not eligible to participate in the Retirement System. The Board of Trustees may structure appointment requirements and term durations for those medical board members. If required, other physicians may be employed to report on special cases. The medical board shall arrange for and pass upon all medical examinations required under the provisions of this Chapter, and shall investigate all essential statements and certificates by or on behalf of a member in connection with an application for disability retirement, and shall report in writing to the Board of Trustees its conclusion and recommendations upon all the matters referred to it.

(l)   Duties of Actuary. - The Board of Trustees shall designate an actuary who shall be the technical adviser of the Board of Trustees on matters regarding the operation of the funds created by the provisions of this Chapter and shall perform such other duties as are required in connection therewith. For purposes of the annual valuation of System assets, the experience studies, and all other actuarial calculations required by this Chapter, all the assumptions used by the System's actuary, including mortality tables, interest rates, annuity factors, and employer contribution rates, shall be set out in the actuary's periodic reports or other materials provided to the Board of Trustees. These materials, once accepted by the Board, shall be considered part of the Plan documentation governing this Retirement System; similarly, the Board's minutes relative to all actuarial assumptions used by the System shall also be considered part of the Plan documentation governing this Retirement System, with the result of precluding any employer discretion in the determination of benefits payable hereunder, consistent with Section 401(a)(25) of the Internal Revenue Code.

(m)   Immediately after the establishment of the Retirement System the actuary shall make such investigation of the mortality, service and compensation experience of the members of the System as he shall recommend and the Board of Trustees shall authorize, and on the basis of such investigation he shall recommend for adoption by the Board of Trustees such tables and such rates as are required in subsection (n), subdivisions (1) and (2), of this section. The Board of Trustees shall adopt tables and certify rates, and as soon as practicable thereafter the actuary shall make a valuation based on such tables and rates of the assets and liabilities of the funds created by this Chapter.

(n)   In 1943, and at least once in each five-year period thereafter, the actuary shall make an actuarial investigation into the mortality, service and compensation experience of the members and beneficiaries of the Retirement System, and shall make a valuation of the assets and liabilities of the funds of the System, and taking into account the result of such investigation and valuation, the Board of Trustees shall:

(1) Adopt for the Retirement System such mortality, service and other tables as shall be deemed necessary; and

(2) Certify the rates of contributions payable by the State of North Carolina on account of new entrants at various ages.

(o) On the basis of such tables and interest assumption rate as the Board of Trustees shall adopt, the actuary shall make an annual valuation of the assets and liabilities of the funds of the System created by this Chapter.

(p) Notwithstanding any law, rule, regulation or policy to the contrary, any board, agency, department, institution or subdivision of the State maintaining lists of names and addresses in the administration of their programs may upon request provide to the Retirement System information limited to social security numbers, current name and addresses of persons identified by the System as members, beneficiaries, and beneficiaries of members of the System. The System shall use such information for the sole purpose of notifying members, beneficiaries, and beneficiaries of members of their rights to and accruals of benefits in the Retirement System. Any social security number, current name and address so obtained and any information concluded therefrom and the source thereof shall be treated as confidential and shall not be divulged by any employee of the Retirement System or of the Department of State Treasurer except as may be necessary to notify the member, beneficiary, or beneficiary of the member of their rights to and accruals of benefits in the Retirement System. Any person, officer, employee or former employee violating this provision shall be guilty of a Class 1 misdemeanor; and if such offending person be a public official or employee, he shall be dismissed from office or employment and shall not hold any public office or employment in this State for a period of five years thereafter.

(q) Fraud Investigations - Access to Persons and Records. In the course of conducting a fraud investigation, the Retirement Systems Division, or authorized representatives who are assisting the Retirement Systems Division staff, shall:

(1) Have ready access to persons and may examine and copy all books, records, reports, vouchers, correspondence, files, personnel files, investments, and any other documentation of any employer. The review of State tax returns

shall be limited to matters of official business, and the Division's report shall not violate the confidentiality provisions of tax laws.

(2)   Have such access to persons, records, papers, reports, vouchers, correspondence, books, and any other documentation that is in the possession of any individual, private corporation, institution, association, board, or other organization that pertain to the following:

a.   Amounts received pursuant to a grant or contract from the federal government, the State, or its political subdivisions.

b.   Amounts received, disbursed, or otherwise handled on behalf of the federal government or the State.

(3)   Have the authority, and shall be provided with ready access, to examine and inspect all property, equipment, and facilities in the possession of any employer agency or any individual, private corporation, institution, association, board, or other organization that were furnished or otherwise provided through grant, contract, or any other type of funding by the employer agency.

With respect to the requirements of sub-subdivision (2)b. of this subsection, providers of social and medical services to a beneficiary shall make copies of records they maintain for services provided to a beneficiary available to the Retirement Systems Division, or to the authorized representatives who are assisting the Retirement Systems Division staff. Copies of the records of social and medical services provided to a beneficiary will permit verification of the health or other status of a beneficiary as required for the payment of benefits under Article 1, Article 4, or Article 6 of this Chapter. The Retirement Systems Division, or authorized representatives who are assisting the Retirement Systems Division staff, shall request records in writing by providing the name of each beneficiary for whom records are sought, the purpose of the request, the statutory authority for the request, and a reasonable period of time for the production of record copies by the provider. A provider may charge, and the Retirement Systems Division, or authorized representatives who are assisting the Retirement Systems Division staff, shall, in accordance with G.S. 90-411, pay a reasonable fee to the provider for copies of the records provided in accordance with this subsection.

(r)   Fraud Investigative Reports and Work Papers. - The Director of the Retirement Systems Division shall maintain for 10 years a complete file of all fraud investigative reports and reports of other examinations, investigations, surveys, and reviews issued under the Director's authority. Fraud investigation work papers and other evidence or related supportive material directly pertaining to the work of the Retirement Systems Division of the Department of State Treasurer shall be retained according to an agreement between the Director of Retirement and State Archives. To promote intergovernmental cooperation and avoid unnecessary duplication of fraud investigative effort, and notwithstanding local unit personnel policies to the contrary, pertinent work papers and other supportive material relating to issued fraud investigation reports may be, at the discretion of the Director of Retirement and unless otherwise prohibited by law, made available for inspection by duly authorized representatives of the State and federal government who desire access to and inspection of such records in connection with some matter officially before them, including criminal investigations. Except as provided in this section, or upon an order issued in Wake County Superior Court upon 10 days' notice and hearing finding that access is necessary to a proper administration of justice, fraud investigation work papers and related supportive material shall be kept confidential, including any information developed as a part of the investigation.

(s) Fraud Reports May Be Anonymous. - The identity of any person reporting fraud, waste, and abuse to the Retirement Systems Division shall be kept confidential and shall not be maintained as a public record within the meaning of G.S. 132-1. (1941, c. 25, s. 6; 1943, c. 719; 1947, c. 259; 1957, c. 541, s. 15; 1965, c. 780, s. 1; 1969, c. 805; c. 1223, s. 17; 1973, c. 241, s. 8; c. 507, s. 5; c. 1114; 1977, c. 564; 1979, c. 376; 1981 (Reg. Sess., 1982), c. 1191, s. 11; 1983 (Reg. Sess., 1984), c. 1034, s. 238; 1987, c. 539, s. 1; 1993, c. 539, s. 972; 1994, Ex. Sess., c. 24, s. 14(c); 1995, c. 490, s. 57; 2012-130, ss. 2(b), 9(b); 2012-185, ss. 2(d), 4(b); 2013-287, s. 4(a).)

§ 135-7. Management of funds.

(a) Vested in Board of Trustees. - The Board of Trustees shall be the trustee of the several funds created by this Chapter as provided in this section and in G.S. 135-8.

(b) Regular Interest Allowance. - The Board of Trustees annually shall allow regular interest on the mean amount for the preceding year in each of the funds with the exception of the expense fund. The amounts so allowed shall be due and payable to said funds, and shall be annually credited thereto by the Board of Trustees from interest and other earnings on the moneys of the Retirement

System. Any additional amount required to meet the interest on the funds of the Retirement System shall be paid from the pension accumulation fund, and any excess of earnings over such amount required shall be paid to the pension accumulation fund. Regular interest shall mean such per centum rate to be compounded annually as shall be determined by the Board of Trustees on the basis of the interest earnings of the System for the preceding year and of the probable earnings to be made, in the judgment of the Board, during the immediate future, such rate to be limited to a minimum of three per centum (3%) and a maximum of four per centum (4%), with the latter rate applicable during the first year of operation of the Retirement System.

(c) Custodian of Funds; Disbursements; Bond of Director. - The State Treasurer shall be the custodian of the several funds and shall invest their assets in accordance with the provisions of G.S. 147-69.2 and 147-69.3.

(d) Deposits to Meet Disbursements. - For the purpose of meeting disbursements for pensions, annuities and other payments there may be kept available cash, not exceeding ten per centum (10%) of the total amount in the several funds of the Retirement System, on deposit with the State Treasurer of North Carolina.

(e) Personal Profit or Acting as Surety Prohibited. - Except as otherwise herein provided, no trustee and no employee of the Board of Trustees shall have any direct interest in the gains or profits of any investment made by the Board of Trustees, nor as such receive any pay or emolument for his service. No trustee or employee of the Board shall, directly or indirectly, for himself or as an agent in any manner use the same, except to make such current and necessary payments as are authorized by the Board of Trustees; nor shall any trustee or employee of the Board of Trustees become an endorser or surety or in any manner an obligor for moneys loaned or borrowed from the Board of Trustees.

(f) Retiree Health Benefit Fund. - The Retiree Health Benefit Fund is established as a fund in which accumulated contributions from employers and any earnings on those contributions shall be used to provide health benefits to retired and disabled employees and their applicable beneficiaries as provided by this Chapter. The Retiree Health Benefit Fund shall be administered in accordance with the provisions of subsection (a) of this section. Employer contributions to the Fund are irrevocable. The assets of the Fund are dedicated to providing health benefits to retired and disabled employees and their applicable beneficiaries as provided by this Chapter and are not subject to the claims of creditors of the employers making contributions to the Fund. However, Fund assets may be used for reasonable expenses to administer the Fund, including costs to conduct required actuarial valuations of State-supported retired employees' health benefits under other post-employment benefit accounting standards set forth by the Governmental Accounting Standards Board of the Financial Accounting Foundation. (1941, c. 25, s. 7; 1957, c. 846, s. 2; 1959, c. 1181, s. 2; 1961, c. 397; 1965, c. 780, s. 1; 1967, c. 720, s. 11; c. 1205; 1971, c. 386, s. 4; 1973, c. 241, s. 9; 1979, c. 467, ss. 14, 15; 2004-124, s. 31.20(a); 2007-323, s. 28.23.)

§§ 135-7.1 through 135-7.2. Repealed by Session Laws 1979, c. 467, ss. 16, 17.

§ 135-8. Method of financing.

(a)   Funds to Which Assets of Retirement System Credited. - All of the assets of the Retirement System shall be credited according to the purpose for which they are held to one of four funds, namely, the annuity savings fund, the annuity reserve fund, the pension accumulation fund, and the pension reserve fund.

(b)   Annuity Savings Fund. - The annuity savings fund shall be a fund in which shall be accumulated contributions from the compensation of members to provide for their annuities. Contributions to any payments from the annuity savings fund shall be made as follows:

(1)   Prior to the first day of July, 1947, each employer shall cause to be deducted from the salary of each member on each and every payroll of such employer for each and every payroll period four per centum (4%) of his actual compensation; and the employer also shall deduct four per centum (4%) of any compensation received by any member for teaching in public schools, or in any of the institutions, agencies or departments of the State, from salaries other than the appropriations from the State of North Carolina. On and after such date the rate so deducted shall be five per centum (5%) of actual compensation except that, with respect to each member who is eligible for coverage under the Social Security Act in accordance with the agreement entered into during 1955 in accordance with the provisions of Article 2 of Chapter 135 of Volume 17 of the General Statutes, as amended, and with respect to members covered under G.S. 135-27, with such coverage retroactive to January 1, 1955, such deduction

shall, commencing with the first day of the period of service with respect to which such agreement is effective, be at the rate of three per centum (3%) of the part of his actual compensation not in excess of the amount taxable to him under the Federal Insurance Contributions Act as from time to time in effect plus five per centum (5%) of the part of his earnable compensation not so taxable; provided that in the case of any member so eligible and receiving compensation from two or more employers such deductions may be adjusted under such rules as the Board of Trustees may establish so as to be as nearly equivalent as practicable to the deductions which would have been made had the member received all of such compensation from one employer. Notwithstanding the foregoing, the Board of Trustees may in its discretion cause such portion as it may determine of deductions made between January 1, 1955, and December 1, 1955, to be transferred into the contribution fund established under G.S. 135-24; such amounts so transferred shall in that event be deemed to be taxes contributed by employees as required under Article 2, Chapter 135 of Volume 17 of the General Statutes as amended, and shall be in lieu of contributions otherwise payable in the same amount as so required.

Notwithstanding the foregoing, effective July 1, 1963, with respect to the period of service commencing on July 1, 1963, and ending December 31, 1965, the rates of such deduction shall be four per centum (4%) of the portion of compensation not in excess of forty-eight hundred dollars ($4,800) and six per centum (6%) of the portion of compensation in excess of forty-eight hundred dollars ($4,800); and with respect to the period of service commencing January 1, 1966, and ending June 30, 1967, the rate of such deductions shall be four per centum (4%) of the portion of compensation not in excess of fifty-six hundred dollars ($5,600) and six per centum (6%) of the portion of compensation in excess of fifty-six hundred dollars ($5,600); and with respect to the period of service commencing July 1, 1967, and ending June 30, 1975, the rate of such deductions shall be five per centum (5%) of the portion of compensation not in excess of fifty-six hundred dollars ($5,600) and six per centum (6%) of the portion of compensation in excess of fifty-six hundred dollars ($5,600). Such rates shall apply uniformly to all members of the Retirement System, without regard to their coverage under the Social Security Act.

Notwithstanding the foregoing, effective July 1, 1975, with respect to the period of service commencing on July 1, 1975, the rate of such deductions shall be six per centum (6%) of the compensation received by any member. Such rates shall apply uniformly to all members of the Retirement System, without regard to their coverage under the Social Security Act.

(2) The deductions provided for herein shall be made notwithstanding that the minimum compensation provided for by law for any member shall be reduced thereby. Every member shall be deemed to consent and agree to the deductions made and provided for herein and shall receipt for his full salary or compensation, and payment of salary or compensation less said deduction shall be a full and complete discharge and acquittance of all claims and demands whatsoever for the services rendered by such person during the period covered by such payment, except as to the benefits provided under this Chapter. The employer shall certify to the Board of Trustees on each and every payroll or in such other manner as the Board of Trustees may prescribe, the amounts to be deducted; and each of said amounts shall be deducted, and when deducted shall be paid into said annuity savings fund, and shall be credited, together with regular interest thereon, to the individual account of the member from whose compensation said deduction was made.

(3) Each board of education of each county and each board of education of each city, and the employer in any department, agency or institution of the State, in which any teacher receives compensation from sources other than appropriations of the State of North Carolina shall deduct from the salaries of these teachers paid from sources other than State appropriations an amount equal to that deducted from the salaries of the teachers whose salaries are paid from State funds, and remit this amount to the State Retirement System. City boards of education and county boards of education in each and every county and city which has employees compensated from other than the State appropriation shall pay to the State Retirement System the same per centum of the compensation that the State of North Carolina pays and shall transmit same to the State Retirement System monthly: Provided, that for the purpose of enabling the boards of education to make such payment, the tax-levying authorities are hereby authorized, empowered and directed to provide the necessary funds therefor. In case the salary is paid in part from State funds and in part from local funds, the local authorities shall not be relieved of providing and remitting the same per centum of the salary paid from local funds as is paid from State funds. In case the entire salary of any teacher, as defined in this Chapter, is paid from county or local funds, the county or city paying such salary shall provide and remit to the Retirement System the same per centum that would be required if the salary were provided by the State of North Carolina.

(4) In addition to contributions deducted from compensation as hereinbefore provided, subject to the approval of the Board of Trustees, any member may redeposit in the annuity savings fund by a single payment an amount equal to the total amount which he previously withdrew therefrom, as provided in this

Chapter. Such amounts so redeposited shall become a part of his accumulated contributions as if such amounts had initially been contributed within the calendar year of such redeposit. In no event, however, shall any member be permitted to redeposit any amount withdrawn after July 1, 1959, except as provided for in G.S. 135-4(e).

(5) The Board of Trustees may approve the purchase of creditable service by any member for leaves of absence or for interrupted service to an employer for the sole purpose of acquiring knowledge, talents, or abilities and to increase the efficiency of service to the employer. This approval shall be made prior to the purchase of the creditable service, is limited to a career total of six years for each member, and may be obtained in the following manner:

a. Approved leave of absence. - Where the employer grants an approved leave of absence, a member may make monthly contributions to the annuity savings fund on the basis of compensation the member was earning immediately prior to such leave of absence. The employer shall make monthly contributions equal to the normal and accrued liability contribution on such compensation or, in lieu thereof, the member may pay into the annuity savings fund monthly an amount equal to the employer's normal and accrued liability contribution when the policy of the employer is not to make such payment.

b. No educational leave policy. - Where the employer has a policy of not granting educational leaves of absence or the member has unsuccessfully petitioned for leave of absence and the member has interrupted service for educational purposes, the member may make monthly contributions into the annuity savings fund in an amount equal to the employee contribution plus the employer normal and accrued liability contribution on the basis of the compensation the member was earning immediately prior to the interrupted service.

c. Educational program prior to July 1, 1981. - Creditable service for leaves of absence or interrupted service for educational purposes prior to July 1, 1981, may be purchased by a member, before or after retirement, who returned as a contributing employee or teacher within 12 months after completing the educational program and completed 10 years of subsequent membership service, by making a lump sum payment into the annuity savings fund equal to the full cost of the service credits calculated on the basis of the assumptions used for purposes of the actuarial valuation of the system's liabilities and shall take into account the retirement allowance arising on account of the additional service credit commencing at the earliest age at which the member could retire on an unreduced retirement allowance as determined by the Board of Trustees upon the advice of the consulting actuary, plus a fee to be determined by the Board of Trustees.

d. Employment in a charter school. - Notwithstanding subparagraph a. of this subdivision, where the employer grants an approved leave of absence for the member to be employed in a charter school or where the member's service is interrupted by employment in a charter school, authorized under Part 6A of Article 16 of Chapter 115C of the General Statutes, the member may make monthly contributions into the annuity savings fund in an amount equal to the employee contribution plus the employer normal and accrued liability contribution on the basis of the compensation the member was earning immediately prior to the interrupted service.

Payments required to be made by the member, the employer, or both under subparagraphs a or b are due by the 15th of the month following the month for which the service credit is allowed and payments made after the due date shall be assessed a penalty, in lieu of interest, of one percent (1%) per month or fraction thereof the payment is made beyond the due date; provided, that these payments shall be made prior to retirement and provided further, that if the member did not become a contributing member within 12 months after completing the educational program and failed to complete three years of subsequent membership service, except in the event of death or disability, any payment made by the member including penalty shall be refunded with regular interest thereon and the service credits cancelled prior to or at retirement.

(6) The contributions of a member, and such interest as may be allowed thereon, paid upon his death or withdrawn by him as provided in this Chapter, shall be paid from the annuity savings fund, and any balance of the accumulated contributions of such a member shall be transferred to the pension accumulation fund.

(b1) Pick Up of Employee Contributions. - Anything within this section to the contrary notwithstanding, effective July 1, 1982, an employer, pursuant to the provisions of section 414(h)(2) of the Internal Revenue Code of 1954 as amended, shall pick up and pay the contributions which would be payable by the employees as members under subsection (b) of this section with respect to the service of employees after June 30, 1982.

The members' contributions picked up by an employer shall be designated for all purposes of the Retirement System as member contributions, except for the determination of tax upon a distribution from the System. These contributions shall be credited to the annuity savings fund and accumulated within the fund in a member's account which shall be separately established for the purpose of accounting for picked-up contributions.

Member contributions picked up by an employer shall be payable from the same source of funds used for the payment of compensation to a member. A deduction shall be made from a member's compensation equal to the amount of his contributions picked up by his employer. This deduction, however, shall not reduce his compensation as defined in subdivision (7a) of G.S. 135-1. Picked up contributions shall be transmitted to the System monthly for the preceding month by means of a warrant drawn by the employer and payable to the Teachers' and State Employees' Retirement System and shall be accompanied by a schedule of the picked-up contributions on such forms as may be prescribed. In the case of a failure to fulfill these conditions, the provisions of subsection (f)(3) of this section shall apply.

The pick up of employee contributions by an employer as provided for hereunder shall be equally applicable to participant contributions required under the optional retirement program as specified in G.S. 135-5.1(c).

(b2) Retroactive Adjustment in Compensation or an Underreporting of Compensation. - A member or beneficiary who is awarded backpay in cases of a denied promotional opportunity or wrongful demotion in which the aggrieved member or beneficiary is granted a promotion or a demotion is reversed retroactively, or in cases in which an employer errs in the reporting of compensation, including the employee and employer contributions, the member or beneficiary and employer may make employee and employer contributions on the retroactive or additional compensation, after submitting clear and convincing evidence of the retroactive promotion or underreporting of compensation, as follows:

(1) Within 90 days of the denial of the promotion or the error in reporting, by the payment of employee and employer contributions that would have been paid; or

(2) After 90 days of the denial of the promotion or the error in reporting, by the payment of the employee and employer contributions that would have been paid plus interest compounded annually at a rate equal to the greater of the average yield on the pension accumulation fund for the preceding calendar year

or the actuarial investment rate-of-return assumption, as adopted by the Board of Trustees.

For members or beneficiaries electing to make the employee contributions on the retroactive adjustment in compensation or on the underreported compensation, the member's or beneficiary's employer, which granted the retroactive promotion or erred in underreporting compensation and contributions, shall make the required employer contributions. Nothing contained in this subsection shall prevent an employer from paying all or a part of the interest assessed on the employee contributions; and to the extent paid by the employer, the interest paid by the employer shall be credited to the pension accumulation fund; provided, however, an employer does not discriminate against any member or beneficiary or group of members or beneficiaries in his employ in paying all or any part of the interest assessed on the employee contributions due.

In the event the retroactive adjustment in compensation or the underreported compensation is for a period that occurs during the four consecutive calendar years that would have produced the highest average annual compensation pursuant to G.S. 135-1(5) the compensation the member or beneficiary would have received during the period shall be included in calculating the member's or beneficiary's average final compensation only in the event the appropriate employee and employer contributions are paid on such compensation.

An employer error in underreporting compensation shall not include a retroactive increase in compensation that occurs during the four consecutive calendar years that would have produced the highest average annual compensation pursuant to G.S. 135-1(5) for reasons other than a wrongfully denied promotional opportunity or wrongful demotion where the member is promoted or the demotion is reversed retroactively.

(c) Annuity Reserve Fund. - The annuity reserve fund shall be the fund in which shall be held the reserves on all annuities in force and from which shall be paid all annuities and all benefits in lieu of annuities, payable as provided in this Chapter. Should a beneficiary retired on account of disability be restored to active service with a compensation not less than his average final compensation at the time of his last retirement his annuity reserve shall be transferred from the annuity reserve fund to the annuity savings fund and credited to his individual account therein.

(d) Pension Accumulation Fund. - The pension accumulation fund shall be the fund in which shall be accumulated all reserves for the payment of all pensions and other benefits payable from contribution made by employers and from which shall be paid all pensions and other benefits on account of members with prior service credit. Contributions to and payments from the pension accumulation fund shall be made as follows:

(1) On account of each member there shall be paid in the pension accumulation fund by employers an amount equal to a certain percentage of the actual compensation of each member to be known as the "normal contribution," and an additional amount equal to a percentage of his actual compensation to be known as the "accrued liability contribution." The rate per centum of such contributions shall be fixed on the basis of the liabilities of the Retirement System as shown by actuarial valuation. Until the first valuation the normal contribution shall be two and fifty-seven one-hundredths percent (2.57%) for teachers, and one and fifty-seven one-hundredths percent (1.57%) for State employees, and the accrued liability contribution shall be two and ninety-four one-hundredths percent (2.94%) for teachers and one and fifty-nine one-hundredths percent (1.59%) of the salary of other State employees.

(2) On the basis of regular interest and of such mortality and other tables as shall be adopted by the Board of Trustees, the actuary engaged by the Board to make each valuation required by this Chapter during the period over which the accrued liability contribution is payable, immediately after making such valuation, shall determine the uniform and constant percentage of the earnable compensation of the average new entrant throughout his entire period of active service which would be sufficient to provide for the payment of any pension payable on his account. The rate per centum so determined shall be known as the "normal contribution" rate. After the accrued liability contribution has ceased to be payable, the normal contribution rate shall be the rate per centum of the earnable salary of all members obtained by deducting from the total liabilities of the pension accumulation fund the amount of the funds in hand to the credit of that fund and dividing the remainder by one per centum of the present value of the prospective future salaries of all members as computed on the basis of the mortality and service tables adopted by the Board of Trustees and regular interest. The normal rate of contribution shall be determined by the actuary after each valuation.

(3) Immediately succeeding the first valuation the actuary engaged by the Board of Trustees shall compute the rate per centum of the total annual compensation of all members which is equivalent to four percent (4%) of the

amount of the total pension liability on account of all members and beneficiaries which is not dischargeable by the aforesaid normal contribution made on account of such members during the remainder of their active service. The rate per centum originally so determined shall be known as the "accrued liability contribution" rate. Such rate shall be increased on the basis of subsequent valuations if benefits are increased over those included in the valuation on the basis of which the original accrued liability contribution rate was determined. Upon certification by the actuary engaged by the Board of Trustees that the accrued liability contribution rate may be reduced without impairing the Retirement System, the Board of Trustees may cause the accrued liability contribution rate to be reduced.

(4)   The total amount payable in each year to the pension accumulation fund shall not be less than the sum of the rate per centum known as the normal contribution rate and the accrued liability contribution rate of the total actual compensation of all members during the preceding year: Provided, however, that, subject to the provisions of subdivision (3) of this subsection the amount of each annual accrued liability contribution shall be at least three percent (3%) greater than the preceding annual accrued liability payment, and that the aggregate payment by employers shall be sufficient, when combined with the amount in the fund, to provide the pensions and other benefits payable out of the fund during the year then current.

(5)   The accrued liability contribution shall be discontinued as soon as the accumulated reserve in the pension accumulation fund shall equal the present value as actuarially computed and approved by the Board of Trustees, of the total liability of such fund less the present value, computed on the basis of the normal contribution rate then in force, of the prospective normal contributions to be received on account of all persons who are at the time members.

(6)   All pensions, and benefits in lieu thereof, with the exception of those payable on account of members who received no prior service allowance, payable from contributions of employer shall be paid from the pension accumulation fund.

(7)   Upon the retirement of a member not entitled to credit for prior service, an amount equal to his pension reserve shall be transferred from the pension accumulation fund to the pension reserve fund.

(e)   Pension Reserve Fund. - The pension reserve fund shall be the fund in which shall be held the reserves on all pensions granted to members not entitled to credit for prior service and from which such pensions and benefits in lieu thereof shall be paid. Should such a beneficiary retired on account of disability be restored to active service with a compensation not less than his average final compensation at the time of his last retirement, the pension thereon shall be transferred from the pension reserve fund to the pension accumulation fund. Should the pension of such disability beneficiary be reduced as a result of an increase in his earning capacity, the amount of the annual reduction in his pension shall be paid annually into the pension accumulation fund during the period of such reduction.

(f)   Collection of Contributions. -

(1)   The collection of members' contributions shall be as follows:

a.   Each employer shall cause to be deducted on each and every payroll of a member for each and every payroll subsequent to the date of establishment of the Retirement System the contributions payable by such member as provided in this Chapter, and the employer shall draw his warrant for the amount so deducted, payable to the Teachers' and State Employees' Retirement System of North Carolina, and shall transmit the same, together with schedule of the contributions, on such forms as prescribed.

(2)   The collection of employers' contributions shall be made as follows:

a.   Upon the basis of each actuarial valuation provided herein there shall be prepared biennially and certified to the Department of Administration a statement of the total amount necessary for the ensuing biennium to the pension accumulation and expense funds, as provided under subsections (d) and (f) of this section, and these funds shall be handled and disbursed in accordance with the State Budget Act, Chapter 143C of the General Statutes.

b.   Until the first valuation has been made and the rates computed as provided in subsection (d) of this section, the amount payable by employers on account of the normal and accrued liability contributions shall be five and fifty-one one-hundredths percent (5.51%) of the payroll of all teachers and three and sixteen one-hundredths percent (3.16%) for other State employees.

c.   Repealed by Session Laws 1993, c. 257, s. 13.

d.   Each board of education in each county and each board of education in each city in which teachers or other employees of the schools receive compensation for services in the public schools from sources other than the appropriation of the State of North Carolina shall pay the Board of Trustees of the State Retirement System such rate of their respective salaries as are paid those of other employees.

e. Each employer shall transmit monthly to the State Retirement System on account of each employee, who is a member of this System, an amount sufficient to cover the normal contribution and the accrued liability contribution of each member employed by such employer for the preceding month.

(3) In the event the employee or employer contributions required under this section are not received by the date set by the Board of Trustees, the Board shall assess the employer with a penalty of 1% per month with a minimum penalty of twenty-five dollars ($25.00). If within 90 days after request therefor by the Board any employer shall not have provided the System with the records and other information required hereunder or if the full accrued amount of the contributions provided for under this section due from members employed by an employer or from an employer other than the State shall not have been received by the System from the chief fiscal officer of such employer within 30 days after the last due date as herein provided, then, notwithstanding anything herein or in the provisions of any other law to the contrary, upon notification by the Board to the State Treasurer as to the default of such employer as herein provided, any distributions which might otherwise be made to such employer from any funds of the State shall be withheld from such employer until notice from the Board to the State Treasurer that such employer is no longer in default.

(g) Merger of Annuity Reserve Fund and Pension Reserve Fund into Pension Accumulation Fund. - Notwithstanding the foregoing, effective at such date not later than December 31, 1959, as the Board of Trustees may determine, the annuity reserve fund and the pension reserve fund shall be merged into and become a part of the pension accumulation fund, provided that such merger shall in no way adversely affect the rights of any members or retired members of the System and further provided the Board of Trustees shall be and hereby is authorized to make such changes in the accounting methods and procedures of the System from time to time as, in its opinion, are in the interest of sound and proper administration of the System.

(h) Repealed by Session Laws 1965, c. 780, s. 1. (1941, c. 25, s. 8; c. 143; 1943, c. 207; 1947, c. 458, ss. 1, 2, 8; 1955, c. 1155, ss. 3-5; 1959, c. 513, s. 4; 1963, c. 687, ss. 4, 5; 1965, c. 780, s. 1; 1967, c. 720, ss. 12, 13; 1969, c. 1223, s. 13; 1971, c. 117, ss. 2, 10; 1975, c. 457, s. 5; c. 879, s. 46; 1977, c. 909;

1981, c. 636, s. 1; c. 1000, ss. 1, 2; 1981 (Reg. Sess., 1982), c. 1282, s. 8; 1985, c. 539, ss. 1, 2; 1991, c. 585, s. 3; c. 718, s. 1; 1993, c. 257, s. 13; 1997-430, s. 11; 2003-359, s. 10; 2006-203, s. 73; 2009-66, s. 7(a); 2010-72, s. 8(a).)

§ 135-9. Exemption from garnishment, attachment, etc.

Except for the applications of the provisions of G.S. 110-136, and G.S. 110-136.3 et seq., and in connection with a court-ordered equitable distribution under G.S. 50-20, the right of a person to a pension, or annuity, or a retirement allowance, to the return of contributions, the pension, annuity or retirement allowance itself, any optional benefit or any other right accrued or accruing to any person under the provisions of this Chapter, and the moneys in the various funds created by this Chapter, are exempt from levy and sale, garnishment, attachment, or any other process whatsoever, and shall be unassignable except as in this Chapter specifically otherwise provided. Application for System approval of a domestic relations order dividing a person's interest under the Retirement System shall be accompanied by an order consistent with the system-designed template order provided on the System's Web site. Notwithstanding any provisions to the contrary, any overpayment of benefits to a member in a State-administered retirement system or the former Disability Salary Continuation Plan or the Disability Income Plan of North Carolina may be offset against any retirement allowance, return of contributions or any other right accruing under this Chapter to the same person, the person's estate, or designated beneficiary. (1941, c. 25, s. 9; 1985, c. 402, s. 1; c. 649, s. 5; 1987, c. 738, s. 29(k); 1989, c. 665, s. 1; c. 792, s. 2.5; 2013-405, s. 4(a).)

§ 135-10. Protection against fraud.

Any person who shall knowingly make any false statement or shall falsify or permit to be falsified any record or records of this Retirement System in any attempt to defraud such System as a result of such act shall be guilty of a Class 1 misdemeanor. Should any change or error in the records result in any member or beneficiary receiving from the Retirement System more or less than he would have been entitled to receive had the records been correct, the Board of Trustees shall correct such error, and as far as practicable, shall adjust the payment in such a manner that the actuarial equivalent of the benefit to which such member or beneficiary was correctly entitled shall be paid. (1941, c. 25, s. 10; 1993, c. 539, s. 973; 1994, Ex. Sess., c. 24, s. 14(c).)

§ 135-10.1. Failure to respond.

If a member fails to respond within 120 days after preliminary option figures and the Form 6-E or Form 7-E are mailed, or if a member fails to respond within 120 days after the effective date of retirement, whichever is later, the Form 6 or Form 7 shall be null and void; the retirement system shall not be liable for any benefits due on account of the voided application, and a new application must be filed establishing a subsequent effective date of retirement. If an applicant for disability retirement fails to furnish requested additional medical information within 90 days following such request, the application shall be declared null and void under the same conditions outlined above, unless the applicant is eligible for early or service retirement in which case the application shall be processed accordingly, using the same effective date as would have been used had the application for disability retirement been approved. The Director of the Retirement Systems Division, acting on behalf of the Board of Trustees, may extend the 120-day limitation provided for in this section when a member has suffered incapacitation such that a reasonable person would not have expected the member to be able to complete the required paperwork within the regular deadline, or when an omission by the Retirement Systems Division prevents the member from having sufficient time to meet the regular deadline. (2005-91, s. 4; 2009-66, s. 4(b); 2010-72, s. 6(a).)

§ 135-11. Application of other pension laws.

Subject to the provisions of Article 2, Chapter 135 of the General Statutes, Volume 17, as amended, no other provisions of law in any other statute which provides wholly or partly at the expense of the State of North Carolina for pensions or retirement benefits for teachers or State employees of the said State, their widows, or other dependents shall apply to members or beneficiaries of the Retirement System established by this Chapter, their widows or other dependents. (1941, c. 25, s. 11; 1955, c. 1155, s. 6.)

§ 135-12. Obligation of maintaining reserves and paying benefits.

The maintenance of annuity reserves and pension reserves as provided for and regular interest creditable to the various funds as provided in G.S. 135-8, and the payment of all pensions, annuities, retirement allowances, refunds and other benefits granted under the provisions of this Chapter, are hereby made obligations of the pension accumulation fund. All income, interest and dividends derived from deposits and investments authorized by this Chapter shall be used for the payment of the said obligations of the said fund. (1941, c. 25, s. 12.)

§ 135-13. Certain laws not repealed; suspension of payments and compulsory retirement.

Nothing in this Chapter shall be construed to repeal or invalidate any of the provisions of Chapter 483 of the Public-Local Laws of 1919, or Chapter 385 of the Public-Local Laws of 1921, as amended, relating to pensions for school teachers in New Hanover County. No payment on account of any benefit granted under the provisions of G.S. 135-5, subsections (a) and (d) inclusive, shall become effective or begin to accrue until the end of one year following the date the System is established nor shall any compulsory retirement be made during such period. (1941, c. 25, s. 13.)

§ 135-14. Pensions of certain former teachers and State employees.

On and after July 1, 1983, special pensions and allowances of certain former teachers and State employees shall be paid out of the Pension Accumulation Fund of the Retirement System, as follows:

(1) Any person who was a teacher or employee, as defined in G.S. 135-1(10) and (25), for 20 or more years, whose separation from service was prior to April 1, 1956, was not due to any dishonorable cause, and who had attained age 65 prior to July 1, 1960, shall upon application be paid an allowance of one hundred seventy-three dollars and twenty-five cents ($173.25) per month.

(2) Any beneficiary who did not qualify for Social Security benefits and had 20 or more years of creditable service and qualified for a minimum eighty-five

dollars ($85.00) per month under the provisions of Chapter 1140 of the 1965 Session Laws, shall be paid the allowance in effect on June 30, 1983.

(3) Any beneficiary who did not qualify for Social Security benefits and who had 15 years but less than 20 years of creditable service and qualified for a benefit of four dollars ($4.00) per month for each year of creditable service under the provisions of Chapter 1199 of the 1965 Session Laws shall be paid the allowance in effect on June 30, 1983.

(4) All the allowances in subsections (1) through (3) of this section may be adjusted by any cost-of-living increases in retirement allowances provided by the General Assembly or by the Board of Trustees. (1943, c. 785; 1953, c. 1132, s. 1; 1955, c. 1199, ss. 1, 2; 1957, cc. 852, 1408, 1412; 1959, c. 538, s. 1; 1979, c. 1057, ss. 1, 2; 1983, c. 761, s. 223.)

§ 135-14.1. Certain school superintendents and assistant superintendents.

Any person who has been a superintendent or assistant superintendent in the public schools of North Carolina for a total of 20 years or more and who was not a superintendent or assistant superintendent in the public schools of this State at the time of the enactment of the Teachers' and State Employees' Retirement System Act, the same being this Chapter, and whose cessation of employment as a superintendent or assistant superintendent was not due to any dishonorable cause shall be entitled to receive benefits under said Retirement Act for such services in the same manner and to the same extent as such 20 years of prior service would have entitled such superintendent or assistant superintendent had he or she been a superintendent or assistant superintendent in the public schools at the time said Retirement Act became effective, and had chosen to become a member of the Retirement System, provided that such former superintendent or assistant superintendent has returned to State service and been employed for at least five years and has reached the age of 65 before July 1, 1957; provided, further, the monthly benefit to such former superintendent or assistant superintendent shall be equal to the minimum provided with respect to teachers under the provisions of G.S. 135-14, as amended. (1957, c. 1431.)

§ 135-15: Repealed by Session Laws 1949, c. 1056, s. 9.

§ 135-16. Employees transferred to North Carolina State Employment Service by act of Congress.

Notwithstanding any provision contained in this Chapter, any employee of the United States Employment Service who was transferred to and became employed by the State of North Carolina, or any of its agencies, on November 16, 1946, by virtue of Public Laws 549, 79th Congress, Chapter 672, 2nd Session, and who was employed by the War Manpower Commission or the United States Employment Service between January 1, 1942, and November 15, 1946, shall be deemed to have been engaged in membership service as defined by this Chapter for any payroll period or periods between such dates: Provided, that any such employee or member on or before January 1, 1948, pays to the Board of Trustees for the benefit of the proper fund or account an amount equal to the accumulated contributions, with interest thereon, that such employee or member would have made during such period if he had been a member of the Retirement System with earnable compensation based on the salary received for such period and as limited by this Chapter: Provided, further that funds are made available by the United States Employment Service, or other federal agency, to the Division of Employment Security for the payment of and the Division of Employment Security pays to the Board of Trustees for the benefit of the proper fund a sum equal to the employer's contributions that would have been paid for such period for members or employees who pay the accumulated contributions provided in this section.

The Board of Trustees is authorized to adopt and issue all necessary rules and regulations for the purpose of administering and enforcing the provisions of this section. (1947, c. 464, s. 1; c. 598, s. 1; 2011-401, s. 3.17.)

§ 135-16.1. Blind or visually impaired employees.

(a)   On July 1, 1971, all blind or visually impaired employees employed by the Department of Health and Human Services shall be enrolled as members of the Teachers' and State Employees' Retirement System. All such employees shall be given full credit for all service theretofore as employees of the Department of Health and Human Services. All retired employees drawing or receiving benefits from and under the private retirement plan purportedly created on December 6, 1966, by the Bureau of Employment for the Blind Division pursuant to a trust agreement purportedly entered into with a private banking institution as trustee shall continue to be paid by the Teachers' and

State Employees' Retirement System benefits in the same amount which they purportedly were entitled to under the private retirement plan and trust agreement, except that such retired persons shall be eligible for such annual cost-of-living increases as may be provided for retirement members of the Teachers' and State Employees' Retirement System under the provisions of this Article.

(b) Upon the enrollment of the employees in the Teachers' and State Employees' Retirement System, the purported private retirement plan and trust agreement hereinabove referred to shall be dissolved and terminated.

(c) Notwithstanding the foregoing, blind persons licensed by the State and operating vending facilities under contract with the Department of Health and Human Services, Division of Services for the Blind and its successors, hereinafter referred to as licensed vendors, so licensed on and after October 1, 1983, shall not be members of the Retirement System. All licensed vendors in service or who are members of the Retirement System before October 1, 1983, shall make an irrevocable election to do one of the following:

(1) Continue contributing membership service as if an employee under the same conditions and requirements as are otherwise provided, and have the rights of a member to all benefits and a retirement allowance;

(2) Receive a return of accumulated contributions with cessation of contributing membership service, under G.S. 135-5(f), and in any event with regular interest regardless of membership service; or

(3) Terminate contributing membership service and be entitled alternatively to the benefits and allowances provided under G.S. 135-3(8) or 135-5(a). (1971, c. 1025, s. 3; 1973, c. 476, s. 143; 1983, c. 867, s. 3; 1997-443, s. 11A.118(a); 2000-121, s. 28.)

§ 135-17. Facility of payment.

In the event of the death of a member or beneficiary not survived by a person designated to receive any return of accumulated contributions or balance thereof, or in the event that the Board of Trustees shall find that a beneficiary is unable to care for his affairs because of illness or accident, any benefit payments due may, unless claim shall have been made therefor by a duly appointed guardian, committee or other legal representative, be paid to the spouse, a child, a parent or other blood relative, or to any person deemed by the Board of Trustees to have incurred expense for such beneficiary or deceased member, and any such payments so made shall be a complete discharge of the liabilities of this Retirement System therefor. (1949, c. 1056, s. 6.)

§ 135-18: Repealed by Session Laws 1969, c. 1223, s. 14.

§ 135-18.1. Transfer of credits from the North Carolina Local Governmental Employees' Retirement System.

(a) Any person who is a member of the Teachers' and State Employees' Retirement System of North Carolina on July 1, 1951, and who was previously a member of the North Carolina Governmental Employees' Retirement System, hereafter in this section referred to as the local system, shall be entitled to transfer to this Retirement System his credits for membership and prior service in the local system as of the date of termination of membership in the local system, notwithstanding that his membership in the local system may have been terminated prior to July 1, 1951: Provided, such member shall deposit in this Retirement System prior to January 1, 1952, the full amount of any accumulated contributions standing to his credit in, or previously withdrawn from, the local system and shall apply to the Board of Trustees of this Retirement System for a transfer of credit from the local system. Any person who becomes a member of this Retirement System on or after July 1, 1951, shall be entitled prior to his retirement to transfer to this Retirement System his credits for membership and prior service in the local system: Provided, the actual transfer of employment is made while his account in the local system is active and such person shall request the local system to transfer his accumulated contributions, interest, and service credits to this Retirement System; provided further, with respect to any person who becomes a member of this Retirement System after July 1, 1969, the local system agrees to transfer to this Retirement System the amount of reserve held in the local system as a result of previous contributions of the employer on behalf of the transferring employee.

(b) The accumulated contributions withdrawn from the local system and deposited in this Retirement System shall be credited to such member's account in the annuity savings fund of this Retirement System and shall be deemed, for the purpose of computing any benefits subsequently payable from the annuity savings fund, to be regular contributions made on the date of such deposit.

(c) Upon the deposit in this Retirement System of the accumulated contributions previously withdrawn from the local system the Board of Trustees of this Retirement System shall request the Board of Trustees of the local system to certify to the period of membership service credit and the regular accumulated contributions attributable thereto and to the period of prior service credit, if any, and the contributions with interest allowable as a basis for prior service benefits in the local system, as of the date of termination of membership in the local system. Credit shall be allowed in this System for the service so certified in determining the member's credited service and, upon his retirement he shall be entitled, in addition to the regular benefits allowable on account of his participation in this Retirement System, to the pension which shall be the actuarial equivalent at age 65 or at retirement, if prior thereto, of the amount of the credit with interest thereon representing contributions attributable to his service credits in the local system.

(d) The Board of Trustees of the Retirement System shall effect such rules as it may deem necessary to prevent any duplication of service, interest or other credits which might otherwise occur. (1951, c. 797; 1961, c. 516, s. 7; 1965, c. 780, s. 1; 1969, c. 1223, s. 15; 1971, c. 117, ss. 16, 17; 1973, c. 241, s. 11.)

§ 135-18.2: Repealed by Session Laws 1959, c. 538, s. 3.

§ 135-18.3. Conditions under which amendments void.

If for any reason the federal-state agreement provided in Article 2 of Chapter 135 of the General Statutes, Volume 17, as amended, is not entered upon, or the referendum authorized therein with respect to positions covered by the Teachers' and State Employees' Retirement System of North Carolina is not held, or the conditions specified in section 218 (d)(3) of this Social Security Act with respect to such referendum if held are not met, this act shall be null and void. (1955, c. 1155, s. 7.)

§ 135-18.4. Reservation of power to change.

The General Assembly reserves the right at any time and from time to time, and if deemed necessary or appropriate by said General Assembly in order to coordinate with any changes, in the benefit and other provisions of the Social Security Act made after January 1, 1955, to modify or amend in whole or in part any or all of the provisions of the Teachers' and State Employees' Retirement System of North Carolina. (1955, c. 1155, s. 8.)

§ 135-18.5. Provision for emergency expenses of integration of System.

For the purpose of meeting the expenses involved in administering the provisions of this Article to June 30, 1959, and in holding the referendum described herein with respect to positions covered under the Teachers' and State Employees' Retirement System of North Carolina as established by Article 1 of Chapter 135 of the General Statutes, Volume 17, as amended, any funds not otherwise provided for such purpose by action of the General Assembly during the session of 1955 or 1957 may be borrowed from the pension accumulation fund of such System; provided, however, that the amount so borrowed and the expenditure thereof shall be subject to the approval of the Board of Trustees of such System and the assistant director of the budget, and that such amounts so borrowed shall be repaid as soon as practicable. (1955, c. 1155, s. 9; 1957, c. 855, s. 9.)

§ 135-18.6. Termination or partial termination; discontinuance of contributions.

In the event of the termination or partial termination of the Retirement System or in the event of complete discontinuance of contributions under the Retirement System, the rights of all affected members to benefits accrued to the date of such termination, partial termination, or discontinuance, to the extent funded as of such date, or the amounts credited to the members' accounts, shall be nonforfeitable and fully vested. (1987; c. 177, s. 1(a), (b).)

§ 135-18.7. Internal Revenue Code compliance.

(a) Notwithstanding any other provisions of law to the contrary, compensation for any calendar year after 1988 in which employee or employer contributions are made and for which annual compensation is used for computing any benefit under this Article shall not exceed the higher of two hundred thousand dollars ($200,000) or the amount determined by the Commissioner of Internal Revenue as the limitation for calendar years after 1989; provided the imposition of the limitation shall not reduce a member's benefit below the amount determined as of December 31, 1988.

Effective January 1, 1996, the annual compensation of a member taken into account for determining all benefits provided under this Article shall not exceed one hundred fifty thousand dollars ($150,000), as adjusted pursuant to section 401(a)(17)(B) of the Internal Revenue Code and any regulations issued under the Code. However, with respect to a person who became a member of the Retirement System prior to January 1, 1996, the imposition of this limitation on compensation shall not reduce the amount of compensation which may be taken into account for determining the benefits of that member under this Article below the amount of compensation which would have been recognized under the provisions of this Article in effect on July 1, 1993.

Effective January 1, 2002, the annual compensation of a person, who became a member of the Retirement System on or after January 1, 1996, taken into account for determining all benefits accruing under this Article for any plan year after December 31, 2001, shall not exceed two hundred thousand dollars ($200,000) or the amount otherwise set by the Internal Revenue Code or determined by the Commissioner of Internal Revenue as the limitation for calendar years after 2002.

All the provisions in this subsection have been enacted to make clear that the Plan shall not base contributions or Plan benefits on annual compensation in excess of the limits prescribed by Section 401(a)(17) of the Internal Revenue Code, as adjusted from time to time, subject to certain federal grandfathering rules.

(b) Notwithstanding any other provisions of law to the contrary, the annual benefit payable on behalf of a member shall, if necessary, be reduced to the extent required by Section 415(b) and with respect to calendar years commencing prior to January 1, 2000, Section 415(e) of the Internal Revenue Code, as adjusted by the Secretary of the Treasury or his delegate pursuant to Section 415(d) of the Code. If a member is a participant under any qualified defined contributions plan that is required to be taken into account for the purposes of the limitation contained in Section 415 of the Internal Revenue Code, the annual benefit payable under this Article shall be reduced to the extent required by Section 415(e) prior to making any reduction under the defined contribution plan provided by the employer. However, with respect to a member who has benefits accrued under this Article but whose benefit had not commenced as of December 31, 1999, the combined plan limitation contained in Section 415(e) of the Internal Revenue Code shall not be applied to such member for calendar years commencing on or after January 1, 2000.

(c) On and after September 8, 2009, and for all Plan years to which the minimum distribution rules of the Internal Revenue Code are applicable, with respect to any member who has terminated employment, the Plan shall comply with federal income tax minimum distribution rules by applying a reasonable and good faith interpretation to Section 401(a)(9) of the Internal Revenue Code.

(d) This subsection applies to distributions and rollovers from the Plan. The Plan does not have mandatory distributions within the meaning of Section 401(a)(31) of the Internal Revenue Code. With respect to distributions from the Plan and notwithstanding any other provision of the Plan to the contrary that would otherwise limit a distributee's election under this Article, a distributee (including, after December 31, 2006, a non-spouse beneficiary if that non-spouse beneficiary elects a direct rollover only to an inherited traditional or Roth IRA as permitted under applicable federal law) may elect, at the time and in the manner prescribed by the Plan administrator, to have any portion of an eligible rollover distribution paid directly to an eligible retirement plan specified by the distributee in a direct rollover. As used in this subsection, an "eligible retirement plan" means an individual retirement account described in Section 408(a) of the Code, an individual retirement annuity described in Section 408(b) of the Code, an annuity plan described in Section 403(a) of the Code, on and after January 1, 2009, a Roth IRA, or a qualified trust described in Section 401(a) of the Code, that accepts the distributee's eligible rollover distribution. Effective on and after January 1, 2002, an eligible retirement plan also means an annuity contract described in Section 403(b) of the Code and an eligible plan under Section 457(b) of the Code that is maintained by a state, political subdivision of a state, or any agency or instrumentality of a state or political subdivision of a state and which agrees to separately account for amounts transferred into that plan from this Plan. As used in this subsection, a "direct rollover" is a payment by the Plan to the eligible retirement plan specified by the distributee. Provided, an eligible rollover distribution is any distribution of all or any portion of the balance to the credit of the distributee, except that an eligible rollover distribution shall not include: any distribution that is one of a series of substantially equal periodic payments (not less frequently than annually) made for the life (or life expectancy) of the distributee or the joint lives (or joint life expectancies) of the distributee and the distributee's designated beneficiary, or for a specified period of 10 years or more; any distribution to the extent such distribution is required under section 401(a)(9) of the Code; and the portion of any distribution that is not includible in gross income (determined without regard to the exclusion for net realized appreciation with respect to employer securities). Effective as of January 1, 2002, and notwithstanding the exclusion of any after-tax portion from such a rollover distribution in the preceding sentence, a portion of a distribution shall not fail to be an eligible rollover distribution merely because the portion consists of after-tax employee contributions which are not includible in gross income. That portion may be transferred, pursuant to applicable federal law, to an individual retirement account or annuity described in Section 408(a) or (b) of the Code, to a qualified defined benefit plan, or to a qualified defined contribution plan described in Section 401(a), 403(a), or 403(b) of the Code that agrees to separately account for amounts so transferred, including separately accounting for the portion of such distribution which is includible in gross income and the portion of such distribution which is not so includible. The definition of eligible retirement plan shall also apply in the case of a distribution to surviving spouse, or to a spouse or former spouse who is the alternate payee under a qualified domestic relations order, as defined in Section 414(p) of the Internal Revenue Code, or a court-ordered equitable distribution of marital property, as provided under G.S. 50-20.1. Effective on and after January 1, 2007, notwithstanding any other provision of this subsection, a nonspouse beneficiary of a deceased member may elect, at the time and in the manner prescribed by the administrator of the Board of Trustees of this Retirement System, to directly roll over any portion of the beneficiary's distribution from the Retirement System; however, such rollover shall conform with the provisions of section 402(c)(11) of the Code. (1989, c. 276, s. 3; 1993, c. 531, s. 6; 1995, c. 361, s. 1; 2002-71, s. 6; 2009-66, s. 1(a); 2012-130, s. 4(c).)

§ 135-18.8. Deduction for payments allowed.

(a) Any beneficiary who is a member of a domiciled employees' or retirees' association that has at least 2,000 members, the majority of whom are active or retired employees of the State may authorize, in writing, the periodic deduction from the beneficiary's retirement benefits a designated lump sum to be paid to the employees' or retirees' association. The authorization shall remain in effect until revoked by the beneficiary. A plan of deductions pursuant to this section shall become void if the employees' or retirees' association engages in collective bargaining with the State, any political subdivision of the State, or any local school administrative unit.

(b) Any beneficiary may also authorize, in writing, the monthly deduction from the beneficiary's retirement benefits of a designated lump sum to be paid to the State Health Plan for any dependent whom the beneficiary wishes to cover under the State Health Plan. In the event that the beneficiary's own State Health Plan coverage is contributory, in whole or in part, the beneficiary may also authorize a designated lump sum to be paid to the State Health Plan on behalf of the beneficiary. In addition, a beneficiary may similarly authorize the deduction for supplemental voluntary insurance benefits, provided that the deduction is authorized by the Department of State Treasurer and is payable to a company with which the Department of State Treasurer has or had an exclusive contractual relationship. Any such authorization shall remain in effect until revoked by the beneficiary. (1998-212, s. 9.24(a); 1999-237, s. 23; 2002-126, s. 6.4(c); 2012-1, s. 2; 2012-178, s. 4(c).)

§ 135-18.9. Transfer of members from the Legislative Retirement System or the Consolidated Judicial Retirement System.

(a) The accumulated contributions, creditable service, and reserves, if any, of a member of the Legislative Retirement System, as provided for in Article 1A of G.S. 120, or the Consolidated Judicial Retirement System, as provided for in Article 4 of G.S. 135, who later becomes a member of the Teachers' and State Employees' Retirement System for a period of five or more years may, upon application of the member, be transferred from the Legislative Retirement System or the Consolidated Judicial Retirement System. The accumulated contributions, creditable service, and reserves of any member whose service as a member of the Legislative Retirement System or the Consolidated Judicial Retirement System is terminated other than by retirement or death and who later becomes a member of the Teachers' and State Employees' Retirement System may, upon application of the member, be transferred from the Legislative Retirement System or the Consolidated Judicial Retirement System to the Teachers' and State Employees' Retirement System. In order to effect the transfer of a member's creditable service from the Legislative Retirement System or the Consolidated Judicial Retirement System to the Teachers' and State Employees' Retirement System, the accumulated contributions of each member credited in the annuity savings fund in the Legislative Retirement

System or the Consolidated Judicial Retirement System shall be transferred and credited to the annuity savings fund in the Teachers' and State Employees' Retirement System.

(b) The Board of Trustees shall effect such rules as it may deem necessary to administer subsection (a) of this section and to prevent any duplication of service credits or benefits that might otherwise occur. (2003-284, s. 30.18(c).)

§ 135-18.10. Forfeiture of retirement benefits for certain felonies committed while serving as elected government official.

(a) Except as provided in G.S. 135-4(gg), the Board of Trustees shall not pay any retirement benefits or allowances, except for a return of member contributions plus interest, to any member who is convicted of any felony under the federal laws listed in subsection (b) of this section or the laws of this State listed in subsection (c) of this section if all of the following apply:

(1) The federal or State offense is committed while serving as an elected government official.

(2) The conduct on which the federal or State offense is based is directly related to the member's service as an elected government official.

(b) The federal offenses covered by this section are as follows:

(1) A felony violation of 18 U.S.C. § 201 (Bribery of public officials and witnesses), 18 U.S.C. § 286 (Conspiracy to defraud the Government with respect to claims), 18 U.S.C. § 287 (False, fictitious or fraudulent claims), 18 U.S.C. § 371 (Conspiracy to commit offense or to defraud United States), 18 U.S.C. § 597 (Expenditures to influence voting), 18 U.S.C. § 599 (Promise of appointment by candidate), 18 U.S.C. § 606 (Intimidation to secure political contributions), 18 U.S.C. § 641 (Public money, property, or records), 18 U.S.C. § 666 (Embezzlement and theft), 18 U.S.C. § 1001 (Statements or entries generally), 18 U.S.C. § 1341 (Frauds and swindles), 18 U.S.C. § 1343 (Fraud by wire, radio, or television), 18 U.S.C. § 1503 (Influencing or injuring officer or juror generally), 18 U.S.C. § 1951 (Interference with commerce by threats or violence), 18 U.S.C. § 1952 (Interstate and foreign travel or transportation in aid of racketeering enterprises), 18 U.S.C. § 1956 (Laundering of monetary

instruments), 18 U.S.C. § 1962 (Prohibited activities), or section 7201 of the Internal Revenue Code (Attempt to evade or defeat tax).

(2)   Reserved for future codification purposes.

(c)   The offenses under the laws of this State covered by this section are as follows:

(1)   A felony violation of Article 29, 30, or 30A of Chapter 14 of the General Statutes (Relating to bribery, obstructing justice, and secret listening) or G.S. 14-228 (Buying and selling offices), or Part 1 of Article 14 of Chapter 120 of the General Statutes (Code of Legislative Ethics), Article 20 or 22 of Chapter 163 of the General Statutes (Relating to absentee ballots, corrupt practices and other offenses against the elective franchise, and regulating of contributions and expenditures in political campaigns).

(2)   Perjury or false information as follows:

a.   Perjury committed under G.S. 14-209 in falsely denying the commission of an act that constitutes an offense within the purview of an offense listed in subdivision (1) of subsection (c) of this section.

b.   Subornation of perjury committed under G.S. 14-210 in connection with the false denial of another as specified by subdivision (2) of this subsection.

c.   Perjury under Article 22A of Chapter 163 of the General Statutes.

(d)   All monies forfeited under this section shall be remitted to the Civil Penalty and Forfeiture Fund. (2007-179, s. 3(a).)

§ 135-18.10A. Forfeiture of retirement benefits for certain felonies related to employment or holding office.

(a)   Except as provided in G.S. 135-4(ii), the Board of Trustees shall not pay any retirement benefits or allowances, except for a return of member contributions plus interest, to any member who is convicted of any felony under federal law or the laws of this State if all of the following apply:

(1)   The offense is committed while the member is in service.

(2) The conduct resulting in the member's conviction is directly related to the member's office or employment.

(b) Subdivision (2) of subsection (a) of this section shall apply to felony convictions where the court finds under G.S. 15A-1340.16(d)(9) or other applicable State or federal procedure that the member's conduct is directly related to the member's office or employment.

(c) If a member or former member whose benefits under the System were forfeited under this section, except for the return of member contributions plus interest, subsequently receives an unconditional pardon of innocence, or the conviction is vacated or set aside for any reason, then the member or former member may seek a reversal of the benefit forfeiture by presenting sufficient evidence to the State Treasurer. If the State Treasurer determines a reversal of the benefit forfeiture is appropriate, then all benefits will be restored upon repayment of all accumulated contributions plus interest. Repayment of all accumulated contributions that have been received by the individual under the forfeiture provisions of this section must be made in a total lump-sum payment with interest compounded annually at a rate of six and one-half percent (6.5%) for each calendar year from the year of forfeiture to the year of repayment. An individual receiving a reversal of benefit forfeiture must receive reinstatement of the service credit forfeited. (2012-193, s. 1.)

§ 135-18.11. Improper receipt of decedent's retirement allowance.

A person is guilty of a Class 1 misdemeanor if the person, with the intent to defraud, receives money as a result of cashing, depositing, or receiving a direct deposit of a decedent's retirement allowance and the person (i) knows that he or she is not entitled to the decedent's retirement allowance, (ii) receives the benefit at least two months after the date of the retiree's or beneficiary's death, and (iii) does not attempt to inform this Retirement System of the retiree's or beneficiary's death. (2011-232, s. 10(a); 2012-185, s. 3(a); 2013-288, s. 9(b).)

Article 2.

Coverage of Governmental Employees under Title II of the Social Security Act.

§ 135-19. Declaration of policy.

In order to extend to employees of the State and its political subdivisions and of the instrumentalities of either, and to the dependents and survivors of such employees, the basic protection accorded to others by the Old Age and Survivors Insurance System embodied in the Social Security Act, it is hereby declared to be the policy of the legislature, subject to the limitation of this Article, that such steps be taken as to provide such protection to employees of the State and local governments on as broad a basis as is permitted under applicable federal law.

It is also the policy of the legislature that the protection afforded employees in positions covered by a retirement system on the date an agreement under this Article is made applicable to service performed in such positions, or receiving periodic benefits under such retirement system at such time, will not be impaired as a result of making the agreement so applicable or as a result of legislative enactment in anticipation thereof. (1951, c. 562, s. 3; 1955, c. 1154, s. 1.)

§ 135-20. Definitions.

For the purposes of this Article:

(1) The term "employee" includes an officer of the State, or one of its political subdivisions or instrumentalities.

(2) The term "employment" means any service performed by an employee in the employ of the State, or any political subdivision thereof, for such employer, except

a. Service which in the absence of an agreement entered into under this Article would constitute "employment" as defined in the Social Security Act; or

b. Service which under the Social Security Act may not be included in an agreement between the State and the Secretary of Health, Education and Welfare entered into under this Article.

Service which under the Social Security Act may be included in an agreement only upon certification by the Governor in accordance with section 218(d)(3) of that act shall be included in the term "employment" if and when the

Governor issues, with respect to such service, a certificate to the Secretary of Health, Education and Welfare pursuant to G.S. 135-29.

(3) The term "Federal Insurance Contributions Act" means Subchapter A of Chapter 9 of the Federal Internal Revenue Code of 1939 and Subchapters A and B of Chapter 21 of the Federal Internal Revenue Code of 1954, as such Codes have been and may from time to time be amended; and the term "employee tax" means the tax imposed by section 1400 of such Code of 1939 and section 3101 of such Code of 1954.

(4) The term "political subdivision" includes an instrumentality of a state, of one or more of its political subdivisions, or of a state and one or more of its political subdivisions, but only if such instrumentality is a juristic entity which is legally separate and distinct from the state or subdivision and only if its employees are not by virtue of their relation to such juristic entity employees of the state or subdivision.

(5) The term "Secretary of Health, Education and Welfare" includes any individual to whom the Secretary of Health, Education and Welfare has delegated any of his functions under the Social Security Act with respect to coverage under such act of employees of states and their political subdivisions, and with respect to any action taken prior to April 11, 1953, includes the Federal Security Administrator and any individual to whom such Administrator has delegated any such function.

(6) The term "Social Security Act" means the act of Congress approved August 14, 1935, Chapter 531, 49 Stat. 620, officially cited as the "Social Security Act," (including regulations and requirements issued pursuant thereto), as such act has been and may from time to time be amended.

(7) The term "State agency" means the director of the Teachers' and State Employees' Retirement System.

(8) The term "wages" means all remuneration for employment as defined herein, including the cash value of all remuneration paid in any medium other than cash, except that such term shall not include that part of such remuneration which, even if it were paid for "employment" within the meaning of the Federal Insurance Contributions Act, would not constitute "wages" within the meaning of that act. (1951, c. 562, s. 3; 1955, c. 1154, ss. 2-4, 12; 1959, c. 1020; 1965, c. 780, s. 1; 1973, c. 108, s. 84.)

§ 135-21. Federal-State agreement; interstate instrumentalities.

(a) The State agency, with the approval of the Governor, is hereby authorized to enter on behalf of the State into an agreement with the Secretary of Health, Education and Welfare, consistent with the terms and provisions of this Article, for the purpose of extending the benefits of the Federal Old Age and Survivors Insurance System to employees of the State or any political subdivision thereof with respect to services specified in such agreement which constitute "employment" as defined in G.S. 135-20. Such agreement may contain such provisions relating to coverage, benefits, contributions, effective date, modification and termination of the agreement, administration, and other appropriate provisions as the State agency and Secretary of Health, Education and Welfare shall agree upon, but, except as may be otherwise required by or under the Social Security Act as to the services to be covered, such agreement shall provide in effect that -

(1) Benefits will be provided for employees whose services are covered by the agreement (and their dependents and survivors) on the same basis as though such services constituted employment within the meaning of Title II of the Social Security Act.

(2) The State will pay to the Secretary of the Treasury, at such time or times as may be prescribed under the Social Security Act, contributions with respect to wages (as defined in G.S. 135-20), equal to the sum of the taxes which would be imposed by the Federal Insurance Contributions Act if the services covered by the agreement constituted employment within the meaning of that act.

(3) Such agreement shall be effective with respect to services in employment covered by the agreement performed after a date specified therein but shall in no event cover any such services performed prior to January 1, 1951.

(4) All services which constitute employment as defined in G.S. 135-20 and are performed in the employ of the State by employees of the State, shall be covered by the agreement.

(5) All services which constitute employment as defined in G.S. 135-20, are performed in the employ of a political subdivision of the State, and are covered by a plan which is in conformity with the terms of the agreement and has been approved by the State agency under G.S. 135-23, shall be covered by the agreement.

(6) As modified, the agreement shall include all services described in either subdivision (4) or subdivision (5) of this subsection and performed by individuals to whom section 218(c)(3)(C) of the Social Security Act is applicable and shall provide that the service of any such individual shall continue to be covered by the agreement in case he thereafter becomes eligible to be a member of a retirement system; and

(7) As modified, the agreement shall include all services described in either subdivision (4) or subdivision (5) of this subsection and performed by individuals in positions covered by a retirement system with respect to which the Governor has issued a certificate to the Secretary of Health, Education and Welfare pursuant to G.S. 135-29.

(b) Any instrumentality jointly created by this State and any other state or states is hereby authorized, upon the granting of like authority by such other state or states,

(1) To enter into an agreement with the Secretary of Health, Education and Welfare whereby the benefits of the Federal Old Age and Survivors Insurance System shall be extended to employees of such instrumentality,

(2) To require its employees to pay (and for that purpose to deduct from their wages) contributions equal to the amounts which they would be required to pay under G.S. 135-22(a) if they were covered by an agreement made pursuant to subsection (a) of this section, and

(3) To make payments to the Secretary of the Treasury in accordance with such agreement, including payments from its own funds, and otherwise to comply with such agreements.

Such agreement shall, to the extent practicable, be consistent with the terms and provisions of subsection (a) and other provisions of this Article.

(c) Pursuant to section 218(d)(6) of the Social Security Act, the Teachers' and State Employees' Retirement System of North Carolina as established by Article 1 of Chapter 135 of the General Statutes, Volume 17, as amended and as the same may be hereafter amended, shall for the purposes of this Article, be deemed to constitute a single retirement system; and, the North Carolina Local Governmental Employees' Retirement System as established by Article 3 of Chapter 128 of the General Statutes, Volume 16, as amended and as the same may be hereafter amended, shall be deemed to constitute a single retirement system with respect to each political subdivision having positions covered thereby. (1951, c. 562, s. 3; 1953, c. 52; 1955, c. 1154, ss. 5-7, 12.)

§ 135-22. Contributions by State employees.

(a) Every employee of the State whose services are covered by an agreement entered into under G.S. 135-21 shall be required to pay for the period of such coverage, into the contribution fund established by G.S. 135-24, contributions, with respect to wages (as defined in G.S. 135-20), equal to the amount of the employee tax which would be imposed by the Federal Insurance Contributions Act if such services constituted employment within the meaning of that act. Such liability shall arise in consideration of the employee's retention in the service of the State, or his entry upon such service, after the enactment of this Article.

(b) The contribution imposed by this section shall be collected by deducting the amount of the contribution from wages as and when paid, but failure to make such deduction shall not relieve the employee from liability for such contribution.

(c) If more or less than the correct amount of the contribution imposed by this section is paid or deducted with respect to any remuneration, proper adjustments, or refund if adjustment is impracticable, shall be made, without interest, in such manner and at such times as the State agency shall prescribe. (1951, c. 562, s. 3; 1955, c. 1154, s. 8.)

§ 135-23. Plans for coverage of employees of political subdivisions.

(a) Each political subdivision of the State is hereby authorized to submit for approval by the State agency a plan for extending the benefits of Title II of the Social Security Act, in conformity with applicable provisions of such act, to employees of such political subdivisions. Each such plan and any amendment thereof shall be approved by the State agency if it finds that such plan or such plan as amended, is in conformity with such requirements as are provided in regulations of the State agency, except that no such plan shall be approved unless -

(1) It is in conformity with the requirements of the Social Security Act and with the agreement entered into under G.S. 135-21.

(2) It provides that all services which constitute employment as defined in G.S. 135-20 and are performed in the employ of the political subdivision by employees thereof, shall be covered by the plan, except that it may exclude services performed by individuals to whom section 218(c)(3)(C) of the Social Security Act is applicable.

(3) It specifies the source or sources from which the funds necessary to make the payments required by subdivision (1) of subsection (c) and by subsection (d) are expected to be derived and contains reasonable assurance that such sources will be adequate for such purpose.

(4) It provides for such methods of administration of the plan by the political subdivision as are found by the State agency to be necessary for the proper and efficient administration of the plan.

(5) It provides that the political subdivision will make such reports, in such form and containing such information, as the State agency may from time to time require, and comply with such provisions as the State agency or the Secretary of Health, Education and Welfare may from time to time find necessary to assure the correctness and verification of such reports.

(6) It authorizes the State agency to terminate the plan in its entirety, in the discretion of the State agency, if it finds that there has been a failure to comply substantially with any provision contained in such plan, such termination to take effect at the expiration of such notice and on such conditions as may be provided by regulations of the State agency and may be consistent with the provisions of the Social Security Act.

(b) The State agency shall not finally refuse to approve a plan submitted by a political subdivision under subsection (a), and shall not terminate an approved plan, without reasonable notice and opportunity for hearing to the political subdivision affected thereby.

(c) (1) Each political subdivision as to which a plan has been approved under this section shall pay into the contribution fund, with respect to wages (as defined in G.S. 135-20), at such time or times as the State agency may by regulation prescribe, contributions in the amounts and at the rates specified in the applicable agreement entered into by the State agency under G.S. 135-21.

(2) Each political subdivision required to make payments under subdivision (1) of this subsection is authorized, in consideration of the employee's retention in, or entry upon, employment after enactment of this Article, to impose upon each of its employees, as to services which are covered by an approved plan, a contribution with respect to his wages (as defined in G.S. 135-20), not exceeding the amount of the employee tax which would be imposed by the Federal Insurance Contributions Act if such services constituted employment within the meaning of that act, and to deduct the amount of such contribution from his wages as and when paid. Contributions so collected shall be paid into the contribution fund in partial discharge of the liability of such political subdivision or instrumentality under subdivision (1) of this subsection. Failure to deduct such contribution shall not relieve the employee or employer of liability therefor.

(d) Delinquent payments due under subdivision (1) of subsection (c), may, with interest at the rate of six per centum (6%) per annum, be recovered by action in the Superior Court of Wake County against the political subdivision liable therefor or may, at the request of the State agency, be deducted from any other moneys payable to such subdivision by any department or agency of the State. (1951, c. 562, s. 3; 1955, c. 1154, ss. 9, 10, 12.)

§ 135-24. Contribution fund.

(a) There is hereby established a special fund to be known as the contribution fund. Such fund shall consist of and there shall be deposited in such fund:

(1) All contributions, interest, and penalties collected under G.S. 135-22 and 135-23;

(2) All moneys appropriated thereto under this Article;

(3) Any property or securities and earnings thereof acquired through the use of moneys belonging to the fund;

(4) Interest earned upon any moneys in the fund; and

(5) All sums recovered upon the bond of the custodian or otherwise for losses sustained by the fund and all other moneys received for the fund from any other source.

All moneys in the fund shall be mingled and undivided. Subject to the provisions of this Article, the State agency is vested with full power, authority and jurisdiction over the fund, including all moneys and property or securities belonging thereto, and may perform any and all acts whether or not specifically designated, which are necessary to the administration thereof and are consistent with the provisions of this Article.

(b) The contribution fund shall be established and held separate and apart from any other funds or moneys of the State and shall be used and administered exclusively for the purpose of this Article. Withdrawals from such fund shall be made for, and solely for

(1) Payment of amounts required to be paid to the Secretary of the Treasury pursuant to an agreement entered into under G.S. 135-21;

(2) Payment of refunds provided for in G.S. 135-22(c); and

(3) Refunds of overpayments, not otherwise adjustable, made by a political subdivision or instrumentality.

(c) From the contribution fund the custodian of the fund shall pay to the Secretary of the Treasury such amounts and at such time or times as may be directed by the State agency in accordance with any agreement entered into under G.S. 135-21 and the Social Security Act.

(d) The Treasurer of the State shall be ex officio treasurer and custodian of the contribution fund and shall administer such fund in accordance with the provisions of this Article and the directions of the State agency and shall pay all warrants drawn upon it in accordance with the provisions of this section and with such regulations as the State agency may prescribe pursuant thereto.

(e) (1) There are hereby authorized to be appropriated biennially to the contribution fund, in addition to the contributions collected and paid into the contribution fund under G.S. 135-22 and 135-23, to be available for the purposes of G.S. 135-24(b) and (c) until expended, such additional sums as are found to be necessary in order to make the payments to the Secretary of the

Treasury which the State is obligated to make pursuant to an agreement entered into under G.S. 135-21.

(2) The State agency shall submit to each regular session of the State legislature, at least 90 days in advance of the beginning of such session, an estimate of the amounts authorized to be appropriated to the contribution fund by subdivision (1) of this subsection for the next appropriation period.

(f) The State agency shall have the authority to promulgate rules and regulations under which the State agency may make a reasonable charge or assessment against any political subdivision whose employees shall be included in any coverage agreement under any plan of coverage of employees as provided by the provisions of this Article. Such charge or assessment shall be determined by the State agency and shall be apportioned among the various political subdivisions of government in a ratable or fair manner, and the funds derived from such charge or assessment shall be used exclusively by the State agency to defray the cost and expense of administering the provisions of this Article. In case of refusal to pay such charge or assessment on the part of any political subdivision as defined in this Article, or in case such charge or assessment remains unpaid for a period of 30 days, the State agency may maintain a suit in the Superior Court of Wake County for the recovery of such charge or assessment. The Superior Court of Wake County is hereby vested with jurisdiction over all such suits or actions. Only such amount shall be assessed against such political subdivision as is necessary to pay its share of the expense of providing supplies, necessary employees and clerks, records and other proper expenses necessary for the administration of this Article by the State agency, including compensation of the State agency for the agency's services. The funds accumulated and derived from such assessments and charges shall be deposited by the State agency in some safe and reliable depository chosen by the State agency, and the State agency shall issue such checks or vouchers as may be necessary to defray the above-mentioned expenses of administration with the right of the representative of any political subdivision to inspect the books and records and inquire into the amounts necessary for such administration. (1951, c. 562, s. 3; 1963, c. 687, s. 6.)

§ 135-25. Rules and regulations.

The State agency shall make and publish such rules and regulations, not inconsistent with the provisions of this Article, as it finds necessary or appropriate to the efficient administration of the functions with which it is charged under this Article. (1951, c. 562, s. 3.)

§ 135-26. Studies and reports.

The State agency shall make studies concerning the problem of old age and survivors insurance protection for employees of the State and local governments and their instrumentalities and concerning the operation of agreements made and plans approved under this Article and shall submit a report to the legislature at the beginning of each regular session, covering the administration and operation of this Article during the preceding biennium, including such recommendations for amendments to this Article as it considers proper. (1951, c. 562, s. 3.)

§ 135-27. Transfers from State to certain association service.

(a) Any member whose service as a teacher or State employee is terminated because of acceptance of a position prior to July 1, 1983, with the North Carolina Education Association, the North Carolina State Employees' Association, North Carolina State Firemen's Association, the North Carolina State Highway Employees Association, North Carolina Teachers' Association and the State Employees' Credit Union, alumni associations of state-supported universities and colleges, local professional associations of teachers and State employees as defined by the Board of Trustees, and North Carolina State School Boards Association may elect to leave his total accumulated contributions in this Retirement System during the period he is in such association employment, by filing with the Board of Trustees at the time of such termination the form provided by it for that purpose.

(b) Any member who files such an election shall remain a member of the Retirement System during the time he is in such association employment and does not withdraw his contributions. Such a member shall be entitled to all the rights and benefits of the Retirement System as though remaining in State service on the basis of the funds accumulated for his credit at the time of such transfer plus any additional accruals on account of future contributions made as hereinafter provided. Such former State employee may restore any such account and pay into the annuity savings fund before July 1, 1960, such amounts as would have been paid after transfer to such service, provided that the association makes contributions to the Retirement System on behalf of such former members in accordance with subsection (c) of this section.

(c) Under such rules as the Board of Trustees shall adopt, the association to which the member has been transferred may agree to contribute to the Retirement System on behalf of such member such current service contributions as would have been made by his employer had he remained in State service with actual compensation equal to the remuneration received from such association; provided the member continues to contribute to the Retirement System. Any period of such association employment on account of which contributions are made by both the association and the member as herein provided shall be credited as membership service under the Retirement System.

(d) The governing board of any association or organization listed in subsection (a), in its discretion, may elect on or before July 1, 1983, by an appropriate resolution of said board, to cause the employees of such association or organization so employed prior to July 1, 1983, to become members of the Teachers' and State Employees' Retirement System. Such Retirement System coverage shall be conditioned on such association's or organization's paying all of the employer's contributions or matching funds from funds of the association or organization and on such board's collecting from its employees the employees' contributions at such rates as may be fixed by law and by the regulations of the Board of Trustees of the Retirement System, all of such funds to be paid to the Retirement System and placed in the appropriate funds. Retroactive coverage of the employees of any such association or organization may also be effected to the extent that such board requests; provided, the association or organization shall pay all of the employer's contributions or matching funds necessary for such purposes; and, provided further, such association or organization shall collect from its employees all employees' contributions necessary for such purpose, computed at such rates and in such amount as the Board of Trustees of the Retirement System shall determine, all of such funds to be paid to the Retirement System, together with such interest as may be due, and placed in the appropriate funds. The provisions of this subsection shall be fully applicable to the North Carolina Symphony Society, Inc.

(e) Notwithstanding the foregoing, employees of the State Employees' Credit Union who are in service and members of the Retirement System on June 30, 1983, shall, on or before October 1, 1983, make an irrevocable election to do one of the following:

(1) Continue contributing membership service under the same conditions and requirements as are otherwise provided, and have the rights of a member to all benefits and a retirement allowance; or

(2) Receive a return of accumulated contributions with cessation of contributing membership service, under G.S. 135-5(f) and in any event with regular interest regardless of membership service; or

(3) Terminate contributing membership service and be entitled alternatively to the benefits and allowances provided under G.S. 135-3(8) or G.S. 135-5(a).

(f) Notwithstanding the foregoing, employees of the State Employees Association of North Carolina, the employees of the North Carolina Association of Educators, and the employees of the North Carolina School Boards Association who are in service and members of the Retirement System on June 30, 1985, shall, on or before October 1, 1985, make an irrevocable election to exercise one of the three options provided in G.S. 135-27(e). (1953, c. 1050, s. 1; 1959, c. 513, s. 5; 1961, c. 516, s. 5; 1967, c. 720, s. 14; 1969, cc. 540, 847, 1227; 1983, c. 412, ss. 4-6; c. 782; 1985, c. 757, s. 200; 2008-194, s. 6(a); 2012-120, s. 1(b).)

§ 135-28. Transfer of members to employment covered by the North Carolina Local Governmental Employees' Retirement System.

(a) Any member whose services as a teacher or State employee are terminated for any reason other than retirement or death, who, while his account remains active, becomes employed by an employer participating in the North Carolina Local Governmental Employees' Retirement System or an employer which brings its employees into participation in said System while his account is active, may elect to leave his total accumulated contributions in the Teachers' and State Employees' Retirement System during the period he is in the employment of such employer, or his account remains active in the local system. This subsection shall be effective retroactively as well as prospectively.

(b) Any such member shall retain all the rights, credits and benefits obtaining to him under this Retirement System at the time of such transfer while he is a member of the local system and does not withdraw his contributions hereunder and in addition, he shall be granted membership service credits under this Retirement System on account of the period of his membership in the local system for the purpose of increasing his years of creditable service hereunder in order to meet any service requirements of any retirement benefit under this Retirement System and, if he is a member in service under the local system, he shall be deemed to be a member in service under this Retirement System if so required by such benefit: Provided, however, that in lieu of transfer of funds from one retirement system to another, such member who is eligible for retirement benefits shall file application therefor with each retirement system to the end that each retirement system shall pay appropriate benefits without transfer of funds between the systems.

(c) Any member who became or becomes employed by an employer of the North Carolina Local Governmental Employees' Retirement System as provided in (a) above shall be entitled to waive the provisions of (b) above and to transfer to the local system his credits for membership and prior service in this System provided such member shall request this System to transfer his accumulated contributions, interest and service credits to the local system. If such request is made, in addition to the member's accumulated contributions, interest and service credits, there shall be transferred to the local system the amount of reserve held in this System as a result of previous employer contributions on behalf of the transferring employee. (1953, c. 1050, s. 2; 1961, c. 516, s. 6; 1965, c. 780, s. 1; 1971, c. 117, ss. 16, 18; 1973, c. 241, s. 12.)

§ 135-28.1. Transfer of members to employment covered by the Uniform Judicial Retirement System.

(a) Any member whose service as a teacher or State employee is terminated other than by retirement or death and, who, while still a member of this Retirement System, becomes a judge participating in the Uniform Judicial Retirement System, may elect to retain his membership in this Retirement System by not withdrawing his accumulated contributions hereunder. Any such member shall retain all the rights, credits and benefits obtaining to him under this Retirement System at the time of such termination of service hereunder while he is a member of the other system and does not withdraw his contributions hereunder.

(b) The provisions of the preceding subsection to the contrary notwithstanding, with respect to each judge or former judge of the district court division of the General Court of Justice who was a member of this Retirement System immediately prior to January 1, 1974, and who becomes a member of the Uniform Judicial Retirement System on or after January 1, 1974, upon his commencement of membership in the other system there shall be paid in a lump sum to his account in the annuity savings fund of the other system the amount of his accumulated contributions under this System that are attributable to contributions made by him hereunder while a judge of said district court division. Upon such payment, the member's accumulated contributions hereunder shall be reduced by the amount of such payment and his period of creditable membership service shall be reduced by the period of service during which such repaid contributions were originally made.

Any member for whom the payment of his accumulated contributions as herein provided reduces the balance of his account in the annuity savings fund to zero and cancels his entire period of creditable service shall no longer be a member of this Retirement System.

In the case of any member who retains his membership in this Retirement System after the payment hereinabove provided and who subsequently becomes eligible for retirement benefits under this Retirement System or whose death results in benefit payments to another beneficiary, the average final compensation used in the computation of the amount of any such benefits shall be computed as of the date of commencement of his membership in the other system on the same basis as if his retirement or death had occurred as of such date of commencement. Moreover, for the sole purpose of increasing his creditable service hereunder in order to meet any applicable service requirements for benefits hereunder, any such member shall be granted membership service credits under this Retirement System on account of (i) the period of membership service cancelled under the first paragraph of this subsection and (ii) the period of his membership in the other system so long as he remains a member hereunder and, if he is a member in service under the other system, he shall be deemed to be a member in service under this Retirement System if so required for any benefit hereunder.

(c) Any member who becomes eligible for benefits under both this Retirement System and the Uniform Judicial Retirement System may file application therefor with each retirement system to the end that each retirement system shall pay appropriate benefits without transfer of funds between the systems except as otherwise provided in subsection (b) above.

(d) The Board of Trustees shall effect such rules as it may deem necessary to administer the provisions of the preceding subsections of this section and to prevent any duplication of service credits or benefits that might otherwise occur.

(e)   When any judge of a district court division of the General Court of Justice shall have made application for disability retirement prior to January 1, 1974, while a member of this Retirement System to become effective after January 1, 1974, and such judge died before January 1, 1974, and there was filed with the application for disability retirement a statement by a physician that such judge was permanently and totally disabled, such person shall be deemed to have complied with all provisions of this Retirement System as of the date of application for disability retirement and no action of the medical board shall be necessary. He shall be presumed to have chosen Option 2 as to retirement benefits and survivor's benefits shall commence immediately and shall also be paid retroactively to the first day of the calendar month following such judge's death.

(f)   Notwithstanding the provisions of subsections (a), (b), (c), (d), and (e) of this section, the accumulated contributions and creditable service of any member whose service as a teacher or employee has been or is terminated other than by retirement or death and who, while still a member of this Retirement System, became or becomes a member, as defined in G.S. 135-53(11), of the Consolidated Judicial Retirement System for a period of five or more years may, upon application of the member, be transferred from this Retirement System to the Consolidated Judicial Retirement System. In order to effect the transfer of a member's creditable service from the Teachers' and State Employees' Retirement System to the Consolidated Judicial Retirement System, there shall be transferred from the Teachers' and State Employees' Retirement System to the Consolidated Judicial Retirement System the sum of (i) the accumulated contributions of the member credited in the annuity savings fund and (ii) the amount of reserve held in the Teachers' and State Employees' Retirement System as a result of previous contributions by the employer on behalf of the transferring member. (1973, c. 640, s. 2; c. 1221; 1999-237, s. 28.24(b).)

§ 135-29. Referenda and certification.

(a)   With respect to employees of the State and any other individuals covered by Article 1 of Chapter 135 of the General Statutes, Volume 17, as amended and as may be hereafter amended, the Governor is empowered to authorize a referendum, and with respect to the employees of any political subdivision he shall authorize a referendum upon request of the governing body of such vision covered by Article 3 of Chapter 128 of the General Statutes,

Volume 16, as amended and as the same may be hereafter amended, or by some other retirement system established either by the State or by the political subdivision; and in either case the referendum shall be conducted, and the Governor shall designate an agency or individual to supervise its conduct, in accordance with the requirements of section 218(d)(3) of the Social Security Act, on the question of whether service in positions covered by a retirement system established by the State or by a political subdivision thereof should be excluded from or included under an agreement under this Article. The notice of referendum required by section 218(d)(3)(C) of the Social Security Act to be given to employees shall contain or shall be accompanied by a statement, in such form and such detail as the agency or the individual designated to supervise the referendum shall deem necessary and sufficient, to inform the employees of the rights which will accrue to them and their dependents and survivors, and the liabilities to which they will be subject, if their services are included under an agreement under this Article.

(b) Upon receiving evidence satisfactory to him that with respect to any such referendum the conditions specified in section 218(d)(3) of the Social Security Act have been met, the Governor or such State official as may be designated by him, shall so certify to the Secretary of Health, Education and Welfare. (1955, c. 1154, s. 11; 1961, c. 516, s. 8.)

§ 135-30. State employees members of Law-Enforcement Officers' Benefit and Retirement Fund.

The federal-state agreement provided in G.S. 135-21 shall be revised and extended to provide that, effective on, or retroactively as of, such date as may be fixed by the Board of Commissioners of the Law-Enforcement Officers' Benefit and Retirement Fund, all or some of the members of said fund who are employees of the State of North Carolina or any of its agencies, shall be covered by the Social Security Act, dependent upon a referendum or referendums held pursuant to federal laws and regulations, at the request of said board, with the approval of the Governor: Provided, that such action shall be subject to the conditions and terms set forth in such agreement and subject to all applicable provisions of Article 2 of Chapter 135 of the General Statutes not inconsistent herewith: Provided, however, that the effecting of social security coverage shall not cause to be reduced or lowered the amount of the contributions to be made to the Law-Enforcement Officers' Benefit and Retirement Fund by any State employee who is a member thereof nor the amount to be contributed by the State to said fund with respect to each State employee member; provided, further, from and after the date the above-described employees become subject to the Social Security Act, there shall be deducted from each such employee's salary for each and every payroll period such sum as may be necessary to pay the amount of contributions of taxes required on his account with respect to social security coverage, and the State, or the appropriate State agency, as an employer, shall pay the amount of contributions or taxes with respect to such person, as may be necessary on his account to effect the above-described social security coverage. (1959, c. 618, s. 1.)

§ 135-31. Split referendums.

The provisions of this Article shall be construed as authorization for the State or political subdivisions or instrumentalities of government which have not heretofore secured social security coverage, and which are otherwise authorized to secure such coverage, to hold any type of referendum with respect thereto which federal law now or hereafter may authorize, and not be restricted to the types of referendums authorized by federal law at the time of the original enactment of this Article. (1959, c. 618, s. 1.)

Article 3.

Other Teacher, Employee Benefits; Child Health Benefits.

Part 1. General Provisions.

§§ 135-32 through 135-33.1: Repealed by Session Laws 1981 (Regular Session, 1982), c. 1398, s. 1.

§ 135-34: Repealed by Session Laws 1987, c. 738, s. 29(l).

§ 135-35: Repealed by Session Laws 1981, c. 859, s. 13.17; 1981 (Regular Session, 1982), c. 1398, s. 1.

§ 135-36: Repealed by Session Laws 1981 (Regular Session, 1982), c. 1398, s. 1.

§§ 135-37 through 135-42.1: Recodified and renumbered as G.S. 135-43 to 135-47.3.

Article 3A.

Other Benefits for Teachers, State Employees, Retired State Employees, and Child Health.

Part 1. General Provisions.

§§ 135-43 through 135-47.3: Recodified as Article 3B of Chapter 135 by Session Laws 2011-85, ss. 2.4 through 2.8, effective January 1, 2012.

§ 135-48: Reserved for future codification purposes.

Article 3B.

State Health Plan for Teachers and State Employees.

Part 1. General Provisions.

§ 135-48.1. General definitions.

As used in this Article unless the context clearly requires otherwise, the following definitions apply:

(1) Benefit period. - The period of time during which charges for covered services provided to a Plan member must be incurred in order to be eligible for payment by the Plan.

(2) Chemical dependency. - The pathological use or abuse of alcohol or other drugs in a manner or to a degree that produces an impairment in personal, social, or occupational functioning and which may, but need not, include a pattern of tolerance and withdrawal.

(3) Claims Processor. - One or more administrators, third-party administrators, or other parties contracting with the Plan to administer Plan benefits.

(4) Comprehensive group health benefit plan. - A comprehensive health benefit plan offered to an individual because of an employment, organizational, or other group affiliation.

(5) Comprehensive health benefit plan. - Health care coverage that consists of inpatient and outpatient hospital and medical benefits, as well as other outpatient medical services, prescription drugs, medical supplies, and equipment that are generally available in the health insurance market.

(6) Covered service; benefit; allowable expense. - Any medically necessary, reasonable, and customary items of service, including prescription drugs, and medical supplies included in the Plan.

(7) Deductible. - The dollar amount that must be incurred for certain covered services in a benefit period before benefits are payable by the Plan.

(8) Dependent. - An eligible Plan member other than the subscriber.

(9) Dependent child. - Subject to the eligibility requirements of subsections (a) and (b) of G.S. 135-48.41, any of the following up to the first month following the dependent child's 26th birthday:

a. A natural or legally adopted child or children of the employee, whether or not the child is living with the employee.

b. A foster child or children of the employee, whether or not the child is living with the employee.

c. A child for which an employee is a court-appointed guardian.

d. A stepchild of a member who is married to the stepchild's natural parent.

e. Repealed by Session Laws 2011-96, s. 3(a), effective July 1, 2011.

(10) Employee or State employee. - Any permanent full-time or permanent part-time regular employee (designated as half-time or more) of an employing unit.

(11) Employing Unit. - A North Carolina School System; Community College; State Department, Agency, or Institution; Administrative Office of the Courts; or Association or Examining Board whose employees are eligible for membership in a State-Supported Retirement System. An employing unit also shall mean a charter school in accordance with Part 6A of Chapter 115C of the General Statutes whose board of directors elects to become a participating employer in the Plan under G.S. 135-48.54. Bona fide fire departments, rescue or emergency medical service squads, and National Guard units are deemed to be employing units for the purpose of providing benefits under this Article.

(12) Firefighter. - A member of the group "eligible firemen" as defined in G.S. 58-86-25.

(13) Health Benefits Representative or HBR. - The employee designated by the employing unit to administer the Plan for the unit and its employees. The HBR is responsible for enrolling new employees and dependents in accordance with the eligibility requirements under this Article, reporting changes, explaining benefits, reconciling group statements, and remitting group fees. The State Retirement System is the Health Benefits Representative for retired State employees.

(14) Plan or State Health Plan. - The North Carolina State Health Plan for Teachers and State Employees. Depending on the context, the term may refer to the entity created in G.S. 153-48.2 [135-48.2] or to the health benefit plans offered by the entity, in which case "Plan" includes all comprehensive health benefit plans offered under the Plan.

(15) Plan member. - A subscriber or dependent who is eligible and currently enrolled in the Plan and for whom a premium is paid.

(16) Predecessor plan. - The Hospital and Medical Benefits for the Teachers' and State Employees' Retirement System of the State of North Carolina and the North Carolina Teachers' and State Employees' Comprehensive Major Medical Plan.

(17) Rescue squad worker. - An "eligible rescue squad worker" as defined in G.S. 58-86-30.

(18) Retired employee (retiree). - Retired teachers, State employees, and members of the General Assembly who are receiving monthly retirement

benefits from any retirement system supported in whole or in part by contributions of the State of North Carolina, so long as the retiree is enrolled.

(19) Subscriber. - A Plan member who is not a dependent. (2008-168, s. 3(e); 2009-16, s. 3(a); 2009-281, s. 1; 2010-120, s. 1; 2011-85, ss. 1.7(a), 1.10(c), 2.6(b), 2.10; 2011-96, s. 3(a); 2011-183, s. 102; 2011-326, s. 19.3; 2012-173, s. 1.)

§ 135-48.2. Undertaking.

(a) The State of North Carolina undertakes to make available a State Health Plan (hereinafter called the "Plan") exclusively for the benefit of eligible employees, eligible retired employees, and certain of their eligible dependents, which will pay benefits in accordance with the terms of this Article. The Plan shall have all the powers and privileges of a corporation and shall be known as the State Health Plan for Teachers and State Employees. The State Treasurer, Executive Administrator, and Board of Trustees shall carry out their duties and responsibilities as fiduciaries for the Plan. The Plan shall administer one or more group health plans that are comprehensive in coverage. The State Treasurer may operate group plans as a preferred provider option, or health maintenance, point-of-service, or other organizational arrangement.

(b) Payroll deduction shall be available for coverage under the Plan for subscribers able to meet the Plan's requirements for payroll deduction. (2008-168, s. 3(c); 2009-16, ss. 2(f), 5(h); 2009-281, s. 1; 2009-313, s. 2; 2010-194, s. 18(b); 2011-85, ss. 2.6(a), 2.10.)

§ 135-48.3. Right to amend.

The General Assembly reserves the right to alter, amend, or repeal this Article. (1981 (Reg. Sess., 1982), c. 1398, s. 6; 1985, c. 732, s. 62; 2008-168, ss. 3(a), (u); 2011-85, s. 2.6(k); 2012-173, s. 5.)

§ 135-48.4: Reserved for future codification purposes.

§ 135-48.5. Health benefit trust funds created.

(a) There are hereby established two health benefit trust funds, to be known as the Public Employee Health Benefit Fund and the Health Benefit Reserve Fund for the payment of hospital and medical benefits. As used in this section, the term "health benefit trust funds" refers to the fund type described under G.S. 143C-1-3(a)(10).

All premiums, fees, charges, rebates, refunds or any other receipts including, but not limited to, earnings on investments, occurring or arising in connection with health benefits programs established by this Article, shall be deposited into the Public Employee Health Benefit Fund. Disbursements from the Fund shall include any and all amounts required to pay the benefits and administrative costs of such programs as may be determined by the Executive Administrator and Board of Trustees.

Any unencumbered balance in excess of prepaid premiums or charges in the Public Employee Health Benefit Fund at the end of each fiscal year shall be used first, to provide an actuarially determined Health Benefit Reserve Fund for incurred but unpresented claims, second, to reduce the premiums required in providing the benefits of the health benefits programs, and third to improve the plan, as may be provided by the General Assembly. The balance in the Health Benefits Reserve Fund may be transferred from time to time to the Public Employee Health Benefit Fund to provide for any deficiency occurring therein.

The Public Employee Health Benefit Fund and the Health Benefit Reserve Fund shall be deposited with the State Treasurer and invested as provided in G.S. 147-69.2 and 147-69.3.

(b) Disbursement from the Public Employee Health Benefit Fund may be made by warrant drawn on the State Treasurer by the Executive Administrator, or the Executive Administrator and Board of Trustees may by contract authorize the Claims Processors to draw the warrant.

(c) Repealed by Session Laws 2012-173, s. 3(b), effective January 1, 2013. (1981 (Reg. Sess., 1982), c. 1398, s. 6; 1985, c. 732, ss. 43, 63; 1985 (Reg. Sess., 1986), c. 1020, s. 20; 1997-468, s. 3; 1998-1, s. 4(d); 2008-107, s. 10.13(a); 2008-168, ss. 1(a), 2(a), (l); 2011-85, s. 2.5(e); 2012-173, s. 3(b).)

§ 135-48.6: Reserved for future codification purposes.

§ 135-48.8. Statements of public interest.

The State of North Carolina deems it to be in the public interest for North Carolina firefighters, rescue squad workers, and members of the National Guard, and certain of their dependents, who are not eligible for any other type of comprehensive group health insurance or other comprehensive group health benefits, and who have been without any form of group health insurance or other comprehensive group health benefit coverage for at least six consecutive months, to be given the opportunity to participate in the benefits provided by the State Health Plan for Teachers and State Employees. Coverage under the Plan shall be voluntary for eligible firefighters, rescue squad workers, and members of the National Guard who elect participation in the Plan for themselves and their eligible dependents. (2008-168, s. 3(c); 2009-16, ss. 2(f), 5(h); 2009-281, s. 1; 2009-313, s. 2; 2010-194, s. 18(b); 2011-85, s. 2.6(a).)

§ 135-48.9: Reserved for future codification purposes.

§ 135-48.10. Confidentiality of information and medical records; provider contracts.

(a)   Any information described in this section that is in the possession of the State Health Plan for Teachers and State Employees or its Claims Processor under the Plan or the Predecessor Plan shall be confidential and shall be exempt from the provisions of Chapter 132 of the General Statutes or any other provision requiring information and records held by State agencies to be made public or accessible to the public. This section shall apply to all information concerning individuals, including the fact of coverage or noncoverage, whether or not a claim has been filed, medical information, whether or not a claim has been paid, and any other information or materials concerning a plan participant. This information may, however, be released to the State Auditor or to the Attorney General in furtherance of their statutory duties and responsibilities, or to such persons or organizations as may be designated and approved by the State Treasurer. Any information so released shall remain confidential as stated above and any party obtaining such information shall assume the same level of responsibility for maintaining such confidentiality as that of the State Health Plan for Teachers and State Employees.

(b) The terms of a contract between the Plan and its third party administrator or between the Plan and its pharmacy benefit manager are a public record under Chapter 132 of the General Statutes. No provision of law, however, shall be construed to prevent or restrict the release of any information in a Plan contract to the State Treasurer, the State Auditor, the Attorney General, the Director of the State Budget, the Plan's Board of Trustees, and the Plan's Executive Administrator solely and exclusively for their use in the furtherance of their duties and responsibilities.

and after (1981, c. 355; 1981 (Reg. Sess., 1982), c. 1398, ss. 3, 4; 1983, c. 922, s. 21.10; 1985, c. 732, s. 38; 1985 (Reg. Sess., 1986), c. 1020, s. 20; 1998-1, s. 4(h); 2007-323, s. 28.22A(c); 2008-107, s. 10.13(m); 2008-168, s. 1(a), (c), (d); 2009-16, s. 5(f); 2009-83, s. 1; 2010-194, s. 18(a); 2011-85, ss. 1.9(a), 2.4(a), 2.10; 2011-326, s. 15(r).)

§ 135-48.11: Reserved for future codification purposes.

§ 135-48.12. Committee on Actuarial Valuation of Retired Employees' Health Benefits.

(a) There is established the Committee on Actuarial Valuation of Retired Employees' Health Benefits. The Committee shall be responsible for collecting data and reviewing assumptions for the sole purpose of conducting required actuarial valuations of State supported retired employees' health benefits under other post-employment benefit accounting standards set forth by the Governmental Accounting Standards Board of the Financial Accounting Foundation.

(b) The Committee on Actuarial Valuation of Retired Employees' Health Benefits shall consist of five members serving ex officio, as follows:

(1) The State Budget Officer, who shall serve as the Chair;

(2) Repealed by Session Laws 2013-373, s. 1, effective October 1, 2013.

(3) The State Controller;

(4) The State Treasurer; and

(5) The Executive Administrator for the State Health Plan for Teachers and State Employees.

(c) A majority of the members of the Committee then serving shall constitute a quorum.

(d) Each member shall be entitled to one vote on the Committee. Three affirmative votes shall be necessary for a decision by the members at any meeting of the Committee.

(e) The Committee shall keep in convenient form such data as is necessary for actuarial valuation of retired employees' health benefits under accounting standards set forth by the Governmental Accounting Standards Board of the Financial Accounting Foundation. The Department of State Treasurer, Retirement Systems Division, the State Health Plan for Teachers and State Employees, and any other State agency, department, or university institution, local public school agency, or local community college institution shall provide any necessary data upon request of the Committee for the purpose of conducting its responsibilities.

(f) The Committee shall designate either the actuary under contract with the Department of State Treasurer, Retirement Systems Division, or the actuary under contract with the State Health Plan for Teachers and State Employees as the technical adviser to the Committee on matters regarding the actuarial valuation of retired employees' health benefits created by the provisions of this Chapter. The technical advisor shall perform such actuarial valuation and other duties as are required under this Chapter.

(g) The Committee shall secure an annual calendar-year actuarial valuation of retired employees' health benefits under accounting standards set forth by the Governmental Accounting Standards Board of the Financial Accounting Foundation.

(h) The Committee shall keep a record of all of its proceedings which shall be open to public inspection. (2007-467, s. 1; 2007-323, s. 28.22A(o); 2008-168, s. 1(a), (c), (f); 2011-85, ss. 2.4(b), 2.10; 2013-373, s. 1.)

§ 135-48.13: Reserved for future codification purposes.

§ 135-48.14: Reserved for future codification purposes.

§ 135-48.15. Whistle-blower protections related to the State Health Plan.

(a) Statement of Public Policy. - It is the policy of this State that persons shall be encouraged to report verbally or in writing to the State Health Plan, Attorney General, or other appropriate authority evidence of activity related to the State Health Plan and involving the following:

(1) A violation of State or federal law, rule, or regulation.

(2) Fraud.

(3) Misappropriation of State resources.

(4) Gross mismanagement, a gross waste of monies, or gross abuse of authority.

Further, it is the policy of this State that persons shall be free of intimidation or harassment when reporting matters of public concern related to the State Health Plan, including offering testimony to or testifying before appropriate legislative panels.

(b) Protection From Retaliation. - No employer shall sue, discharge, threaten, or otherwise discriminate against an employee regarding the employee's compensation, terms, conditions, location, or privileges of employment because the employee, or a person acting on behalf of the employee, reports or is about to report, verbally or in writing, any activity described in subsection (a) of this section, unless the employee knows or has reason to believe that the report is inaccurate. No other employee of an employer shall retaliate against another employee because the employee, or a person acting on behalf of the employee, reports or is about to report, verbally or in writing, any activity described in subsection (a) of this section. No person shall sue, terminate a contract, threaten, or otherwise discriminate against a reporting person regarding the reporting person's compensation or terms of contract because the reporting person, or a person acting on behalf of the reporting person, reports or is about to report, verbally or in writing, any activity described in subsection (a) of this section, unless the reporting person knows or has reason to believe that the report is inaccurate.

(c)   Relief for Violation. - Any person injured by a violation of subsection (b) of this section may maintain an action in superior court for damages, an injunction, or other remedies provided in this section against the person who committed the violation within one year after the occurrence of the alleged violation of this Article.

(d)   Remedies. - A court, in rendering a judgment in an action brought pursuant to this section, may order an injunction, damages, reinstatement of the employee, the payment of back wages or payments owed under a contract, full reinstatement of fringe benefits and seniority rights, costs, reasonable attorneys' fees, or any combination of these. If an application for a permanent injunction is granted, the person maintaining the action shall be awarded costs and reasonable attorneys' fees. If in an action for damages the court finds that the person maintaining the action was injured by a willful violation of subsection (b) of this section, the court shall award as damages three times the amount of actual damages plus costs and reasonable attorneys' fees against the individual or individuals found to be in violation of subsection (b) of this section.

(e)   Unrelated Unfavorable Action. - It shall not be a violation of this Article for a person to discharge or take any other unfavorable action with respect to an employee who has engaged in protected activity as set forth under this Article if the person proves by the greater weight of the evidence that it would have taken the same unfavorable action in the absence of the protected activity of the employee. (2012-192, s. 3.)

§ 135-48.16: Reserved for future codification purposes.

§ 135-48.17: Reserved for future codification purposes.

§ 135-48.18: Reserved for future codification purposes.

§ 135-48.19: Reserved for future codification purposes.

Part 2. Administrative Structure.

§ 135-48.20. Board of Trustees established.

(a) There is established the Board of Trustees of the State Health Plan for Teachers and State Employees.

(b) The Board of Trustees of the State Health Plan for Teachers and State Employees shall consist of 10 members.

(c) The State Treasurer shall be an ex officio member of the Board and shall serve as its Chair, but shall only vote in order to break a tie vote.

(d) The Director of the Office of State Budget and Management shall be an ex officio nonvoting member of the Board.

(e) Two members shall be appointed by the Governor. Terms shall be for two years. Vacancies shall be filled by the Governor.

(f) Two members shall be appointed by the State Treasurer. Terms shall be for two years. Vacancies shall be filled by the State Treasurer.

(g) Two members shall be appointed by the General Assembly upon the recommendation of the Speaker of the House of Representatives in accordance with G.S. 120-121. Terms shall be for two years. Vacancies shall be filled in accordance with G.S. 120-122.

(h) Two members shall be appointed by the General Assembly upon the recommendation of the President Pro Tempore of the Senate in accordance with G.S. 120-121. Terms shall be for two years. Vacancies shall be filled in accordance with G.S. 120-122.

(i) In making appointments, the appointing authorities shall ensure that one of the appointees under subsection (e) of this section, one of the appointees under subsection (f) of this section, and one of the appointees under subsection (g) of this section, and one of the appointees under subsection (h) of this section are one of the following:

(1) An employee of a State department, agency, or institution;

(2) A teacher employed by a North Carolina public school system;

(3) A retired employee of a State department, agency, or institution; or

(4) A retired teacher from a North Carolina public school system.

In making appointments to the Board under this section, each appointing authority shall consult with all other appointing authorities prior to making its own appointments to ensure that the Board includes members of each of the groups listed in subdivisions (1) through (4) of this subsection.

(j) In making appointments, the appointing authorities shall appoint individuals from the following areas of expertise:

(1) Actuarial science.

(2) Health economics.

(3) Health benefits and administration.

(4) Health law and policy.

In making appointments to the Board under this section, each appointing authority shall consult with all other appointing authorities prior to making its own appointments to ensure that each of the areas of expertise listed in subdivisions (1) through (4) of this subsection is represented by at least one member of the Board.

(k) Each appointing authority may remove any member appointed by that appointing authority.

(l) The members of the Board of Trustees shall receive one hundred dollars ($100.00) per day, except employees eligible to enroll in the Plan, whenever the full Board of Trustees holds a public session, and travel allowances under G.S. 138-6 when traveling to and from meetings of the Board of Trustees or hearings under G.S. 135-48.24, but shall not receive any subsistence allowance or per diem under G.S. 138-5, except when holding a meeting or hearing where this section does not provide for payment of one hundred dollars ($100.00) per day.

(m) No member of the Board of Trustees may serve more than three consecutive two-year terms. (1981 (Reg. Sess., 1982), c. 1398, s. 6; 1983, c. 922, s. 1; 1985, c. 732, ss. 2-5, 8, 11, 42, 59, 60; 1985 (Reg. Sess., 1986), c. 1020, s. 1; 1987, c. 857, s. 2; 1995, c. 490, s. 56; 2002-126, s. 28.16(a); 2007-323, s. 28.22A(b); 2008-168, ss. 1(a), 2(a), (e); 2011-85, ss. 2.5(a), 2.10; 2011-96, s. 6(a).)

§ 135-48.21. Board officers, quorum, meetings.

(a) Besides the Chair, the Board of Trustees shall elect from its own membership such officers as it sees fit.

(b) A majority of the voting members of the Board of Trustees in office shall constitute a quorum. Decisions of the Board of Trustees shall be made by a majority vote of the Trustees present, except as otherwise provided in this Article.

(c) The Board shall meet at least quarterly. Meetings may also be called by the Chair, or at the written request of three members. (1981 (Reg. Sess., 1982), c. 1398, s. 6; 1987, c. 857, s. 3; 2008-168, ss. 1(a), 2(a), (f); 2009-16, s. 5(c); 2011-85, ss. 2.5(b), 2.10.)

§ 135-48.22. Board powers and duties.

The Board of Trustees shall have the following powers and duties:

(1) Approve benefit programs, as provided in G.S. 135-48.30(a)(2).

(2) Approve premium rates, co-pays, deductibles, and coinsurance percentages and maximums for the Plan, as provided in G.S. 135-48.30(a)(2).

(3) Oversee administrative reviews and appeals, as provided in G.S. 135-48.24.

(4) Approve large contracts, as provided in G.S. 135-48.33(a).

(5) Consult with and advise the State Treasurer as required by this Article and as requested by the State Treasurer.

(6) Develop and maintain a strategic plan for the Plan. (2011-85, s. 2.10; 2012-173, s. 4(a).)

§ 135-48.23. Executive Administrator.

(a) The Plan shall have an Executive Administrator and a Deputy Executive Administrator. The Executive Administrator and the Deputy Executive Administrator positions are exempt from the provisions of Chapter 126 of the General Statutes as provided in G.S. 126-5(c1).

(b) The Executive Administrator shall be appointed by the State Treasurer. The term of employment and salary of the Executive Administrator shall be set by the State Treasurer after consultation with the Board of Trustees.

The Executive Administrator may be removed from office by the State Treasurer after consultation with the Board of Trustees, and any vacancy in the office of Executive Administrator may be filled by the State Treasurer.

(c) The Executive Administrator shall appoint the Deputy Executive Administrator and may employ such clerical and professional staff, and such other assistance as may be necessary to assist the Executive Administrator, the Board of Trustees, and the State Treasurer in carrying out their duties and responsibilities under this Article. The Executive Administrator may designate managerial, professional, or policy-making positions as exempt from the North Carolina Human Resources Act. The Executive Administrator may also negotiate, renegotiate and execute contracts with third parties in the performance of the Executive Administrator's duties and responsibilities under this Article; provided any contract negotiations, renegotiations and execution with a Claims Processor, with an optional alternative comprehensive health benefit plan, or program thereunder, authorized under G.S. 135-48.2, with a preferred provider of institutional or professional hospital and medical care, or with a pharmacy benefit manager shall be done only after consultation with the State Treasurer.

(d) The Executive Administrator shall quarterly make reports and recommendations on the Plan to the President Pro Tempore of the Senate and the Speaker of the House of Representatives. (1985, c. 732, s. 10; 1985 (Reg. Sess., 1986), c. 1020, s. 20; 1987, c. 857, s. 5; 1991, c. 427, s. 2; 2000-141, s. 2; 2001-446, s. 6; 2004-124, s. 31.27(a); 2005-276, ss. 29.33(c), 29.34(a); 2007-323, s. 28.22A(l); 2008-168, ss. 1(a), 2(a), (h), 2.2; 2011-85, ss. 2.1(a), 2.5(c), 2.10; 2013-382, s. 9.1(c).)

§ 135-48.24. Administrative review.

(a) If, after exhaustion of internal appeal handling as outlined in the contract with the Claims Processor any person is aggrieved, the Claims Processor shall bring the matter to the attention of the Executive Administrator and Board of Trustees, which shall promptly decide whether the subject matter of the appeal is a determination subject to external review under Part 4 of Article 50 of Chapter 58 of the General Statutes. The Executive Administrator and Board of Trustees shall inform the aggrieved person and the aggrieved person's provider of the decision and shall provide the aggrieved person notice of the aggrieved person's right to appeal that decision as provided in this subsection. If the Executive Administrator and Board of Trustees decide that the subject matter of the appeal is not a determination subject to external review, then the Executive Administrator and Board of Trustees may make a binding decision on the matter in accordance with procedures established by the Executive Administrator and Board of Trustees. The Executive Administrator and Board of Trustees shall provide a written summary of the decisions made pursuant to this section to all employing units, all health benefit representatives, all relevant health care providers affected by a decision, and to any other parties requesting a written summary and approved by the Executive Administrator and Board of Trustees to receive a summary immediately following the issuance of a decision. A decision by the Executive Administrator and Board of Trustees that a matter raised on internal appeal is a determination subject to external review as provided in subsection (b) of this section may be contested by the aggrieved person under Chapter 150B of the General Statutes. The person contesting the decision may proceed with external review pending a decision in the contested case under Chapter 150B of the General Statutes.

(b) The State Treasurer, in consultation with the Board of Trustees, shall adopt and implement utilization review and internal grievance procedures that are substantially equivalent to those required under G.S. 58-50-61 and G.S. 58-50-62. External review of determinations shall be conducted in accordance with Part 4 of Article 50 of Chapter 58 of the General Statutes. As used in this section, "determination" is a decision by the State Treasurer, or the Plan's designated utilization review organization administrated by or under contract with the Plan that an admission, availability of care, continued stay, or other health care service has been reviewed and, based upon information provided, does not meet the Plan's requirements for medical necessity, appropriateness, health care setting, or level of care or effectiveness, and the requested service is therefore denied, reduced, or terminated.

(c) Repealed by Session Laws 2011-398, s. 49, effective January 1, 2012, and applicable to contested cases commenced on or after that date. (1981

(Reg. Sess., 1982), c. 1398, s. 6; 1985, c. 732, s. 53; 1985 (Reg. Sess., 1986), c. 1020, s. 20; 1991, c. 427, s. 6; 2001-446, s. 5(e); 2008-168, ss. 1(a), 2(a), (n); 2011-85, ss. 2.5(g), 2.10; 2011-398, s. 49.)

§ 135-48.25. Rules.

The State Treasurer, in consultation with the Board of Trustees, may adopt rules to implement this Article. The State Treasurer shall provide to all employing units, all health benefit representatives, all relevant health care providers affected by a rule, and to any other persons requesting a written description and approved by the State Treasurer written notice and an opportunity to comment not later than 30 days prior to adopting, amending, or rescinding a rule, unless immediate adoption of the rule without notice is necessary in order to fully effectuate the purpose of the rule. Rules of the Board of Trustees shall remain in effect until amended or repealed by the State Treasurer. The State Treasurer shall provide a written description of the rules adopted under this section to all employing units, all health benefit representatives, all relevant health care providers affected by a rule, and to any other persons requesting a written description and approved by the State Treasurer on a timely basis. Rules adopted by the State Treasurer to implement this Article are not subject to Article 2A of Chapter 150B of the General Statutes. (1981 (Reg. Sess., 1982), c. 1398, s. 6; 1985, c. 732, s. 54; 1991, c. 427, s. 7; 1997-278, s. 3; 1997-468, s. 5; 1998-1, s. 4(f); 2001-253, s. 1(r); 2008-168, ss. 1(a), 2(a), (o); 2011-85, ss. 2.5(h), 2.10.)

§ 135-48.26: Reserved for future codification purposes.

§ 135-48.27. Reports to the General Assembly; General Assembly access to information.

In addition to the reports required by G.S. 135-48.23(d), the State Treasurer, the Executive Administrator, and Board of Trustees shall report to the General Assembly at such times and in such forms as shall be designated by the President Pro Tempore of the Senate and the Speaker of the House of Representatives. Employees of the Legislative Services Commission designated by the Legislative Services Officer (i) shall have access to all records related to the Plan of the State Treasurer, the Board of Trustees, the

Executive Administrator, the Claims Processor, and the Plan and (ii) shall be entitled to attend all meetings, including executive sessions, of the Board of Trustees. (1981 (Reg. Sess., 1982), c. 1398, s. 6; 1985, c. 732, ss. 55, 55.1; 1985 (Reg. Sess., 1986), c. 1020, s. 7; 2008-168, ss. 1(a), (c), 2(c); 2011-85, ss. 2.4(d), 2.10; 2012-194, s. 30.)

§ 135-48.28. Auditing of the Plan.

The State Health Plan for Teachers and State Employees and the Claims Processor shall be subject to the oversight of the State Auditor pursuant to Article 5A of Chapter 147 of the General Statutes. (1981 (Reg. Sess., 1982), c. 1398, s. 6; 1983, c. 913, s. 24; 1985, c. 732, s. 46; 1985 (Reg. Sess., 1986), c. 1020, p. 20; 2007-323, s. 28.22A(o); 2007-345, s. 12; 2008-168, ss. 1(a), (c), 2(g); 2011-85, ss. 2.4(c), 2.10.)

Part 3. Plan Operation.

§ 135-48.30. Powers and duties of the State Treasurer.

(a)   The State Treasurer shall have the following powers and duties:

(1)   Administer and operate the State Health Plan for Teachers and State Employees in accordance with G.S. 135-48.2 and the provisions of this Article.

(2)   Set benefits, premium rates, co-pays, deductibles, and coinsurance percentages and maximums, subject to approval by the Board of Trustees. In setting premium rates, the State Treasurer may set a partially contributory rate of zero dollars, subject to approval by the Board of Trustees.

(3)   Set the allowable charges for medical and prescription drug benefits, as necessary.

(4)   Design and implement coordination of benefits policies.

(5)   May offer wellness incentives.

(6) Set administrative and medical policies that are not in direct conflict with this Article.

(7) Adopt and implement, in consultation with the Board of Trustees, utilization review and internal grievance procedures that are substantially equivalent to those required under G.S. 58-50-61 and G.S. 58-50-62. External review of determinations shall be conducted in accordance with Part 4 of Article 50 of Chapter 58 of the General Statutes.

(8) Implement and administer pharmacy and medical utilization management programs and programs to detect and address utilization abuse of benefits.

(9) Establish and operate fraud detection and audit programs.

(10) Expend funds for any independent audit.

(11) Establish procedures to require prior medical approval and implement the procedures after consultation with the Board of Trustees.

(12) Prepare and submit to the Governor and the General Assembly cost estimates for the Plan, including those required by Article 15 of Chapter 120 of the General Statutes.

(13) Disclose to the Governor and the General Assembly changes or additions to the health benefits programs and health care cost containment programs offered under the Plan, together with statements of financial and actuarial effects as required by Article 15 of Chapter 120 of the General Statutes.

(14) Secure and maintain tax qualification of the Plan under any applicable provisions of the Internal Revenue Code.

(15), (16) Repealed by Session Laws 2012-173, s. 3(c), effective January 1, 2013.

(17) Optionally offer Medicare-related options under G.S. 135-48.38.

(b) The State Treasurer may delegate his or her powers and duties under this section to the Executive Administrator, the Board of Trustees, and employees of the Plan. In delegating powers or duties, however, the State

Treasurer maintains the responsibility for the performance of those powers or duties. (2011-85, s. 2.10; 2012-173, s. 3(c), 4(b).)

§ 135-48.31: Reserved for future codification purposes.

§ 135-48.32. Contracts to provide benefits.

The Plan benefits shall be provided under contracts between the Plan and the claims processors selected by the Plan. The State Treasurer may contract with a pharmacy benefits manager to administer pharmacy benefits under the Plan. Such contracts shall include the applicable provisions of this Article and the description of the Plan in the request for proposal, and shall be administered by the respective claims processor or Pharmacy Benefits Manager, which will determine benefits and other questions arising thereunder. The contracts necessarily will conform to applicable State law. If any of the provisions of this Article and the request for proposals must be modified for inclusion in the contract because of State law, such modification shall be made. The State Treasurer shall ensure that the terms of the contract between the Plan and the Plan's Claims Processing Contractor, the Pharmacy Benefit Manager, and the Disease Management Contractor require the contractor to provide the following:

(1)   Detailed billing by each entity showing itemized cost information, including individual administrative services provided;

(2)   Transactional data; and

(3)   The cost to the Plan for each administrative function performed by the contractor. (2008-168, s. 3(c); 2009-16, ss. 2(f), 5(h); 2009-281, s. 1; 2009-313, s. 2; 2010-194, s. 18(b); 2011-85, ss. 2.6(a), 2.10.)

§ 135-48.33. Contracting provisions; large contract review by Board of Trustees and Attorney General, auditing, no cost plus contracts.

(a)   The Board of Trustees must approve all Plan contracts in excess of five hundred thousand dollars ($500,000), including contracts with an initial cost of less than five hundred thousand dollars ($500,000), but that may exceed five hundred thousand dollars ($500,000) during the term of the contract.

(b) The Plan shall: (i) submit all proposed contracts for supplies, materials, printing, equipment, and contractual services that exceed one million dollars ($1,000,000) authorized by this Article to the Attorney General or the Attorney General's designee for review as provided in G.S. 114-8.3; and (ii) include in all proposed contracts to be awarded by the Plan under this section a standard clause which provides that the State Auditor and internal auditors of the Plan may audit the records of the contractor during and after the term of the contract to verify accounts and data affecting fees and performance. The Plan shall not award a cost plus percentage of cost agreement or contract for any purpose. (2008-168, s. 3(c); 2009-16, ss. 2(f), 5(h); 2009-281, s. 1; 2009-313, s. 2; 2010-194, s. 18(b); 2011-85, ss. 2.6(a), 2.10; 2011-326, s. 15(s).)

§ 135-48.34. Contracts not subject to Article 3 of Chapter 143 of the General Statutes.

The design, adoption, and implementation of the preferred provider contracts, networks, and optional alternative comprehensive health benefit plans, and programs available under the optional alternative plans, as authorized under G.S. 135-48.2, are not subject to the requirements of Article 3 of Chapter 143 of the General Statutes, but are subject to the requirements of G.S. 135-48.33. (2011-85, s. 2.10.)

§ 135-48.35. Contract disputes not contested case under the Administrative Procedure Act, Chapter 150B of the General Statutes.

A dispute involving the performance, terms, or conditions of a contract between the Plan and an entity under contract with the Plan is not a contested case under Article 3 of Chapter 150B of the General Statutes. (2001-192, s. 2; 2008-168, ss. 1(a), (c), 2(d); 2011-85, s. 2.4(e).)

§ 135-48.36: Reserved for future codification purposes.

§ 135-48.37. Liability of third person; right of subrogation; right of first recovery.

(a) The Plan shall have the right of subrogation upon all of the Plan member's right to recover from a liable third party for payment made under the

Plan, for all medical expenses, including provider, hospital, surgical, or prescription drug expenses, to the extent those payments are related to an injury caused by a liable third party. The Plan member shall do nothing to prejudice these rights. The Plan has the right to first recovery on any amounts so recovered, whether by the Plan or the Plan member, and whether recovered by litigation, arbitration, mediation, settlement, or otherwise. Notwithstanding any other provision of law to the contrary, the recovery limitation set forth in G.S. 28A-18-2 shall not apply to the Plan's right of subrogation of Plan members.

(b) If the Plan is precluded from exercising its right of subrogation, it may exercise its rights of recovery against any third party who was overpaid. If the Plan recovers damages from a liable third party in excess of the claims paid, any excess will be paid to the member, less a proportionate share of the costs of collection.

(c) In the event a Plan member recovers any amounts from a liable third party to which the Plan is entitled under this section, the Plan may recover the amounts directly from the Plan member. The Plan has a lien, for not more than the value of claims paid related to the liability of the third party, on any damages subsequently recovered against the liable third party. If the Plan member fails to pursue the remedy against a liable third party, the Plan is subrogated to the rights of the Plan member and is entitled to enforce liability in the Plan's own name or in the name of the Plan member for the amount paid by the Plan.

(d) In no event shall the Plan's lien exceed fifty percent (50%) of the total damages recovered by the Plan member, exclusive of the Plan member's reasonable costs of collection as determined by the Plan in the Plan's sole discretion. The decision by the Plan as to the reasonable cost of collection is conclusive and is not a "final agency decision" for purposes of a contested case under Chapter 150B of the General Statutes. Notice of the Plan's lien or right to recovery shall be presumed when a Plan member is represented by an attorney, and the attorney shall disburse proceeds pursuant to this section. (2004-124, s. 31.25; 2006-264, s. 66(a); 2008-168, ss. 1(a), 3(a), (t); 2011-85, ss. 2.6(j), 2.10.)

§ 135-48.38. Persons eligible for Medicare; optional participation in other Medicare products.

(a) Benefits payable for covered expenses under this Plan will be reduced by any benefits payable for the same covered expenses under Medicare, so that

Medicare will be the primary carrier except where compliance with federal law specifies otherwise.

(b)   For those participants eligible for Medicare, the Plan will be administered on a "carve out" basis. The provisions of the Plan are applied to the charges not paid by Medicare (Parts A & B). In other words, those charges not paid by Medicare would be subject to the deductible and coinsurance of the Plan just as if the charges not paid by Medicare were the total bill.

(c)   For those individuals eligible for Part A (at no cost to them), benefits under this program will be reduced by the amounts to which the covered individuals would be entitled to under Parts A and B of Medicare, even if they choose not to enroll for Part B.

(d)   Notwithstanding the foregoing provisions of this section or any other provisions of the Plan, the State Treasurer may enter into negotiations with the Centers for Medicare and Medicaid Services, U.S. Department of Health and Human Services, in order to secure a more favorable coordination of the Plan's benefits with those provided by Medicare, including but not limited to, measures by which the Plan would provide Medicare benefits for all of its Medicare-eligible members in return for adequate payments from the federal government in providing such benefits. Should such negotiations result in an agreement favorable to the Plan and its Medicare-eligible members, the State Treasurer may, after consultation with the Board of Trustees, implement such an agreement which shall supersede all other provisions of the Plan to the contrary related to its payment of claims for Medicare-eligible members.

(e)   Notwithstanding subsections (a), (b), and (c) of this section, the State Treasurer may contract for coverage in lieu of current Plan medical and prescription drug benefits for Medicare retirees or to supplement Medicare benefits and may, after consultation with the Board of Trustees, implement such an agreement, which shall supersede all other provisions of the Plan to the contrary related to its payment of claims for Medicare-eligible members. (1981 (Reg. Sess., 1982), c. 1398, s. 6; 1985 (Reg. Sess., 1986), c. 1020, s. 18; 1987, c. 857, s. 21; 1989, c. 752, s. 22(o); 2008-168, ss. 1(a), 3(a), (o); 2011-85, ss. 2.6(g), 2.10.)

§ 135-48.39: Reserved for future codification purposes.

Part 4. Eligibility and Enrollment.

§ 135-48.40. Categories of eligibility.

(a) Noncontributory Coverage. - The following persons are eligible for coverage under the Plan, on a noncontributory basis, subject to the provisions of G.S. 135-48.43:

(1) Retired teachers, State employees, members of the General Assembly, and retired State law enforcement officers who retired under the Law Enforcement Officers' Retirement System prior to January 1, 1985. Except as otherwise provided in this subdivision, on and after January 1, 1988, a retiring employee or retiree must have completed at least five years of contributory retirement service with an employing unit prior to retirement from any State-supported retirement system in order to be eligible for group benefits under this Part as a retired employee or retiree. For employees first hired on and after October 1, 2006, and members of the General Assembly first taking office on and after February 1, 2007, future coverage as retired employees and retired members of the General Assembly is subject to a requirement that the future retiree have 20 or more years of retirement service credit in order to be covered by the provisions of this subdivision.

(2) Surviving spouses of:

a. Deceased retired employees, provided the death of the former plan member occurred prior to October 1, 1986; and

b. Deceased teachers, State employees, and members of the General Assembly who are receiving a survivor's alternate benefit under any of the State-supported retirement programs, provided the death of the former plan member occurred prior to October 1, 1986.

(b) Partially Contributory Coverage. - The following persons are eligible for coverage under the Plan, on a partially contributory basis, subject to the provisions of G.S. 135-48.43:

(1) (Effective until January 1, 2015) All permanent full-time employees of an employing unit who meet either of the following conditions:

a. Paid from general or special State funds.

b. Paid from non-State funds and in a group for which his or her employing unit has agreed to provide coverage.

Employees of State agencies, departments, institutions, boards, and commissions not otherwise covered by the Plan who are employed in permanent job positions on a recurring basis and who work 30 or more hours per week for nine or more months per calendar year are covered by the provisions of this subdivision.

(1) (Effective January 1, 2015) All full-time employees of an employing unit. For the purposes of this section, the full-time status of an employee will be determined by the employing unit in accordance with section 4980H of the Internal Revenue Code and the applicable regulations, as amended.

(2) Repealed by Session Laws 2013-324, s. 2, effective July 23, 2013.

(3) Retired teachers, State employees, members of the General Assembly, and retired State law enforcement officers who retired under the Law Enforcement Officers' Retirement System prior to January 1, 1985. Except as otherwise provided in this subdivision, on and after January 1, 1988, a retiring employee or retiree must have completed at least five years of contributory retirement service with an employing unit prior to retirement from any State-supported retirement system in order to be eligible for group benefits under this Part as a retired employee or retiree. For employees first hired on and after October 1, 2006, and members of the General Assembly first taking office on and after February 1, 2007, future coverage as retired employees and retired members of the General Assembly is subject to a requirement that the future retiree have 20 or more years of retirement service credit in order to be covered by the provisions of this subdivision.

(4) Surviving spouses of:

a. Deceased retired employees, provided the death of the former plan member occurred prior to October 1, 1986; and

b. Deceased teachers, State employees, and members of the General Assembly who are receiving a survivor's alternate benefit under any of the State-supported retirement programs, provided the death of the former plan member occurred prior to October 1, 1986.

(5) Employees of the General Assembly, not otherwise covered by this section, as determined by the Legislative Services Commission, except for legislative interns and pages.

(6) Members of the General Assembly.

(7) Notwithstanding the provisions of subsection (e) of this section, employees on official leave of absence while completing a full-time program in school administration in an approved program as a Principal Fellow in accordance with Article 5C of Chapter 116 of the General Statutes.

(8) Notwithstanding the provisions of G.S. 135-48.44, employees formerly covered by the provisions of this section, other than retired employees, who have been employed for 12 or more months by an employing unit, or who have completed a contract term of employment of 10 or 11 months and whose employing unit is a local school administrative unit, and whose jobs are eliminated because of a reduction, in total or in part, in the funds used to support the job or its responsibilities, provided the employees were covered by the Plan at the time of separation from service resulting from a job elimination. Employees covered by this subsection shall be covered for a period of up to 12 months following a separation from service because of a job elimination. An employee formerly covered by the provisions of this section shall not be eligible for coverage under this subdivision if the employee is provided health benefit coverage on a non-contributory basis by a subsequent employer.

(9) Any member enrolled pursuant to subdivision (1) or (2) of this subsection who is on approved leave of absence with pay or receiving workers' compensation.

(10) Employees on approved Family and Medical Leave.

(c) One-Half Contributory Coverage. - The following persons are eligible for coverage under the Plan, on a one-half contributory basis, subject to the provisions of G.S. 135-48.43:

(1) A school employee in a job-sharing position as described in G.S. 115C-326.5. If these employees elect to participate in the Plan, the employing unit shall pay fifty percent (50%) of the Plan's total employer premiums. Individual employees shall pay the balance of the total premiums not paid by the employing unit.

(2) Employees and members of the General Assembly with 10 but less than 20 years of retirement service credit provided the employees were first hired on or after October 1, 2006, and the members first took office on or after February 1, 2007. For such future retirees, the State shall pay fifty percent (50%) of the Plan's total employer premiums. Individual retirees shall pay the balance of the total premiums not paid by the State.

(d) Fully Contributory Coverage. - The following persons shall be eligible for coverage under the Plan, on a fully contributory basis, subject to the provisions of G.S. 135-48.43:

(1) Former members of the General Assembly who enroll before October 1, 1986.

(2) For enrollments after September 30, 1986, former members of the General Assembly if covered under the Plan at termination of membership in the General Assembly. To be eligible for coverage as a former member of the General Assembly, application must be made within 30 days of the end of the term of office. Only members of the General Assembly covered by the Plan at the end of the term of office are eligible. If application is not made within the specified time period, the member forfeits eligibility.

(3) Surviving spouses of deceased former members of the General Assembly who enroll before October 1, 1986.

(4) Employees of the General Assembly, not otherwise covered by this section, as determined by the Legislative Services Commission, except for legislative interns and pages.

(5) For enrollments after September 30, 1986, surviving spouses of deceased former members of the General Assembly, if covered under the Plan at the time of death of the former member of the General Assembly.

(6) All permanent part-time employees (designated as half-time or more) of an employing unit who meet the conditions outlined in sub-subdivision (b)(1)a. of this section and who are not covered by the provisions of subdivision (b)(1) of this section.

(7) The spouses and eligible dependent children of enrolled teachers, State employees, retirees, former members of the General Assembly, former employees covered by the provisions of subdivision (b)(8) of this section,

Disability Income Plan beneficiaries, enrolled continuation members, and members of the General Assembly. Spouses of surviving dependents are not eligible, nor are dependent children if they were not covered at the time of the member's death. Surviving spouses may cover their dependent children provided the children were enrolled at the time of the member's death or enroll within 90 days of the member's death.

(8) Blind persons licensed by the State to operate vending facilities under contract with the Department of Health and Human Services, Division of Services for the Blind and its successors, who are:

a. Operating such a vending facility;

b. Former operators of such a vending facility whose service as an operator would have made these operators eligible for an early or service retirement allowance under Article 1 of this Chapter had they been members of the Retirement System; and

c. Former operators of such a vending facility who attain five or more years of service as operators and who become eligible for and receive a disability benefit under the Social Security Act upon cessation of service as an operator.

Spouses, dependent children, surviving spouses, and surviving dependent children of such members are not eligible for coverage.

(9) Surviving spouses of deceased retirees and surviving spouses of deceased teachers, State employees, and members of the General Assembly provided the death of the former Plan member occurred after September 30, 1986, and the surviving spouse was covered under the Plan at the time of death.

(10) Any eligible dependent child of the deceased retiree, teacher, State employee, member of the General Assembly, former member of the General Assembly, or Disability Income Plan beneficiary, provided the child was covered at the time of death of the retiree, teacher, State employee, member of the General Assembly, former member of the General Assembly, or Disability Income Plan beneficiary, (or was in posse at the time and is covered at birth under this Part), or was covered under the Plan on September 30, 1986. An eligible surviving dependent child can remain covered until age 26 or indefinitely if certified as incapacitated under G.S. 135-44.41(b) [135-48.41(b)].

(11) Retired teachers, State employees, and members of the General Assembly with less than 10 years of retirement service credit, provided the teachers and State employees were first hired on or after October 1, 2006, and the members first took office on or after February 1, 2007.

(12) Notwithstanding the provisions of G.S. 135-48.44, former employees covered by the provisions of this section and their spouses and eligible dependent children who were covered by the Plan at the time of the former employees' separation from service pursuant to this section, following expiration of the former employees' coverage provided by this section. Election of coverage under this subdivision shall be made within 90 days after the termination of coverage provided under this section.

(13) The following persons, their eligible spouses, and eligible dependent children, provided that the person seeking coverage as a subscriber (i) is not eligible for another comprehensive group health benefit plan and (ii) has been without coverage under a comprehensive group health benefit plan for at least six consecutive months:

a. Firefighters.

b. Rescue squad workers.

c. Persons receiving a pension from the North Carolina Firemen and Rescue Squad Workers' Pension Fund.

d. Members of the North Carolina National Guard.

e. Retirees of the North Carolina National Guard with 20 years of service.

For the purposes of this subdivision, Medicare benefits, Civilian Health and Medical Program of the Uniformed Services (CHAMPUS) benefits, and other Uniformed Services benefits shall be considered comprehensive group health benefit plans. The Plan may require certification of persons seeking coverage under this subdivision. (1981 (Reg. Sess., 1982), c. 1398, s. 6; 1983, c. 499; c. 761, ss. 252-255; c. 867, s. 4; c. 922, s. 5; 1985, c. 400, ss. 5, 6; 1985 (Reg. Sess., 1986), c. 1020, s. 29(a)-(l); 1987, c. 738, ss. 29(n), 36(a), 36(b); c. 809, ss. 3, 4; c. 857, ss. 11(a), 11.1, 11.2, 12; 1989, c. 752, s. 22(e), (f); 1989 (Reg. Sess., 1990), c. 1074, s. 22(a); 1993, c. 321, s. 85(b); 1995, c. 278, s. 1; c. 507, ss. 7.21(a)-(c), 7.28(a)-(c); 1997-443, s. 11A.118(a); 1997-512, ss. 17, 19-27; 1999-237, s. 28.29(f); 2000-141, ss. 6(a), (b); 2000-184, ss. 1(a),(b), 3; 2001-

487, s. 86(a); 2002-174, s. 4; 2003-358, s. 4; 2004-124, s. 31.21(b); 2004-199, s. 34(b); 2005-276, s. 29.31(e); 2006-174, ss. 1, 2, 3; 2007-323, s. 28.22A(g1), (o); 2007-345, s. 12; 2008-168, ss. 1(a), 3(a), (f); 2008-194, s. 6(b); 2009-16, s. 3(b); 2009-281, s. 1; 2009-570, s. 43.2; 2009-571, s. 3(a), (d); 2010-72, s. 3(a); 2010-136, ss. 1, 2; 2011-85, ss. 1.6(b), 2.6(c), 2.10; 2011-96, s. 2(a); 2013-324, ss. 1, 2.)

§ 135-48.41. Additional eligibility provisions.

(a) A foster child is covered as a dependent child (i) if living in a regular parent-child relationship with the expectation that the employee will continue to rear the child into adulthood, (ii) if at the time of enrollment, or at the time a foster child relationship is established, whichever occurs first, the employee applies for coverage for such child and submits evidence of a bona fide foster child relationship, identifying the foster child by name and setting forth all relevant aspects of the relationship, (iii) if the claims processor accepts the foster child as a participant through a separate written document identifying the foster child by name and specifically recognizing the foster child relationship, and (iv) if at the time a claim is incurred, the foster child relationship, as identified by the employee, continues to exist. Children placed in a home by a welfare agency which obtains control of, and provides for maintenance of the child, are not eligible participants.

(b) A dependent child shall not be eligible for coverage under the Plan if the dependent child is eligible for employer based health care outside of the State Health Plan for Teachers and State Employees, other than a parent's claim. Coverage of a dependent child may be extended beyond the 26th birthday if the dependent is physically or mentally incapacitated to the extent that he or she is incapable of earning a living and (i) such handicap developed or began to develop before the dependent's 19th birthday, or (ii) such handicap developed or began to develop before the dependent's 26th birthday if the dependent was covered by the Plan in accordance with G.S. 135-48.40(d)(7).

(c) No person shall be eligible for coverage as a dependent if eligible as an employee or retired employee, except when a spouse is eligible on a fully contributory basis. In addition, no person shall be eligible for coverage as a dependent of more than one employee or retired employee at the same time.

(d) Former employees who are receiving disability retirement benefits or disability income benefits pursuant to Article 6 of Chapter 135 of the General Statutes or who are approved for those benefits but not in receipt of the benefits due to lump-sum payouts of vacation, bonus, and sick leave, provided the former employee has at least five years of contributory retirement service with an employing unit of a State-supported retirement system, shall be eligible for the benefit provisions of this Plan, as set forth in this Part, on a noncontributory or partially contributory basis. Such coverage shall terminate as of the end of the month in which such former employee is no longer eligible for disability retirement benefits or disability income benefits pursuant to Article 6 of this Chapter.

(e) Employees on official leave of absence without pay may elect to continue this group coverage at group cost provided that they pay the full employee and employer contribution through the employing unit during the leave period.

(f) For the support of the benefits made available to any member vested at the time of retirement, their spouses or surviving spouses, and the surviving spouses of employees who are receiving a survivor's alternate benefit under G.S. 135-5(m) of those associations listed in G.S. 135-27(a), licensing and examining boards under G.S. 135-1.1, the North Carolina State Art Society, Inc., and the North Carolina Symphony Society, Inc., each association, organization or board shall pay to the Plan the full cost of providing these benefits under this section as determined by the State Health Plan for Teachers and State Employees. In addition, each association, organization or board shall pay to the Plan an amount equal to the cost of the benefits provided under this section to presently retired members of each association, organization or board since such benefits became available at no cost to the retired member. This subsection applies only to those individuals employed prior to July 1, 1983, as provided in G.S. 135-27(d).

(g) An eligible surviving spouse and any eligible surviving dependent child of a deceased retiree, teacher, State employee, member of the General Assembly, former member of the General Assembly, or Disability Income Plan beneficiary shall be eligible for group benefits under this section without waiting periods for preexisting conditions provided coverage is elected within 90 days after the death of the former plan member. Coverage may be elected at a later time, during an annual enrollment period, but members 19 years of age and older may be subject to the 12-month waiting period for preexisting conditions and will be effective the first day of the month following receipt of the application.

(h) No person shall be eligible for coverage as an employee or retired employee or as a dependent of an employee or retired employee upon a finding by the State Treasurer or by a court of competent jurisdiction that the employee or dependent knowingly and willfully made or caused to be made a false statement or false representation of a material fact in a claim for reimbursement of medical services under the Plan or in any representation or attestation to the Plan.

The State Treasurer may make an exception to the provisions of this subsection when persons subject to this subsection have had a cessation of coverage for a period of five years and have made a full and complete restitution to the Plan for all fraudulent claim amounts. Nothing in this subsection shall be construed to obligate the State Treasurer to make an exception as allowed for under this subsection.

(i) Any employee receiving benefits pursuant to Article 6 of this Chapter when the employee has less than five years of retirement membership service, or an employee on leave without pay due to illness or injury for up to 12 months, is entitled to continued coverage under the Plan for the employee and any eligible dependents by paying one hundred percent (100%) of the cost. (1981 (Reg. Sess., 1982), c. 1398, s. 6; 1983, c. 499; c. 761, ss. 252-255; c. 867, s. 4; c. 922, s. 5; 1985, c. 400, ss. 5, 6; 1985 (Reg. Sess., 1986), c. 1020, s. 29(a)-(l); 1987, c. 738, ss. 29(n), 36(a), 36(b); c. 809, ss. 3, 4; c. 857, ss. 11(a), 11.1, 11.2, 12; 1989, c. 752, s. 22(e), (f); 1989 (Reg. Sess., 1990), c. 1074, s. 22(a); 1993, c. 321, s. 85(b); 1995, c. 278, s. 1; c. 507, ss. 7.21(a)-(c), 7.28(a)-(c); 1997-443, s. 11A.118(a); 1997-512, ss. 17, 19-27; 1999-237, s. 28.29(f); 2000-141, ss. 6(a), (b); 2000-184, ss. 1(a),(b), 3; 2001-487, s. 86(a); 2002-174, s. 4; 2003-358, s. 4; 2004-124, s. 31.21(b); 2004-199, s. 34(b); 2005-276, s. 29.31(e); 2006-174, ss. 1, 2, 3; 2007-323, s. 28.22A(g1), (o); 2007-345, s. 12; 2008-168, ss. 1(a), 3(a), (f); 2008-194, s. 6(b); 2009-16, s. 3(b); 2009-281, s. 1; 2009-570, s. 43.2; 2009-571, s. 3(a), (d); 2010-72, s. 3(a); 2010-136, ss. 1, 2; 2011-85, ss. 1.7(b), 2.6(c), 2.10; 2011-96, s. 3(b); 2011-294, s. 1; 2012-173, s. 2(a).)

§ 135-48.42. Enrollment.

(a) Except as otherwise required by applicable federal law, new employees must be given the opportunity to enroll or decline enrollment for themselves and their dependents within 30 days from the date of employment or from first becoming eligible on a partially contributory basis. Coverage may become effective on the first day of the month following date of entry on payroll or on the first day of the following month. New employees age 19 and older not enrolling themselves and their dependents age 19 and older within 30 days, or not adding dependents when first eligible as provided herein may enroll during annual enrollment, but may be subject to a 12-month waiting period for preexisting health conditions, except for employees who elect to change their coverage in accordance with rules established by the State Treasurer for optional or alternative plans available under the Plan. Children born to covered employees having coverage type (2) or (3), as outlined in G.S. 135-48.43(d) shall be automatically covered at the time of birth without any waiting period for preexisting health conditions. Children born to covered employees having coverage type (1) shall be automatically covered at birth without any waiting period for preexisting health conditions so long as the claims processor receives notification within 30 days of the date of birth that the employee desires to change from coverage (1) to coverage type (2) or (3), provided that the employee pays any additional premium required by the coverage type selected retroactive to the first day of the month in which the child was born.

(b) Except as otherwise required by applicable federal law, newly acquired dependents (spouse/child) age 19 and older enrolled within 30 days of becoming an eligible dependent will not be subject to the 12-month waiting period for preexisting conditions. A dependent can become first eligible due to marriage, adoption, legal guardianship, entering a foster child relationship, and at the beginning of each legislative session (applies only to enrolled legislators). Effective date for newly acquired dependents if application was made within the 30 days can be the first day of the following month. Effective date for an adopted child can be date of adoption, or date of placement in the adoptive parents' home, or the first of the month following the date of adoption or placement. Firefighters, rescue squad workers, and members of the National Guard, and their eligible dependents, are subject to the same terms and conditions as are new employees and their dependents covered by this subdivision. Enrollments in these circumstances must occur within 30 days of eligibility to enroll.

(c) Eligible employees younger than age 19 and dependents younger than age 19 may be enrolled during annual enrollment and shall not be subject to any waiting period for a preexisting condition.

(d) When an eligible or enrolled member applies to enroll the member's eligible dependent child or spouse, the member shall provide the documentation required by the Plan to verify the dependent's eligibility for coverage.

(e) Eligible employees and retirees may only change their elections, including adding or removing dependents, during the Plan year due to a qualifying event as defined under federal law. (2008-168, s. 3(g); 2009-16, s. 3(c), (g); 2009-281, s. 1; 2011-85, ss. 1.7(c), 2.6(d), 2.10; 2011-96, ss. 2(d)(1), 3(c); 2012-173, s. 2(b); 2013-324, s. 3.)

§ 135-48.43. Effective dates of coverage.

(a) Eligible Employees and Retired Employees. - Employees and retirees who otherwise satisfy the eligibility requirements set forth in G.S. 135-48.40 will be offered coverage with the following effective dates:

(1) Employees and retired employees covered under the Predecessor Plan will continue to be covered, subject to the terms hereof.

(2) (Effective until January 1, 2015) New employees may apply for coverage to be effective on the first day of the month following employment, or on a like date the following month if the employee has enrolled.

(2) (Effective January 1, 2015) New employees may apply for coverage to be effective on the first day of the month following the date that the employee is determined by the employing unit to be a full-time employee as defined in G.S. 135-48.40(b)(1) or, if later, the first day of any applicable stability periods established by the employing unit in accordance with section 4980H of the Internal Revenue Code and the applicable regulations, as amended.

(3) Employees not enrolling or adding dependents when first eligible in accordance with G.S. 135-48.42 may enroll later during annual enrollment, except employees who elect to change their coverage in accordance with rules adopted by the State Treasurer for optional alternative plans offered under the Plan.

(4) Members of the General Assembly, beginning with the 1985 Session, shall become first eligible with the convening of each Session of the General Assembly, regardless of a Member's service during previous Sessions.

Members and their dependents enrolled when first eligible after the convening of each Session of the General Assembly will not be subject to any waiting periods for preexisting health conditions. Members of the 1983 Session of the General Assembly, not already enrolled, shall be eligible to enroll themselves and their dependents on or before October 1, 1983, without being subject to any waiting periods for preexisting health conditions.

(b)   Waiting Periods and Preexisting Conditions. -

(1)   New employees and dependents age 19 and older enrolling when first eligible are subject to no waiting period for preexisting conditions under the Plan.

(2)   Employees age 19 and older not enrolling or not adding dependents age 19 and older when first eligible may enroll later during annual enrollment, but enrollees age 19 or older may be subject to a twelve-month waiting period for preexisting conditions except as provided in subdivision (a)(3) of this section. The waiting period under this subdivision is subject to applicable federal law.

(3)   Retiring employees and dependents enrolled when first eligible after an employee's retirement are subject to no waiting period for preexisting conditions under the Plan. Retiring employees not enrolled or not adding dependents age 19 and older when first eligible after an employee's retirement may enroll at a later time during annual enrollment, but may be subject to a 12-month waiting period for preexisting conditions except as provided in subdivision (a)(3) of this section.

(4)   Employees and dependents enrolling or reenrolling within 12 months after a termination of enrollment or employment that were not enrolled at the time of this previous termination, regardless of the employing units involved, shall not be considered as newly-eligible employees or dependents for the purposes of waiting periods and preexisting conditions. Employees and dependents transferring from optional prepaid alternative plans available under the Plan; employees and dependents immediately returning to service from an employing unit's approved periods of leave without pay for illness, injury, educational improvement, workers' compensation, parental duties, or for military reasons; employees and dependents immediately returning to service from a reduction in an employing unit's work force; retiring employees and dependents reenrolled in accordance with subdivision (3) of this subsection; formerly-enrolled dependents reenrolling as eligible employees; formerly-enrolled employees reenrolling as eligible dependents; and employees and dependents

reenrolled without waiting periods and preexisting conditions under specific rules adopted by the State Treasurer in the best interests of the Plan shall not be considered reenrollments for the purpose of this subdivision. Furthermore, employees accepting permanent, full-time appointments who had previously worked in a part-time or temporary position and their qualified dependents shall not be covered by waiting periods and preexisting conditions under this division provided enrollment as a permanent, full-time employee is made when the employee and his dependents are first eligible to enroll.

(5) To administer the 12-month waiting period for preexisting conditions for employees age 19 and older and dependents age 19 and older under this Article, the Plan must give credit against the 12-month period for the time a person was covered under a previous plan if the previous plan's coverage was continuous to a date not more than 63 days before the effective date of coverage. As used in this subdivision, a "previous plan" means any policy, certificate, contract, or any other arrangement provided by any accident and health insurer, any hospital or medical service corporation, any health maintenance organization, any preferred provider organization, any multiple employer welfare arrangement, any self-insured health benefit arrangement, any governmental health benefit or health care plan or program, or any other health benefit arrangement. Waiting periods for preexisting conditions administered under this Article are subject to applicable federal law.

(c) Dependents of Employees and Retired Employees. -

(1) Dependents of employees and retired employees who have family coverage under the Predecessor Plan will continue to be covered subject to the terms hereof.

(2) Employees who have dependents may apply for family coverage at the time they enroll as provided in subdivisions (a)(2) and (a)(3) of this section and such dependents will be covered under the Plan beginning the same date as such employees.

(3) Employees and retired employees may change from one category of coverage to a different category of coverage without a waiting period for preexisting conditions, and, as applicable, dependents will be covered under the Plan the first of the month or the first of the second month following the dependent's eligibility for coverage, provided written application is submitted to the Health Benefits Representative within 30 days of becoming eligible.

(4) Employees or retired employees who wish to change to employee only coverage shall give written notice to their Health Benefits Representative within 30 days after any change in the status of dependents, (resulting from death, divorce, etc.) that requires a change in contract category. The effective date will be the first of the month following the dependent's ineligibility event. If notification was not made within the 30 days following the dependent's ineligibility event, the dependent will be retroactively removed the first of the month following the dependent's ineligibility event, and the coverage category change will be the first of the month following written notification, except in cases of death, in which case the coverage category change will be made retroactive to the first of the month following the death.

(5) Employees not adding dependents age 19 and older when first eligible may enroll later during annual enrollment, but dependents may be subject to a 12-month waiting period for preexisting health conditions except as provided in subdivision (a)(3) of this section.

(6) Employees or retired employees who wish to change to employee only coverage even though their dependents continue to be eligible, shall give written notification to their Health Benefits Representative. Except as otherwise required by applicable federal law, the date of this category change will be the first of the month following written notification or any first of the month thereafter as desired by the employee.

(7) The effective date for newborns or adopted children will be date of birth, date of adoption, or placement with adoptive parent provided member is currently covered under employee and family or employee and child coverage. If the member wishes to add a newborn or adopted child and is currently enrolled in employee only coverage, the member must submit application for coverage and a coverage type change within 30 days of the child's birth or date of adoption or placement. Effective date for the coverage category change is the first of the month in which the child is born, adopted, or placed. Adopted children may also be covered the first of the month following placement or adoption.

(d) Categories of Coverage Available. - There are four categories of coverage which an employee or retiree may elect.

(1) Employee Only. - Covers enrolled employees only. Maternity benefits are provided to employee only.

(2) Employee and Child. - Covers enrolled employee and all eligible dependent children. Maternity benefits are provided to the employee only.

(3) Employee and Family. - Covers employee and spouse, and all eligible dependent children. Maternity benefits are provided to employee or enrolled spouse.

(4) Employee and Spouse. - Covers employee and spouse only. Maternity benefits are provided to the employee or the employee's enrolled spouse.

(e) Firefighters, rescue squad workers, and members of the National Guard are subject to the same terms and conditions of this section as are employees. Eligible dependents of firefighters, rescue squad workers, and members of the National Guard are subject to the same terms and conditions of this section as are dependents of employees.

(f) If any provision of this section is in conflict with applicable federal law, federal law shall control to the extent of the conflict. (1981 (Reg. Sess., 1982), c. 1398, s. 6; 1983, c. 499; c. 761, ss. 252-255; c. 867, s. 4; c. 922, s. 5; 1985, c. 400, ss. 5, 6; 1985 (Reg. Sess., 1986), c. 1020, ss. 5(b), 20; 1987, c. 857, s. 13; 1991, c. 427, ss. 10-12; 1996, 2nd Ex. Sess., c. 18, s. 28.23(b); 1997-512, ss. 28-31, 40; 1999-237, s. 28.29(g); 2007-323, s. 28.22A(h); 2008-168, ss. 1(a), 3(a), (h); 2009-16, ss. 3(d), 5(a); 2009-281, s. 1; 2011-85, ss. 1.7(d), 2.6(e), 2.10; 2011-96, ss. 2(d)(2), 3(d); 2012-173, s. 2(c); 2013-324, s. 4.)

§ 135-48.44. Cessation of coverage.

(a) Coverage under this Plan of an employee and his or her surviving spouse or eligible dependent children or of a retired employee and his or her surviving spouse or eligible dependent children shall cease on the earliest of the following dates:

(1) The last day of the month in which an employee or retired employee dies. Provided such surviving spouse or eligible dependent children were covered under the Plan at the time of death of the former employee or retired employee, or were covered on September 30, 1986, any such surviving spouse or eligible dependent children may then elect to continue coverage under the Plan by submitting written application to the Claims Processor and by paying the cost for such coverage when due at the applicable fees. Such coverage shall

cease on the last day of the month in which such surviving spouse or eligible dependent children die, except as provided by this Article.

(2) The last day of the month in which an employee's employment with the State is terminated as provided in subsection (d) of this section.

(3) The last day of the month in which a divorce becomes final.

(4) The last day of the month in which an employee or retired employee requests cancellation of coverage.

(5) The last day of the month in which a covered individual enters active military service.

(6) The last day of the month in which a covered individual is found to have knowingly and willfully made or caused to be made a false statement or false representation of a material fact in a claim for reimbursement of medical services under the Plan. The State Treasurer may make an exception to the provisions of this subdivision when persons subject to this subdivision have had a cessation of coverage for a period of five years and have made a full and complete restitution to the Plan for all fraudulent claim amounts. Nothing in this subdivision shall be construed to obligate the State Treasurer to make an exception as allowed for under this subdivision.

(7) The last day of the month in which an employee who is Medicare-eligible selects Medicare to be the primary payer of medical benefits. Coverage for a Medicare-eligible spouse of an employee shall also cease the last day of the month in which Medicare is selected to be the primary payer of medical benefits for the Medicare-eligible spouse. Such members are eligible to apply for conversion coverage.

(8) The last day of the month in which a covered individual is found to be ineligible for coverage.

(b) Coverage under this Plan as a dependent child ceases when the child ceases to be a dependent child as defined by G.S. 135-48.1 except, coverage may continue under this Plan for a period of not more than 36 months after loss of dependent status on a fully contributory basis provided the dependent child was covered under the Plan at the time of loss of dependent status.

(c) Coverage under the Plan as a surviving dependent child whether covered as a dependent of a surviving spouse, or as an individual member (no living parent), ceases when the child ceases to be a dependent child as defined by G.S. 135-48.1, except coverage may continue under the Plan on a fully contributory basis for a period of not more than 36 months after loss of dependent status.

(d) Termination of employment shall mean termination for any reason, including layoff and leave of absence, except as provided in subdivisions (a)(1) and (2) of this section, but shall not, for purposes of this Plan, include retirement upon which the employee is granted an immediate service or disability pension under and pursuant to a State-supported Retirement System.

(1) In the event of termination for any reason other than death, coverage under the Plan for an employee and his or her eligible spouse or dependent children, provided the eligible spouse or dependent children were covered under the Plan at termination of employment may be continued for a period of not more than 18 months following termination of employment on a fully contributory basis. Employees who were covered under the Plan at termination of employment may be continued for a period of not more than 18 months or 29 months if determined to be disabled under the Social Security Act, Title II, OASDI or Title XVI, SSI.

(2) In the event of approved leave of absence without pay, other than for active duty in the Armed Forces of the United States, coverage under this Plan for an employee and his or her dependents may be continued during the period of such leave of absence by the employee's paying one hundred percent (100%) of the cost.

(3) If employment is terminated in the second half of a calendar month and the covered individual has made the required contribution for any coverage in the following month, that coverage will be continued to the end of the calendar month following the month in which employment was terminated.

(4) Employees paid for less than 12 months in a year, who are terminated at the end of the work year and who have made contributions for the non-work months, will continue to be covered to the end of the period for which they have made contributions, with the understanding that if they are not employed by another State-covered employer under this Plan at the beginning of the next work year, the employee will refund to the ex-employer the amount of the employer's cost paid for them during the non-paycheck months.

(5) Any employee receiving benefits pursuant to Article 6 of this Chapter when the employee has less than five years of retirement membership service, or an employee on leave of absence without pay due to illness or injury for up to 12 months, is entitled to continued coverage under the Plan for the employee and any eligible dependents by the employee's paying one hundred percent (100%) of the cost.

(e) A legally divorced spouse and any eligible dependent children of a covered employee or retired employee may continue coverage under this Plan for a period of not more than 36 months following the first of the month after a divorce becomes final on a fully contributory basis, provided the former spouse and any eligible dependent children were covered under the Plan at the time a divorce became final.

(f) A legally separated spouse of a covered employee or retired employee may continue coverage under this Plan for a period not to exceed 36 months from the separation date on a fully contributory basis, provided the separated spouse was covered under the Plan at the time of separation and provided the covered employee's or retired employee's actions result in the loss of coverage for the separated spouse. Eligible dependent children may also continue coverage if covered under the Plan at time of separation, provided the employee's or retired employee's actions result in the loss of coverage for the dependent children.

(g) Whenever this section gives a right to continuation coverage, such coverage must be elected within the time allowed by applicable federal law.

(h) Continuation coverage under this Plan shall not be continued past the occurrence of any one of the following events:

(1) The termination of the Plan.

(2) Failure of a Plan member to pay monthly in advance any required premiums.

(3) A person becomes a covered employee or a dependent of a covered employee under any group health plan and that group health plan has no restrictions or limitations on benefits.

(4) A person becomes eligible for Medicare benefits on or after the effective date of the continuation coverage.

(5)   The person was determined to be no longer disabled, provided the 18-month coverage was extended to 29 months due to having been determined to be disabled under the Social Security Act, Title II, OASDI or Title XVI, SSI.

(6)   The person reaches the maximum applicable continuation period of 18, 29, or 36 months.

(i)   Notice requirements concerning continuation coverage shall be developed by the Plan.

(j)   The spouse and any eligible dependent children of a covered employee may continue coverage under the Plan on a fully contributory basis for a period not to exceed 36 months from the date the employee becomes eligible for Medicare benefits which results in a loss of coverage under the Plan, provided that the spouse and eligible dependent children were covered under the Plan at the time the employee became eligible for Medicare benefits which results in a loss of coverage under the Plan. (1981 (Reg. Sess., 1982), c. 1398, s. 6; 1983, c. 922, ss. 17, 19-21; 1985, c. 732, ss. 13, 34; 1985 (Reg. Sess., 1986), c. 1020, ss. 19, 29(m)-(x); 1987, c. 738, s. 29(o); 1989, c. 752, s. 22(p); 1991, c. 427, s. 42; 1995, c. 278, s. 2; 1997-512, ss. 32-35; 2000-184, s. 4; 2008-168, ss. 1(a), 3(a), (q); 2008-187, s. 49.5; 2009-16, s. 3(f); 2011-85, ss. 2.6(h), 2.10; 2011-183, s. 103; 2012-194, s. 31.)

§ 135-48.45. Conversion.

(a)   Upon a cessation of group coverage under the Plan and/or eligibility for group coverage under the Plan, an employee or dependent shall be entitled to a conversion to nongroup coverage without the necessity of a physical examination. Such conversion coverage shall include hospitalization, surgical, and medical benefits as contained in the major medical and alternative plan conversion provisions of Article 53 of Chapter 58 of the General Statutes. The State Treasurer in his or her sole discretion shall approve the conversion coverage, which shall be administered by the Claims Processor through an insurance contract arranged by the Claims Processor, or administered as otherwise directed by the State Treasurer. An eligible employee or dependent must apply for conversion coverage within 30 days after termination of group eligibility.

(b) The State Treasurer shall provide for the continuation of conversion privilege exercised under the predecessor plan, on a fully contributory basis. The State Treasurer shall consult with the Board of Trustees before taking action under this subsection. (1981 (Reg. Sess., 1982), c. 1398, s. 6; 1983, c. 922, s. 21.6; 1985, c. 732, ss. 30, 56; 1985 (Reg. Sess., 1986), c. 1020, s. 20; 2008-168, ss. 1(a), 3(a), (r); 2011-85, ss. 2.6(i), 2.10.)

§ 135-48.46: Reserved for future codification purposes.

§ 135-48.47: Reserved for future codification purposes.

§ 135-48.48: Reserved for future codification purposes.

§ 135-48.49: Reserved for future codification purposes.

Part 5. Coverage Mandates and Exclusions; Other Mandates.

§ 135-48.50. Coverage mandates.

The Plan shall provide coverage subject to the following coverage mandates:

(1) Abortion coverage. - The Plan shall not provide coverage for abortions for which State funds could not be used under G.S. 143C-6-5.5. The Plan shall, however, provide coverage for subsequent complications or related charges arising from an abortion not covered under this subdivision.

(2) Immunizations. - The Plan shall pay one hundred percent (100%) of allowable medical charges for immunizations for the prevention of contagious diseases as generally accepted medical practices would dictate when directed by a credentialed provider as determined by the claims processor.

(3) Insulin. - Prescription benefits shall be provided for insulin even though a prescription is not required.

(4) Mental health parity. - Benefits for the treatment of mental illness and chemical dependency are covered by the Plan and shall be subject to the same deductibles, durational limits, and coinsurance factors as are benefits for physical illness generally. Nothing in this subdivision, however, shall prohibit the

Plan from requiring the most cost-effective treatment setting to be utilized by a person undergoing necessary care and treatment for chemical dependency.

(5) [Reserved.]

(6) Permissive coverage extension. - If a covered service becomes excluded from coverage under the Plan, the Executive Administrator and Claims Processor may, in the event of exceptional situations creating undue hardships or adverse medical conditions, allow persons enrolled in the Plan to remain covered by the Plan's previous coverage for up to three months after the effective date of the change in coverage, provided the persons so enrolled had been undergoing a continuous plan of specific treatment initiated within three months prior to the effective date of the change in coverage.

(7) Reconstructive surgery. - Charges for cosmetic surgery or treatment required for correction of damage caused by accidental injury sustained by the covered individual while coverage under this plan is in force on his or her account or to correct congenital deformities or anomalies shall not be excluded if they otherwise qualify as covered medical expenses. Reconstructive breast surgery following mastectomy, as those terms are defined in G.S. 58-51-62, shall be covered. (2011-85, s. 2.10; 2011-145, s. 29.23(c); 2012-194, s. 32.)

§ 135-48.51. Coverage and operational mandates related to Chapter 58 of the General Statutes.

The following provisions of Chapter 58 of the General Statutes apply to the State Health Plan:

(1) G.S. 58-3-191, Managed care reporting and disclosure requirements.

(2) G.S. 58-3-221, Access to nonformulary and restricted access prescription drugs.

(3) G.S. 58-3-223, Managed care access to specialist care.

(4) G.S. 58-3-225, Prompt claim payments under health benefit plans.

(5) G.S. 58-3-235, Selection of specialist as primary care provider.

(6) G.S. 58-3-240, Direct access to pediatrician for minors.

(7) G.S. 58-3-245, Provider directories.

(8) G.S. 58-3-250, Payment obligations for covered services.

(9) G.S. 58-3-265, Prohibition on managed care provider incentives.

(10) G.S. 58-3-280, Coverage for the diagnosis and treatment of lymphedema.

(11) G.S. 58-3-285, Coverage for hearing aids.

(12) G.S. 58-50-30, Right to choose services of certain providers.

(13) G.S. 58-67-88, Continuity of care. (2011-85, s. 2.10; 2012-129, s. 2; 2013-296, s. 3; 2013-324, s. 5.)

§ 135-48.52. General limitations and exclusions.

The Plan shall not provide coverage for or pay any benefits for any of the following:

(1) Charges to the extent paid, or which the individual is entitled to have paid, or to obtain without cost, in accordance with any government laws or regulations except Medicare. If a charge is made to any such person which he or she is legally required to pay, any benefits under this Plan will be computed in accordance with its provisions, taking into account only such charge. "Any government" includes the federal, State, provincial, or local government, or any political subdivision thereof, of the United States, Canada, or any other country.

(2) Charges for services rendered in connection with any occupational injury or disease arising out of and in the course of employment with any employer, if (i) the employer furnishes, pays for or provides reimbursement for such charges, or (ii) the employer makes a settlement payment for such charges, or (iii) the person incurring such charges waives or fails to assert his or her rights respecting such charges.

(3) Charges for any services rendered as a result of injury or sickness due to an act of war, declared or undeclared, which act shall have occurred after the effective date of a person's coverage under the Plan.

(4) Charges for any services with respect to which there is no legal obligation to pay. For the purposes of this item, any charge which exceeds the charge that would have been made if a person were not covered under this Plan shall, to the extent of such excess, be treated as a charge for which there is no legal obligation to pay; and any charge made by any person for anything which is normally or customarily furnished by such person without payment from the recipient or user thereof shall also be treated as a charge for which there is no legal obligation to pay.

(5) Charges during a continuous hospital confinement which commenced prior to the effective date of the person's coverage under this Plan.

(6) Charges for services unless a claim is filed within 18 months from the date of service.

(7) Charges for sexual dysfunction or hair growth drugs or for nonmedically necessary drugs used for cosmetic purposes. (2011-85, s. 2.10.)

§ 135-48.54. Optional participation for charter schools operated by private nonprofit corporations.

(a) The board of directors of each charter school operated by a private nonprofit corporation shall elect whether to become a participating employer in the Plan in accordance with this Article. This election shall be in writing, shall be made no later than 30 days after October 28, 1998, and shall be filed with the Plan and with the State Board of Education. For each charter school employee who is employed on or before the date the board makes the election, membership in the Plan is effective as of the date the board makes the election. For each charter school employee who is employed after the date the board makes the election, membership in the Plan is effective as of the date of that employee's entry into eligible service. This subsection applies only to charter schools that received State Board of Education approval under G.S. 115C-238.29D in 1997 or 1998.

(b) No later than 30 days after both parties have signed the written charter under G.S. 115C-238.29E, the board of directors of a charter school operated by a private nonprofit corporation shall elect whether to become a participating employer in the Plan in accordance with this Article. This election shall be in writing and filed with the Plan and the State Board of Education. This election is effective for each charter school employee as of the date of that employee's entry into eligible service. This subsection applies to charter schools that receive State Board of Education approval under G.S. 115C-238.29D after 1998.

(c) A board's election to become a participating employer in the Plan under this section is irrevocable and shall require all eligible employees of the charter school to participate.

(d) If a charter school's board of directors does not elect to become a participating employer in the Plan under this section, that school's employees and the dependents of those employees are not eligible for any benefits under the Plan on account of employment with a charter school.

(e) The board of directors of each charter school shall notify each of its employees as to whether the board elected to become a participating employer in the Plan under this section. This notification shall be in writing and shall be provided within 30 days of the board's election or at the time an initial offer for employment is made, whichever occurs last. If the board did not elect to become a participating employer in the Plan, the notice shall include a statement that the employee shall have no legal recourse against the board or the State for any possible benefit under the Plan. The employee shall provide written acknowledgment of the employee's receipt of the notification under this subsection. (1998-212, s. 9.14A(e); 2008-168, ss. 1(a), 3(a), (i); 2011-85, ss. 2.6(f), 2.10.)

§ 135-48.55. Interest charged to charter schools on late premiums.

The total amount of premiums due the Plan from charter schools as employing units, including amounts withheld from the compensation of Plan members, that is not remitted to the Plan by the fifteenth day of the month following the due date of remittance shall be assessed interest of one and one-half percent (1 ½%) of the amount due the Plan, per month or fraction thereof, beginning with the sixteenth day of the month following the due date of the remittance. The interest authorized by this section shall be assessed until the premium payment plus the accrued interest amount is remitted to the Plan. The remittance of premium payments under this section shall be presumed to have been made if the remittance is postmarked in the United States mail on a date not later than the fifteenth day of the month following the due date of the remittance. (1981 (Reg. Sess., 1982), c. 1398, s. 6; 1985, c. 732, s. 52; 1991, c. 427, s. 5; 1997-468, s. 4; 1998-1, s. 4(e); 1999-237, s. 28.29(h); 2003-69, s. 2; 2004-124, s. 31.21(c); 2005-276, s. 29.31(e); 2007-323, s. 28.22A(m), (m1), (o); 2007-345, ss. 11, 12; 2008-107, s. 10.13(a); 2008-168, ss. 1(a), 2(a), (m); 2009-281, s. 1; 2009-571, s. 3(c); 2011-85, s. 2.5(f).)

§ 135-48.56. Education of covered active and retired employees.

It is the intent of the General Assembly that active employees and retired employees covered under the Plan and its successor Plan shall have several opportunities in each fiscal year to attend presentations conducted by Plan management staff providing detailed information about benefits, limitations, premiums, co-payments, and other pertinent Plan matters. To this end, the Plan's management staff shall conduct multiple presentations each year to Plan members and association groups representing active and retired employees across all geographic regions of the State. Regional meetings shall be held in locations that afford reasonably convenient access to Plan members. The presentations shall be designed not only to present information about the Plan but also to hear and respond to Plan members' questions and concerns. (1981 (Reg. Sess., 1982), c. 1398, s. 6; 1983, c. 922, s. 2; 1985, c. 732, ss. 7, 9, 23, 24, 50, 51; 1985 (Reg. Sess., 1986), c. 1020, ss. 3, 20; 1987, c. 857, ss. 6, 7; 1987 (Reg. Sess., 1988), c. 1091, s. 5; 1989, c. 752, s. 22(a); 1991, c. 427, s. 3; 1993 (Reg. Sess., 1994), c. 679, s. 10.3; 1997-468, s. 2; 1997-519, s. 3.15; 1998-1, s. 4(c); 2000-141, s. 3; 2001-253, ss. 1(a), 1(q); 2001-487, s. 85.5; 2006-249, s. 4(b); 2007-323, s. 28.22(i); 2008-107, s. 10.13(a); 2008-168, ss. 1(a), 2(a), (k), (j); 2009-16, s. 5(b); 2011-85, s. 2.5(d); 2011-326, s. 27.)

§ 135-48.57. Payments for county or city ambulance service.

Allowable payments for services provided by a county or city ambulance service shall be paid directly or shall be co-payable to the county or city ambulance service provider. As used in this subsection, "county or city ambulance service" means ambulance services provided by a county or county-franchised ambulance service supplemented by county funds, or a municipally owned and operated ambulance service or by an ambulance service supplemented by municipal funds. (1981, c. 355; 1981 (Reg. Sess., 1982), c. 1398, ss. 3, 4; 1983, c. 922, s. 21.10; 1985, c. 732, s. 38; 1985 (Reg. Sess., 1986), c. 1020, s. 20; 1998-1, s. 4(h); 2007-323, s. 28.22A(c); 2008-107, s. 10.13(m); 2008-168, s. 1(a), (c), (d); 2009-16, s. 5(f); 2009-83, s. 1; 2010-194, s. 18(a); 2011-85, s. 2.4(a).)

§ 135-48.58. Premiums for firefighters, rescue squad workers, and members of National Guard.

In setting premiums for firefighters, rescue squad workers, and members of the National Guard, and their eligible dependents, the Plan shall establish rates separate from those affecting other members of the Plan. These separate premium rates shall include rate factors for incurred but unreported claim costs, for the effects of adverse selection from voluntary participation in the Plan, and for any other actuarially determined measures needed to protect the financial integrity of the Plan for the benefit of its served employees, retired employees, and their eligible dependents. (1981 (Reg. Sess., 1982), c. 1398, s. 6; 1985, c. 732, s. 52; 1991, c. 427, s. 5; 1997-468, s. 4; 1998-1, s. 4(e); 1999-237, s. 28.29(h); 2003-69, s. 2; 2004-124, s. 31.21(c); 2005-276, s. 29.31(e); 2007-323, s. 28.22A(m), (m1), (o); 2007-345, ss. 11, 12; 2008-107, s. 10.13(a); 2008-168, ss. 1(a), 2(a), (m); 2009-281, s. 1; 2009-571, s. 3(c); 2011-85, ss. 2.5(f), 2.10.)

§ 135-48.59: Reserved for future codification purposes.

Part 6. Long-Term Care Benefits.

§ 135-48.60: Repealed by Session Laws 2012-173, s. 3(d), effective January 1, 2013.

§ 135-48.61: Repealed by Session Laws 2012-173, s. 3(d), effective January 1, 2013.

§ 135-48.62: Repealed by Session Laws 2012-173, s. 3(d), effective January 1, 2013.

§ 135-49: Reserved for future codification purposes.

Article 4.

Consolidated Judicial Retirement Act.

§ 135-50. Short title and purpose.

(a) This Article shall be known and may be cited as the "Consolidated Judicial Retirement Act."

(b) The purpose of this Article is to improve the administration of justice by attracting and retaining the most highly qualified talent available within the State to the positions of justice and judge, district attorney and solicitor, public defender, the Director of Indigent Defense Services, and clerk of superior court, within the General Court of Justice. (1973, c. 640, s. 1; 1983 (Reg. Sess., 1984), c. 1031, ss. 2, 3; 2005-276, s. 29.30A(a); 2005-345, s. 42; 2007-323, s. 28.21B(a); 2008-107, s. 26.24(a).)

§ 135-51. Scope.

(a) This Article provides consolidated retirement benefits for all justices and judges, district attorneys, and solicitors who are serving on January 1, 1974, and who become such thereafter; and for all clerks of superior court who are so serving on January 1, 1975, and who become such after that date; and for all public defenders who are serving on July 1, 2007, and who become public defenders after that date; and for the Director of Indigent Defense Services who is serving on July 1, 2008, and those who become Director of Indigent Defense Services after that date.

(b) For justices and judges of the appellate and superior court divisions of the General Court of Justice who so served prior to January 1, 1974, the provisions of this Article supplement and, under certain circumstances, replace the provisions of Articles 6 and 8, as the case may be, of Chapter 7A of the General Statutes.

For district attorneys and judges of the district court of the General Court of Justice who so served prior to January 1, 1974, the provisions of this Article supplement and, under certain circumstances, replace the provisions of Article 1 of this Chapter.

For clerks of superior court of the General Court of Justice who so served prior to January 1, 1975, the provisions of this Article supplement and, under certain circumstances, replace the provisions of Article 1 of this Chapter.

(c) The retirement benefits of any person who becomes a justice or judge, district attorney, or solicitor on and after January 1, 1974, or clerk of superior court on and after January 1, 1975, or public defender on or after July 1, 2007, or the Director of Indigent Defense Services on or after July 1, 2008, shall be determined solely in accordance with the provisions of this Article. (1973, c. 640, s. 1; 1983 (Reg. Sess., 1984), c. 1031, s. 4; 2005-276, s. 29.30A(b); 2005-345, s. 42; 2007-323, s. 28.21B(b); 2008-107, s. 26.24(b).)

§ 135-52. Application of Article 1; administration.

(a) References in Article 1 of this Chapter to the provisions of "this Chapter" shall not necessarily apply to this Article. However, except as otherwise provided in this Article, the provisions of Article 1 are applicable and shall apply to and govern the administration of the Retirement System established hereby. Not in limitation of the foregoing, the provisions of G.S. 135-5(h), 135-5(n), 135-9, 135-10, 135-12 and 135-17 are specifically applicable to the Retirement System established hereby.

(b) The provisions of this Article shall be administered by the Board of Trustees of the Teachers' and State Employees' Retirement System. (1973, c. 640, s. 1.)

§ 135-53. Definitions.

The following words and phrases as used in this Article, unless a different meaning is plainly required by the context, shall have the following meanings:

(1) "Accumulated contributions" with respect to any member shall mean the sum of all the amounts deducted from the compensation of the member pursuant to G.S. 135-68 since he last became a member and credited to his account in the annuity savings fund, plus any amount standing to his credit pursuant to G.S. 135-67(c) as a result of a prior period of membership, plus any amounts credited to his account pursuant to G.S. 135-28.1(b) or 135-56(b), together with regular interest on all such amounts computed as provided in G.S. 135-7(b).

(2) "Actuarial equivalent" shall mean a benefit of equal value when computed upon the bases of such mortality tables as shall be adopted by the Board of Trustees, and regular interest.

(2a) "Average final compensation" shall mean the average annual compensation of a member during the 48 consecutive calendar months of membership service producing the highest such average.

(3) "Beneficiary" shall mean any person in receipt of a retirement allowance or other benefit as provided in this Article.

(4) "Board of Trustees" shall mean the Board of Trustees established by G.S. 135-6.

(4a) "Clerk of superior court" shall mean the clerk of superior court provided for in G.S. 7A-100(a).

(5) "Compensation" shall mean all salaries and wages derived from public funds which are earned by a member of the Retirement System for his service as a justice or judge, or district attorney, or clerk of superior court, or public defender, or the Director of Indigent Defense Services. Effective July 1, 2009, "compensation" also means payment of military differential wages. "Compensation" shall not include local supplementation as authorized under G.S. 7A-300.1 for Judicial Department employees.

(6) "Creditable service" shall mean for any member the total of his prior service plus his membership service.

(6a) "Director of Indigent Defense Services" shall mean the Director of Indigent Defense Services as provided for in G.S. 7A-498.6.

(6b) "District attorney" shall mean the district attorney or solicitor provided for in G.S. 7A-60.

(7) "Filing" when used in reference to an application for retirement shall mean the receipt of an acceptable application on a form provided by the Retirement System.

(8) "Final compensation" shall mean for any member the annual equivalent of the rate of compensation most recently applicable to him.

(9) "Judge" shall mean any justice or judge of the General Court of Justice and the administrative officer of the courts.

(10) "Medical board" shall mean the board of physicians provided for in G.S. 135-6.

(11) "Member" shall mean any person included in the membership of the Retirement System as provided in this Article.

(12) "Membership service" shall mean service as a judge, district attorney, clerk of superior court, public defender, or the Director of Indigent Defense Services rendered while a member of the Retirement System.

(13) "Previous system" shall mean, with respect to any member, the retirement benefit provisions of Article 6 and Article 8 of Chapter 7A of the General Statutes, to the extent that such Article or Articles were formerly applicable to the member, and in the case of judges of the district court division, district attorney, public defender, the Director of Indigent Defense Services, and and clerk of superior court of the General Court of Justice, the Teachers' and State Employees' Retirement System.

(14) "Prior service" shall mean service rendered by a member, prior to his membership in the Retirement System, for which credit is allowable under G.S. 135-56.

(14a) "Public defender" means a public defender provided for in G.S. 7A-498.7, the appellate defender provided for in G.S. 7A-498.8, the capital defender, and the juvenile defender.

(15) "Regular interest" shall mean interest compounded annually at such a rate as shall be determined by the Board of Trustees in accordance with G.S. 135-7(b).

(16) "Retirement" under this Chapter shall mean the commencement of monthly retirement benefits, along with the termination of employment and the complete separation from active service with no intent or agreement, expressed or implied, to return to service. A retirement allowance under the provisions of this Chapter may only be granted upon retirement of a member. In order for a member's retirement to become effective in any month, the member must perform no work, including part-time, temporary, substitute, or contractor work, at any time during the same month immediately following the effective first day of retirement.

(17) "Retirement allowance" shall mean the periodic payments to which a beneficiary becomes entitled under the provisions of this Article.

(18) "Retirement System" shall mean the "Consolidated Judicial Retirement System" of North Carolina, as established in this Article.

(19) "Year" as used in this Article shall mean the regular fiscal year beginning July 1 and ending June 30 in the following calendar year, unless otherwise defined by regulation of the Board of Trustees. (1973, c. 640, s. 1; 1983 (Reg. Sess., 1984), c. 1031, ss. 5-10; 1999-237, s. 28.24(f); 2005-276, s. 29.30A(c); 2005-345, s. 42; 2007-323, s. 28.21B(c); 2008-107, s. 26.24(c); 2009-66, s. 6(g); 2010-31, s. 29.7(e); 2013-288, s. 4(c).)

§ 135-54. Name and date of establishment.

A Retirement System is hereby established and placed under the management of the Board of Trustees for the purpose of providing retirement allowances and other benefits under the provisions of this Article for justices and judges, district attorneys, public defenders, the Director of Indigent Defense Services, and clerks of superior court of the General Court of Justice of North Carolina, and their survivors. This Retirement System is a governmental plan, within the meaning of Section 414(d) of the Internal Revenue Code. Therefore, the nondiscrimination rules of Sections 401(a)(5) and 401(a)(26) of the Code do not apply. The Retirement System so created shall be established as of January 1, 1974.

The Retirement System shall have the power and privileges of a corporation and shall be known as the "Consolidated Judicial Retirement System of North Carolina," and by such name all of its business shall be transacted.

Consistent with Section 401(a)(1) of the Internal Revenue Code, all contributions from participating employers and participating employees to this Retirement System shall be made to funds held in trust through trust instruments that have the purposes of distributing trust principal and income to retired members and their beneficiaries and of paying other definitely determinable benefits under this Chapter, after meeting the necessary expenses of administering this Retirement System. Neither the trust corpus nor income from this trust can be used for purposes other than the exclusive benefit of members or their beneficiaries, except that employer contributions made to the trust under a good faith mistake of fact may be returned to an employer, where the refund can occur within less than one year after the mistaken contribution was made, consistent with the rule adopted by the Board of Trustees. The Retirement System shall have a consolidated Plan document, consisting of relevant statutory provisions in this Chapter, associated regulations in the North Carolina Administrative Code, substantive and procedural information on the official forms used by the Retirement System, and policies and minutes of the Board of Trustees. (1973, c. 640, s. 1; 1983 (Reg. Sess., 1984), c. 1031, s. 11; 2005-276, s. 29.30A(d); 2005-345, s. 42; 2007-323, s. 28.21B(d); 2008-107, s. 26.24(d); 2012-130, s. 7(d).)

§ 135-55. Membership.

(a)   The membership of the Retirement System shall consist of:

(1)   All judges and district attorneys in office on January 1, 1974;

(2)   All persons who become judges and district attorneys or reenter service as judges and district attorneys after January 1, 1974;

(3)   All clerks of superior court in office on January 1, 1975;

(4)   All persons who become clerks of superior court or reenter service as clerks of superior court after January 1, 1975;

(5)   All public defenders in office on July 1, 2007;

(6) All persons who become public defenders or reenter service as public defenders after July 1, 2007;

(7) The Director of Indigent Defense Services on July 1, 2008; and

(8) All persons who become the Director of Indigent Defense Services or reenter service as the Director of Indigent Defense Services after July 1, 2008.

(b) The membership of any person in the Retirement System shall cease upon:

(1) The withdrawal of his accumulated contributions after he is no longer a judge, district attorney, public defender, the Director of Indigent Defense Services, or clerk of superior court, or

(2) His retirement under the provisions of the Retirement System, or

(3) His death. (1973, c. 640, s. 1; 1983 (Reg. Sess., 1984), c. 1031, ss. 12, 13; 2005-276, s. 29.30A(e); 2005-345, s. 42; 2007-323, s. 28.21B(e); 2008-107, s. 26.24(e).)

§ 135-56. Creditable service.

(a) Subject to such rules and regulations as the Board of Trustees shall adopt with regard to the verification of a judge's prior service, the prior service of a judge shall consist of his service rendered prior to January 1, 1974, as a justice of the Supreme Court, judge of the Court of Appeals, judge of the superior court, judge of the district court division of the General Court of Justice, as administrative officer of the courts, or as a solicitor or district attorney.

(b) When membership ceases as a result of a member's withdrawal of his accumulated contributions, the prior service and previous membership service of the member shall no longer be considered to be creditable service; provided, however, that if a member whose creditable service has been cancelled in accordance with this subsection subsequently returns to membership for a period of five years, he may thereafter repay in a lump sum the amount withdrawn plus regular interest thereon from the date of withdrawal through the date of repayment and thereby increase his creditable service by the amount of creditable service lost when he withdrew his accumulated contributions.

(c) On and after January 1, 1984, the creditable service of a member who was a member of the former Uniform Solicitorial or Uniform Clerks of Superior Court Retirement Systems at the time of merger of those Systems into this Consolidated Judicial Retirement System and whose accumulated contributions are transferred from those Systems to this System, includes service that was creditable in the Uniform Solicitorial and Uniform Clerks of Superior Court Retirement Systems; and membership service with those Retirement Systems is membership service with this Retirement System.

(d) Any member may purchase creditable service for service as a judge, district attorney, or clerk of superior court, when not otherwise provided for in this section, and as a judge of any lawfully constituted court of this State inferior to the superior court, not to include service as a magistrate, justice of the peace or mayor's court judge. The member, after the transfer of any accumulated contributions from the Teachers' and State Employees' Retirement System or Local Governmental Employees' Retirement System, shall pay an amount equal to the full cost of the service credits calculated on the basis of the assumptions used for purposes of the actuarial valuation of the System's liabilities, taking into account the additional retirement allowance arising on account of the additional service credit commencing at the earliest age at which the member could retire with an unreduced retirement allowance as determined by the Board of Trustees upon the advice of the consulting actuary. Notwithstanding the foregoing provisions of this subsection that provide for the purchase of service credits, the terms "full cost", "full liability", and "full actuarial cost" include assumed annual post-retirement allowance increases, as determined by the Board of Trustees, from the earliest age at which a member could retire on an unreduced service allowance.

(e) Any member may purchase creditable service for service as a member of the General Assembly not otherwise creditable under this section, provided the service is not credited in the Legislative Retirement Fund nor the Legislative Retirement System, and further provided the member pays a lump sum amount equal to the full cost of the additional service credits calculated on the basis of the assumptions used for the purposes of the actuarial valuation of the System's liabilities, taking into account the additional retirement allowance arising on account of the additional service credits commencing at the earliest age at which a member could retire on an unreduced retirement allowance as determined by the Board of Trustees upon the advice of the consulting actuary, plus an administrative fee to be set by the Board of Trustees. Notwithstanding the foregoing provisions of this subsection that provide for the purchase of service credits, the terms "full cost", "full liability", and "full actuarial cost" include assumed annual post-retirement allowance increases, as determined by the Board of Trustees, from the earliest age at which a member could retire on an unreduced service allowance.

(f) The creditable service of a member who was a member of the Local Governmental Employees' Retirement System, the Teachers' and State Employees' Retirement System, or the Legislative Retirement System and whose accumulated contributions and reserves are transferred from that System to this System, includes service that was creditable in the Local Governmental Employees' Retirement System, the Teachers' and State Employees' Retirement System, or the Legislative Retirement System, and membership service with those Retirement Systems is membership service with this Retirement System.

(g) If a member who has not vested in this System on July 1, 2007, is convicted of an offense listed in G.S. 135-75.1 for acts committed after July 1, 2007, then that member shall forfeit all benefits under this System. If a member who has vested in this System on July 1, 2007, is convicted of an offense listed in G.S. 135-75.1 for acts committed after July 1, 2007, then that member is not entitled to any creditable service that accrued after July 1, 2007. No member shall forfeit any benefit or creditable service earned from a position not as a justice, judge, district attorney, or clerk of superior court.

(h) On and after July 1, 2007, the creditable service of a member who was a public defender and a member of the Teachers' and State Employees' Retirement System at the time of transfer of membership from the previous system to this System shall include service as a public defender that was creditable in the previous system immediately prior to July 1, 2007. The accumulated contributions, creditable service, and reserves, if any, of a member as a public defender shall be transferred from the previous system to this System in the same manner as prescribed under G.S. 135-28.1 as it pertained to judges of the district court division of the General Court of Justice.

(i) On and after July 1, 2008, the creditable service of a member who is the Director of Indigent Defense Services and a member of the Teachers' and State Employees' Retirement System at the time of transfer of membership from the previous system to this System shall include service as the Director of Indigent Defense Services beginning July 1, 2004, that was creditable in the previous system immediately prior to July 1, 2008. The accumulated contributions, creditable service, and reserves, if any, of a member as the Director of Indigent Defense Services beginning July 1, 2004, shall be transferred from the previous system to this System in the same manner as prescribed under G.S. 135-28.1 as it pertained to judges of the district court division of the General Court of Justice.

(j) If a member who is in service and has not vested in this System on December 1, 2012, is convicted of an offense listed in G.S. 135-75.1A for acts committed after December 1, 2012, then that member shall forfeit all benefits under this System, except for a return of member contributions plus interest. If a member who is in service and has vested in this System on December 1, 2012, is convicted of an offense listed in G.S. 135-75.1A for acts committed after December 1, 2012, then that member is not entitled to any creditable service that accrued after December 1, 2012. (1973, c. 640, s. 1; 1977, c. 936; 1983 (Reg. Sess., 1984), c. 1031, ss. 14, 15; 1985, c. 649, s. 1; 1989, c. 255, s. 21(a); 1999-237, s. 28.24(c); 2003-284, s. 30.18(f); 2007-179, s. 4(b); 2007-323, s. 28.21B(h); 2008-107, s. 26.24(h); 2012-193, s. 6.)

§ 135-56.01. Reciprocity of creditable service with other State-administered retirement systems.

(a) Only for the purpose of determining eligibility for benefits accruing under this Article, creditable service standing to the credit of a member of the Legislative Retirement System, Teachers' and State Employees' Retirement System, or the Local Governmental Employees' Retirement System shall be added to the creditable service standing to the credit of a member of this System; provided, that in the event a person is a retired member of any of the foregoing retirement systems, such creditable service standing to the credit of the retired member prior to retirement shall be likewise counted. In no instance shall service credits maintained in the aforementioned retirement systems be added to the creditable service in this System for application of this System's benefit accrual rate in computing a service retirement benefit unless specifically authorized by this Article.

(b) A person who was a former member of this System and who has forfeited his creditable service in this System by receiving a return of contributions and who has creditable service in the Legislative Retirement System, Teachers' and State Employees' Retirement System, or the Local Government Employees' Retirement System may count such creditable service for the purpose of restoring the creditable service forfeited in this System under the terms and conditions as set forth in this Article and reestablish membership in this System.

(c) Creditable service under this section shall not be counted twice for the same period of time whether earned as a member, purchased, or granted as prior service credits. (1989 (Reg. Sess., 1990), c. 1066, s. 35(d); 1997-456, s. 27.)

§ 135-56.1: Repealed by Session Laws 1983 (Regular Session, 1984), c. 1031, s. 16.

§ 135-56.2. Creditable service for other employment.

Any member may purchase creditable service for service as a State teacher or employee, as defined under G.S. 135-1(10) and (25), and for service as an employee of local government, as defined under G.S. 128-21(10). A member, upon the completion of 10 years of membership service, may also purchase creditable service for periods of federal employment, provided that the member is not receiving any retirement benefits resulting from this federal employment, and provided that the member is not vested in the particular federal retirement system to which the member may have belonged while a federal employee. The member, after the transfer of any accumulated contributions from the Teachers' and State Employees' Retirement System or Local Governmental Employees' Retirement System, shall pay an amount equal to the full cost of the service credits calculated on the basis of the assumptions used for purposes of the actuarial valuation of the Retirement System's liabilities, taking into account the additional retirement allowance arising on account of the additional service credits commencing at the earliest age at which the member could retire with an unreduced retirement allowance as determined by the Board of Trustees upon the advice of the consulting actuary, plus an administrative fee as set by the Board of Trustees. As an alternative to transferring any accumulated contributions from the Teachers' and State Employees' Retirement System or the Local Governmental Employees' Retirement System to the Consolidated Judicial Retirement System, a member may irrevocably elect to transfer these contributions to the Supplemental Retirement Income Plan of North Carolina as determined by the Plan's Board of Trustees and the Department of State Treasurer in accordance with the provisions of G.S. 135-94(a)(4). Notwithstanding the foregoing provisions of this section that provide for the purchase of service credits, the terms "full cost", "full liability", and "full actuarial cost" include assumed annual post-retirement allowance increases, as determined by the Board of Trustees, from the earliest age at which a member could retire on an unreduced service allowance. (1983 (Reg. Sess., 1984), c. 1041; 1985, c. 348, s. 1; c. 749, s. 2; 1989, c. 255, s. 21(b).)

§ 135-56.3. Repayments and Purchases.

(a) Purchase of Service Credits Through Rollover Contributions From Certain Other Plans. - Notwithstanding any other provision of this Article, and without regard to any limitations on contributions otherwise set forth in this Article, a member, who is eligible to restore or purchase membership or creditable service pursuant to the provisions of this Article, may, subject to such rules and regulations established by the Board of Trustees, purchase such service credits through rollover contributions to the Annuity Savings Fund from (i) an annuity contract described in Section 403(b) of the Internal Revenue Code, (ii) an eligible plan under Section 457(b) of the Internal Revenue Code which is maintained by a state, political subdivision of a state, or any agency or instrumentality of a state or political subdivision of a state, (iii) an individual retirement account or annuity described in Section 408(a) or 408(b) of the Internal Revenue Code that is eligible to be rolled over and would otherwise be includible in gross income, or (iv) a qualified plan described in Section 401(a) or 403(a) of the Internal Revenue Code. Notwithstanding the foregoing, the Retirement System shall not accept any amount as a rollover contribution unless such amount is eligible to be rolled over to a qualified trust in accordance with applicable law and the member provides evidence satisfactory to the Retirement System that such amount qualifies for rollover treatment. Unless received by the Retirement System in the form of a direct rollover, the rollover contribution must be paid to the Retirement System on or before the 60th day after the date it was received by the member.

Purchase of Service Credits Through Plan-to-Plan Transfers. - Notwithstanding any other provision of this Article, and without regard to any limitations on contributions otherwise set forth in this Article, a member, who is eligible to restore or purchase membership or creditable service pursuant to the provisions of this Article, may, subject to such rules and regulations established by the Board of Trustees, purchase such service credits through a direct transfer to the Annuity Savings Fund of funds from (i) an annuity contract described in Section 403(b) of the Internal Revenue Code or (ii) an eligible plan under Section 457(b) of the Code which is maintained by a state, political subdivision of a state, or any agency or instrumentality of a state or political subdivision of a state.

(b) (See note) Purchase of Service Credits Through Plan-to-Plan Transfers. - Notwithstanding any other provision of this Article, and without regard to any limitations on contributions otherwise set forth in this Article, a member, who is eligible to restore or purchase membership or creditable service pursuant to the provisions of this Article, may, subject to such rules and regulations established by the Board of Trustees, purchase such service credits through a direct transfer to the Annuity Savings Fund of funds from (i) the Supplemental Retirement Income Plans A, B, or C of North Carolina or (ii) any other defined contribution plan qualified under Section 401(a) of the Internal Revenue Code which is maintained by the State of North Carolina, a political subdivision of a state, or any agency or instrumentality of a state or political subdivision of a state. (2002-71, s. 7.)

§ 135-57. Service retirement.

(a) Any member on or after January 1, 1974, who became a member prior to August 1, 2011, and who has attained his fiftieth birthday and five years of membership service may retire upon electronic submission or written application to the board of trustees setting forth at what time, as of the first day of a calendar month, not less than one day nor more than 120 days subsequent to the execution and filing thereof, he desires to be retired.

(a1) Any member who became a member on or after August 1, 2011, and who has attained the member's fiftieth birthday and 10 years of membership service may retire upon electronic submission or written application to the Board of Trustees setting forth at what time, as of the first day of a calendar month, not less than one day nor more than 120 days subsequent to the execution and filing thereof, the member desires to be retired.

(b) Any member who is a justice or judge of the General Court of Justice shall be automatically retired as of the first day of the calendar month coinciding with or next following the later of January 1, 1974, or his attainment of his seventy-second birthday; provided, however, that no judge who is a member on January 1, 1974, shall be forced to retire under the provisions of this subsection at an earlier date than the last day that he is permitted to remain in office under the provisions of G.S. 7A-4.20.

(c) Any member who terminates service on or after January 1, 1974, having accumulated five or more years of creditable service and having become a member prior to August 1, 2011, may retire under the provisions of subsection (a) above, provided that he shall not have withdrawn his accumulated contributions prior to the effective date of his retirement, and the requirement of subsection (a) that the member be in service shall not apply.

(c1) Any member having accumulated 10 or more years of creditable service and having become a member on or after August 1, 2011, may retire under the provisions of subsection (a1) above, provided that the member shall not have withdrawn the member's accumulated contributions prior to the effective date of the member's retirement, and the requirement of subsection (a1) that the member be in service shall not apply.

(d) Any member who was in service October 8, 1981, who had attained 50 years of age, may retire upon electronic submission or written application to the board of trustees setting forth at what time, as of the first day of a calendar month, not less than one day nor more than 120 days subsequent to the execution and filing thereof, he desires to be retired. (1973, c. 640, s. 1; 1981, c. 378, s. 6; 1983, c. 761, s. 230; 1987, c. 513, s. 1; 1991 (Reg. Sess., 1992), c. 873, s. 2; 2007-431, s. 4; 2009-66, ss. 3(e), 12(i), (j); 2011-232, s. 8.)

§ 135-58. Service retirement benefits.

(a) Any member who retires under the provisions of subsection (a) or subsection (c) of G.S. 135-57 before July 1, 1990, after he either has attained his sixty-fifth birthday or has completed 24 years or more of creditable service shall receive an annual retirement allowance, payable monthly, which shall commence on the effective date of his retirement and shall be continued on the first day of each month thereafter during his lifetime, the amount of which shall be computed as the sum of (1), (2) and (3) following, provided that in no event shall the annual allowance payable to any member be greater than an amount which, when added to the allowance, if any, to which he is entitled under the Teachers' and State Employees' Retirement System, the Legislative Retirement System or the North Carolina Local Governmental Employees' Retirement System (prior in any case to any reduction for early retirement or for an optional mode of payment) would total three fourths of his final compensation:

(1) Four percent (4%) of his final compensation, multiplied by the number of years of his creditable service rendered as a justice of the Supreme Court or judge of the Court of Appeals;

(2) Three and one-half percent (3 ½%) of his final compensation, multiplied by the number of years of his creditable service rendered as a judge of the superior court or as administrative officer of the courts;

(3) Three percent (3%) of his final compensation, multiplied by the number of years of his creditable service rendered as a judge of the district court, district attorney, or clerk of superior court.

(a1) Any member who retires under the provisions of subsection (a) or subsection (c) of G.S. 135-57 on or after July 1, 1990, but before July 1, 1999, after he either has attained his 65th birthday or has completed 24 years or more of creditable service shall receive an annual retirement allowance, payable monthly, which shall commence on the effective date of his retirement and shall be continued on the first day of each month thereafter during his lifetime, the amount of which shall be computed as the sum of (1), (2), and (3) following, provided that in no event shall the annual allowance payable to any member be greater than an amount which, when added to the allowance, if any, to which he is entitled under the Teachers' and State Employees' Retirement System, the Legislative Retirement System or the North Carolina Local Governmental Employees' Retirement System (prior in any case to any reduction for early retirement or for an optional mode of payment) would total three-fourths of his final compensation:

(1) Four and two-hundredths percent (4.02%) of his final compensation, multiplied by the number of years of his creditable service rendered as a justice of the Supreme Court or judge of the Court of Appeals;

(2) Three and fifty-two hundredths percent (3.52%) of his final compensation, multiplied by the number of years of his creditable service rendered as a judge of the superior court or as administrative officer of the courts;

(3) Three and two-hundredths percent (3.02%) of his final compensation, multiplied by the number of years of his creditable service rendered as a judge of the district court, district attorney, or clerk of superior court.

(a2) Any member who retires under the provisions of G.S. 135-57(a) or G.S. 135-57(c) on or after July 1, 1999, but before July 1, 2001, after the member has either attained the member's 65th birthday or has completed 24 years or more of creditable service, shall receive an annual retirement allowance, payable monthly, which shall commence on the effective date of the member's retirement and shall be continued on the first day of each month thereafter during the member's lifetime, the amount of which shall be computed as the sum of the amounts in subdivisions (1), (2), (3), (4), and (5) following, provided that in no event shall the annual allowance payable to any member be greater than an amount which, when added to the allowance, if any, to which the member is entitled under the Teachers' and State Employees' Retirement System, the Legislative Retirement System, or the Local Governmental Employees' Retirement System (prior in any case to any reduction for early retirement or for an optional mode of payment) would total three-fourths of the member's final compensation:

(1) Four and two-hundredths percent (4.02%) of the member's final compensation, multiplied by the number of years of creditable service rendered as a justice of the Supreme Court or judge of the Court of Appeals;

(2) Three and fifty-two hundredths percent (3.52%) of the member's final compensation, multiplied by the number of years of creditable service rendered as a judge of the superior court or as Administrative Officer of the Courts;

(3) Three and two-hundredths percent (3.02%) of the member's final compensation, multiplied by the number of years of creditable service, rendered as a judge of the district court, district attorney, or clerk of superior court;

(4) A service retirement allowance computed in accordance with the service retirement provisions of Article 3 of Chapter 128 of the General Statutes using an average final compensation as defined in G.S. 135-53(2a) and creditable service equal to the number of years of the member's creditable service that was transferred from the Local Governmental Employees' Retirement System to this System as provided in G.S. 135-56; and

(5) A service retirement allowance computed in accordance with the service retirement provisions of Article 1 of this Chapter using an average final compensation as defined in G.S. 135-53(2a) and creditable service equal to the number of years of the member's creditable service that was transferred from the Teachers' and State Employees' Retirement System to this System as provided in G.S. 135-56.

(a3)   Any member who retires under the provisions of G.S. 135-57(a) or G.S. 135-57(c) on or after July 1, 2001, but before January 1, 2004, after the member has either attained the member's 65th birthday or has completed 24 years or more of creditable service, shall receive an annual retirement allowance, payable monthly, which shall commence on the effective date of the member's retirement and shall be continued on the first day of each month thereafter during the member's lifetime, the amount of which shall be computed as the sum of the amounts in subdivisions (1), (2), (3), (4), and (5) following, provided that in no event shall the annual allowance payable to any member be greater than an amount which, when added to the allowance, if any, to which the member is entitled under the Teachers' and State Employees' Retirement System, the Legislative Retirement System, or the Local Governmental Employees' Retirement System (prior in any case to any reduction for early retirement or for an optional mode of payment) would total three-fourths of the member's final compensation:

(1)   Four and two-hundredths percent (4.02%) of the member's final compensation, multiplied by the number of years of creditable service rendered as a justice of the Supreme Court or judge of the Court of Appeals;

(2)   Three and fifty-two hundredths percent (3.52%) of the member's final compensation, multiplied by the number of years of creditable service rendered as a judge of the superior court or as Administrative Officer of the Courts;

(3)   Three and two-hundredths percent (3.02%) of the member's final compensation, multiplied by the number of years of creditable service, rendered as a judge of the district court, district attorney, or clerk of superior court;

(4)   A service retirement allowance computed in accordance with the service retirement provisions of Article 3 of Chapter 128 of the General Statutes using an average final compensation as defined in G.S. 135-53(2a) and creditable service equal to the number of years of the member's creditable service that was transferred from the Local Governmental Employees' Retirement System to this System as provided in G.S. 135-56; and

(5)   A service retirement allowance computed in accordance with the service retirement provisions of Article 1 of this Chapter using an average final compensation as defined in G.S. 135-53(2a) and creditable service, including any sick leave standing to the credit of the member, equal to the number of years of the member's creditable service that was transferred from the

Teachers' and State Employees' Retirement System to this System as provided in G.S. 135-56.

(a4) Any member who retires under the provisions of G.S. 135-57(a) or G.S. 135-57(c) on or after January 1, 2004, but before July 1, 2007, after the member has either attained the member's 65th birthday or has completed 24 years or more of creditable service, shall receive an annual retirement allowance, payable monthly, which shall commence on the effective date of the member's retirement and shall be continued on the first day of each month thereafter during the member's lifetime, the amount of which shall be computed as the sum of the amounts in subdivisions (1), (2), (3), (4), and (5) of this subsection, provided that in no event shall the annual allowance payable to any member be greater than an amount which, when added to the allowance, if any, to which the member is entitled under the Teachers' and State Employees' Retirement System, the Legislative Retirement System, or the Local Governmental Employees' Retirement System (prior in any case to any reduction for early retirement or for an optional mode of payment), would total three-fourths of the member's final compensation:

(1) Four and two hundredths percent (4.02%) of the member's final compensation, multiplied by the number of years of creditable service rendered as a justice of the Supreme Court or judge of the Court of Appeals;

(2) Three and fifty-two hundredths percent (3.52%) of the member's final compensation, multiplied by the number of years of creditable service rendered as a judge of the superior court or as Administrative Officer of the Courts;

(3) Three and two hundredths percent (3.02%) of the member's final compensation, multiplied by the number of years of creditable service rendered as a judge of the district court, district attorney, or clerk of superior court;

(4) A service retirement allowance computed in accordance with the service retirement provisions of Article 3 of Chapter 128 of the General Statutes using an average final compensation as defined in G.S. 135-53(2a) and creditable service equal to the number of years of the member's creditable service that was transferred from the Local Governmental Employees' Retirement System to this System as provided in G.S. 135-56; and

(5) A service retirement allowance computed in accordance with the service retirement provisions of Article 1 of this Chapter of the General Statutes using an average final compensation as defined in G.S. 135-53(2a) and creditable

service, including any sick leave standing to the credit of the member, equal to the number of years of the member's creditable service that was transferred from the Teachers' and State Employees' Retirement System or the Legislative Retirement System to this System as provided in G.S. 135-56.

(a5) Any member who retires under the provisions of G.S. 135-57(a) or G.S. 135-57(c) on or after July 1, 2007, but before July 1, 2008, after the member has either attained the member's 65th birthday or has completed 24 years or more of creditable service, shall receive an annual retirement allowance, payable monthly, which shall commence on the effective date of the member's retirement and shall be continued on the first day of each month thereafter during the member's lifetime, the amount of which shall be computed as the sum of the amounts in subdivisions (1), (2), (3), (4), and (5) of this subsection, provided that in no event shall the annual allowance payable to any member be greater than an amount which, when added to the allowance, if any, to which the member is entitled under the Teachers' and State Employees' Retirement System, the Legislative Retirement System, or the Local Governmental Employees' Retirement System (prior in any case to any reduction for early retirement or for an optional mode of payment), would total three-fourths of the member's final compensation:

(1) Four and two hundredths percent (4.02%) of the member's final compensation, multiplied by the number of years of creditable service rendered as a justice of the Supreme Court or judge of the Court of Appeals;

(2) Three and fifty-two hundredths percent (3.52%) of the member's final compensation, multiplied by the number of years of creditable service rendered as a judge of the superior court or as Administrative Officer of the Courts;

(3) Three and two hundredths percent (3.02%) of the member's final compensation, multiplied by the number of years of creditable service rendered as a judge of the district court, district attorney, clerk of superior court, or public defender;

(4) A service retirement allowance computed in accordance with the service retirement provisions of Article 3 of Chapter 128 of the General Statutes using an average final compensation as defined in G.S. 135-53(2a) and creditable service equal to the number of years of the member's creditable service that was transferred from the Local Governmental Employees' Retirement System to this System as provided in G.S. 135-56; and

(5)   A service retirement allowance computed in accordance with the service retirement provisions of Article 1 of this Chapter using an average final compensation as defined in G.S. 135-53(2a) and creditable service, including any sick leave standing to the credit of the member, equal to the number of years of the member's creditable service that was transferred from the Teachers' and State Employees' Retirement System or the Legislative Retirement System to this System as provided in G.S. 135-56.

(a6)   Any member who retires under the provisions of G.S. 135-57(a) or G.S. 135-57(c) on or after July 1, 2008, after the member has either attained the member's 65th birthday or has completed 24 years or more of creditable service, shall receive an annual retirement allowance, payable monthly, which shall commence on the effective date of the member's retirement and shall be continued on the first day of each month thereafter during the member's lifetime, the amount of which shall be computed as the sum of the amounts in subdivisions (1), (2), (3), (4), and (5) of this subsection, provided that in no event shall the annual allowance payable to any member be greater than an amount which, when added to the allowance, if any, to which the member is entitled under the Teachers' and State Employees' Retirement System, the Legislative Retirement System, or the Local Governmental Employees' Retirement System (prior in any case to any reduction for early retirement or for an optional mode of payment), would total three-fourths of the member's final compensation:

(1)   Four and two hundredths percent (4.02%) of the member's final compensation, multiplied by the number of years of creditable service rendered as a justice of the Supreme Court or judge of the Court of Appeals;

(2)   Three and fifty-two hundredths percent (3.52%) of the member's final compensation, multiplied by the number of years of creditable service rendered as a judge of the superior court or as Administrative Officer of the Courts;

(3)   Three and two hundredths percent (3.02%) of the member's final compensation, multiplied by the number of years of creditable service rendered as a judge of the district court, district attorney, clerk of superior court, public defender, or the Director of Indigent Defense Services;

(4)   A service retirement allowance computed in accordance with the service retirement provisions of Article 3 of Chapter 128 of the General Statutes using an average final compensation as defined in G.S. 135-53(2a) and creditable service equal to the number of years of the member's creditable service that

was transferred from the Local Governmental Employees' Retirement System to this System as provided in G.S. 135-56; and

(5) A service retirement allowance computed in accordance with the service retirement provisions of Article 1 of this Chapter using an average final compensation as defined in G.S. 135-53(2a) and creditable service, including any sick leave standing to the credit of the member, equal to the number of years of the member's creditable service that was transferred from the Teachers' and State Employees' Retirement System or the Legislative Retirement System to this System as provided in G.S. 135-56.

(b) Any member who retires under the provisions of subsection (a) or subsection (c) of G.S. 135-57 before he either has attained his sixty-fifth birthday or has completed 24 years of creditable service shall receive an annual retirement allowance, payable monthly, which shall commence on the effective date of his retirement and shall be continued on the first day of each month thereafter during his lifetime, the amount of which shall be determined in the same manner and be subject to the same maximum limitation as provided for in subsection (a) above except that the allowance so computed shall be reduced by one quarter of one percent (¼ of 1%) thereof for each month by which the member's retirement date precedes the first day of the month coincident with or next following the earlier of

(1) The member's sixty-fifth birthday or

(2) The date the member would have completed 24 years of creditable service if he had been in membership service from his retirement date until such date.

For the sole purpose of determining whether a member has completed the required 24 years of creditable service referred to in this subsection (b) or the date on which he would have completed such period of creditable service if he had remained in membership service, in the case of a member of the Teachers' and State Employees' Retirement System who became a member of this Retirement System under circumstances described in G.S. 135-28.1, and who at the time of his retirement hereunder is in service and has retained his membership in the Teachers' and State Employees' Retirement System as provided for in G.S. 135-28.1, his creditable service shall be taken as the sum of his creditable service hereunder plus the amount of creditable service remaining to his credit in such other system as provided for in G.S. 135-28.1.

(c) The foregoing subsections of this section to the contrary notwithstanding, in no event will the retirement allowance payable at any time to a retired member who was a member of a previous system immediately prior to January 1, 1974, prior to any reduction of such allowance in accordance with G.S. 135-61, be less than the retirement allowance to which he would have been entitled under the terms of such previous system if this Article had not been enacted.

(d) Commencing with the payment for the month of January 1974, the retirement allowance of each retired member of a previous system who was in receipt of a retirement allowance thereunder as of January 1, 1974, shall be paid from the assets of the Retirement System in the same amount as would have been applicable for January 1974, if this Article had not been enacted.

(e) Notwithstanding any other provision to the contrary, in no event will the retirement allowance payable at any time to a retired member who was a member of a previous system immediately prior to January 1, 1974, prior to any reduction of such allowance in accordance with G.S. 135-61, be greater than the retirement allowance to which he would have been entitled under the terms of such previous system if this Article had not been enacted or than the retirement allowance to which he would have been entitled under this Article if he had not been entitled to benefits under the terms of such previous system, whichever is larger. (1973, c. 640, s. 1; 1977, c. 1120, s. 2; 1983 (Reg. Sess., 1984), c. 1031, ss. 17, 18; c. 1109, ss. 13.14, 13.15; 1985, c. 649, s. 7; 1989 (Reg. Sess., 1990), c. 1077, ss. 6, 7; 1999-237, s. 28.24(d), (e); 2001-424, s. 32.29(a), (b); 2003-284, s. 30.18(g), (h); 2005-276, s. 29.30A(f), (g); 2005-345, s. 42; 2007-323, s. 28.21B(f), (g); 2008-107, s. 26.24(f), (g).)

§ 135-59. Disability retirement.

(a) Upon application by or on behalf of the member, any member in service who has completed five or more years of creditable service and who has not attained his sixty-fifth birthday may be retired by the Board of Trustees, on the first day of any calendar month, not less than one day nor more than 120 days next following the date of filing such application, on a disability retirement allowance; provided, that the medical board, after a medical examination of such member, shall certify that such member is mentally or physically incapacitated for the further performance of duty, that such incapacity was incurred at the time of active employment and has been continuous thereafter, that such incapacity is likely to be permanent, and that such member should be retired; and, provided further, that if a member is removed by the Supreme Court for mental or physical incapacity under the provisions of G.S. 7A-376, no action is required by the medical board under this section and, provided further, the medical board shall determine if the member is able to engage in gainful employment and, if so, the member shall still be retired and the disability retirement allowance as a result thereof shall be reduced as in G.S. 135-60(d). Provided further, that the medical board shall not certify any member as disabled who:

(1)   Applies for disability retirement based upon a mental or physical incapacity which existed when the member first established membership in the system; or

(2)   Is in receipt of any payments on account of the same disability which existed when the member first established membership in the system.

The Board of Trustees shall require each employee upon enrolling in the Retirement System to provide information on the membership application concerning any mental or physical incapacities existing at the time the member enrolls.

Notwithstanding the foregoing to the contrary, any beneficiary who commenced retirement with an early or service retirement benefit has the right, within three years of this retirement, to convert to an allowance with disability retirement benefits without modification of any election of optional allowance previously made; provided, the beneficiary presents clear and convincing evidence that the beneficiary would have met all applicable requirements for disability retirement benefits while still in service as a member. The allowance on account of disability retirement benefits to the beneficiary shall be retroactive to the effective date of early or service retirement.

(b)   Notwithstanding the foregoing, the surviving spouse of a deceased member who has met all other requirements for disability retirement benefits, except whose death occurred before the first day of the calendar month in which the member's disability retirement allowance was due and payable, and who was the designated beneficiary for a return of accumulated contributions and the final compensation death benefit as provided in G.S. 135-63, shall be paid in lieu of the return of accumulated contributions and the final compensation death benefit a monthly allowance equal to a reduced retirement allowance provided by a fifty percent (50%) joint and survivorship option, plus the allowance payable to a former member's surviving spouse, in the manner prescribed under G.S. 135-64 as though the former member had commenced retirement the first day of the month following his death. (1973, c. 640, s. 1; 1981, c. 689, s. 3; c. 940, s. 2; 1985, c. 479, ss. 192(b), 194; 1987, c. 513, s. 1; 2009-66, s. 3(f).)

§ 135-60. Disability retirement benefits.

(a) Upon retirement for disability in accordance with G.S. 135-59, a member shall receive a disability retirement allowance computed and payable as provided for service retirement in G.S. 135-58(a2) except that the member's creditable service shall be taken as the creditable service he would have had had he continued in service to the earliest date he could have retired on an unreduced service retirement allowance as a member in the same division of the General Court of Justice in which he was serving on his disability retirement date.

(b) Once each year during the first five years following retirement of a member on a disability retirement allowance, and once in every three-year period thereafter, the Board of Trustees may, and upon his application shall, require any disability beneficiary who has not yet attained his sixtieth birthday to undergo a medical examination, such examination to be made at the place of residence of the beneficiary or other place mutually agreed upon, by a physician or physicians designated by the Board of Trustees. Should any disability beneficiary who has not yet attained his sixtieth birthday refuse to submit to at least one medical examination in any such year by a physician or physicians designated by the Board of Trustees, his allowance may be discontinued until his withdrawal of such refusal, and should his refusal continue for one year, it shall be assumed that he is no longer disabled.

(c) Should the medical board certify to the Board of Trustees that a disability beneficiary prior to his sixty-fifth birthday has recovered to the extent that he would not satisfy the requirements for disability retirement if he were an active member of the Retirement System, or if his disability shall be assumed to have terminated in accordance with subsection (b) above, his disability retirement allowance shall thereupon cease, he shall be restored as a member of the Retirement System, and the period during which he was in receipt of a disability retirement allowance shall not be included in his creditable service.

(d) The Board of Trustees shall determine whether a disability beneficiary is engaged in or is able to engage in a gainful occupation paying more than the difference, as hereinafter indexed, between his disability retirement allowance and the gross compensation earned as an employee during the 12 consecutive months in the final 48 months of service prior to retirement producing the highest gross compensation excluding any compensation received on account of termination. If the disability beneficiary is earning or is able to earn more than the difference, the portion of his disability retirement allowance not provided by his contributions shall be reduced to an amount which, together with the portion of the disability retirement allowance provided by his contributions and the amount earnable by him shall equal the amount of his gross compensation prior to retirement. This difference shall be increased on January 1 of each year by the ratio of the Consumer Price Index to the Index one year earlier, calculated to the nearest tenth of one percent (1/10th of 1%). Should the earning capacity of the disability beneficiary later change, the portion of his disability retirement allowance not provided by his contributions may be further modified. In lieu of the reductions on account of a disability beneficiary earning more than the aforesaid difference, he may elect to convert his disability retirement allowance to a service retirement allowance calculated on the basis of his final compensation and creditable service at the time of disability retirement and his age at the time of conversion to service retirement. This election is irrevocable. (1973, c. 640, s. 1; 1981, c. 975, s. 4; c. 980, s. 5; 1983 (Reg. Sess., 1984), c. 1031, s. 19; 1999-237, s. 28.24(g).)

§ 135-61. Election of optional allowance.

Any member who retires under the provisions of this Article shall have the right to elect to have his allowance payable under any one of the optional forms provided for in G.S. 135-5(g), subject to the conditions therein contained, in lieu of the allowance that would otherwise be payable. (1973, c. 640, s. 1.)

§ 135-62. Return of accumulated contributions.

(a) Should a member cease membership service otherwise than by death or retirement under the provisions of this Article, he shall, upon submission of an application, be paid, not earlier than 60 days from the date of termination of service, his contributions and, if he has attained at least five years of membership service or if termination of his membership service is involuntary as certified by the employer, the accumulated regular interest thereon, provided that he has not in the meantime returned to service as a judge. Upon payment of such accumulated contributions his membership in the Retirement System shall cease and, if he thereafter again becomes a member, no credit shall be allowed for any service previously rendered, except as otherwise provided in G.S. 135-56(b). Any such payment of a member's accumulated contributions shall be in full and complete discharge of any rights in or to any benefits otherwise payable under this Article.

(b)   Repealed by Session Laws 1993, c. 531, s. 7. (1973, c. 640, s. 1; 1981, c. 672, s. 4; 1983, c. 467; 1983 (Reg. Sess., 1984), c. 1031, s. 20; 1993, c. 531, s. 7.)

§ 135-63. Benefits on death before retirement.

(a)   Upon receipt of proof, satisfactory to the Board of Trustees, of the death of a member in service, there shall be paid in a lump sum to such person as the member shall have nominated by electronic submission prior to completing 10 years of service in a form approved by the Board of Trustees or by written designation duly acknowledged and filed with the Board of Trustees, if such person is living at the time of the member's death, otherwise to the member's legal representatives, a death benefit equal to the sum of (i) the member's accumulated contributions, plus (ii) the member's final compensation; provided, however, that if the member has attained his fiftieth birthday with at least five years of membership service at his date of death, and if the designated recipient of the death benefits is the member's spouse who survives him, and if the spouse so elects, then the lump-sum death benefit provided for herein shall consist only of a payment equal to the member's final compensation and there shall be paid to the surviving spouse an annual retirement allowance, payable monthly, which shall commence on the first day of the calendar month coinciding with or next following the death of the member and shall be continued on the first day of each month thereafter until the remarriage or death of the spouse. The amount of any such retirement allowance shall be equal to one half of the amount of the retirement allowance to which the member would have been entitled had he retired under the provisions of G.S. 135-57(a) on the first day of the calendar month coinciding with or next following his date of death, reduced by two percent (2%) thereof for each full year, if any, by which the age of the member at his date of death exceeds that of his spouse. If the retirement allowance to the spouse shall terminate on the remarriage or death of the spouse before the total of the retirement allowance payments made equals the amount of the member's accumulated contributions at date of death, the excess of such accumulated contributions over the total of the retirement allowances paid to the spouse shall be paid in a lump sum to such person as the member shall have nominated by electronic submission in a form approved by the Board of Trustees or by written designation duly acknowledged and filed with the Board of Trustees, if such person is living at the time such payment falls due, otherwise to the former member's legal representatives.

(b) There shall be paid to the surviving unremarried spouse of any former judge who died in service prior to January 1, 1974, and after his forty-ninth birthday an annual retirement allowance which shall commence on January 1, 1974, and shall be continued on the first day of each month thereafter until the remarriage or death of the spouse. The amount of any such retirement allowance shall be computed in accordance with the provisions of subsection (a) above as if the provisions of this Article had been in effect on the date of death of the former judge, and the final compensation of such former judge had been equal to the rate of annual compensation in effect on December 31, 1973, for the office held by the former judge at the time of his death.

(c) Upon receipt of proof, satisfactory to the Board of Trustees, of the death of a member not in service, there shall be paid in a lump sum to such person as the member shall have nominated by electronic submission prior to completing 10 years of service in a form approved by the Board of Trustees or by written designation duly acknowledged and filed with the Board of Trustees, if such person is living at the time of the member's death, otherwise to the member's legal representatives, a death benefit equal to the member's accumulated contributions.

(d) Notwithstanding the provisions of G.S. 7A-376, there shall be paid to the surviving spouse of any former judge whose death occurred prior to July 1, 1983, who had not withdrawn his contributions pursuant to G.S. 135-62, an annual retirement allowance which shall commence on July 1, 1983, and shall be continued on the first day of each month thereafter until the death or remarriage of the spouse. If the spouse dies or remarries before the total of the retirement allowance paid equals the amount of the former judge's accumulated contributions, the excess of the accumulated contributions over the total of the retirement allowance paid to the spouse shall be paid in a lump sum to the person the spouse has nominated by written designation duly acknowledged and filed with the Board of Trustees, if the person is living at the time the payment falls due, otherwise to the spouse's legal representative. The amount of any such retirement allowance shall be computed in accordance with the provisions of subsection (a) above. This subsection does not authorize allowances to surviving spouses of former judges convicted of crimes related to the performance of their judicial duties.

(e) For purposes of this subsection, a participant whose employment is interrupted by reason of service in the Uniformed Services, as that term is defined in section 4303(16) of the Uniformed Services Employment and Reemployment Rights Act, Public Law 103-353, shall be deemed to be "in service" until the last day of such service in the Uniformed Services. If the participant does not return immediately after that service to employment with a covered employer in this System, then the participant shall be deemed "in service" until the date on which the participant was first eligible to be separated or released from his or her involuntary military service. (1973, c. 640, s. 1; c. 1385; 1983, c. 761, ss. 231, 234; 2009-66, ss. 6(c), 11(a), (b).)

§ 135-64. Benefits on death after retirement.

(a) In the event of the death of a former member while in receipt of a retirement allowance pursuant to his retirement under the provisions of G.S. 135-57, or after a former member's sixty-fifth birthday while in receipt of a retirement allowance pursuant to his retirement under the provisions of G.S. 135-59, there shall be paid to the former member's surviving spouse, if any, an annual retirement allowance, payable monthly, which shall commence on the first day of the calendar month next following the date of death of the former member and shall be continued on the first day of each month thereafter until the remarriage or death of the spouse. The amount of any such allowance shall be equal to one half of the allowance that was payable to the former member for the month immediately prior to his month of death, or which would have been so payable had an optional mode of payment not been elected under the provisions of G.S. 135-61, reduced by two percent (2%) thereof for each full year, if any, by which the age of the former member at date of death exceeds that of his spouse.

(b) In the event of the death of a former member prior to his sixty-fifth birthday while in receipt of a retirement allowance pursuant to his retirement under the provisions of G.S. 135-59, there shall be paid to the former member's surviving spouse, if any, an annual retirement allowance, payable monthly, which shall commence on the first day of the calendar month next following the date of death of the former member and shall be continued on the first day of each month thereafter until the remarriage or death of the spouse. The amount of any such allowance shall be equal to one half of the allowance to which the former member would have been entitled under the provisions of G.S. 135-58 if he had remained in service from his disability retirement date to his date of death with no change in his final compensation or status and had then retired, reduced by two percent (2%) thereof for each full year, if any, by which the age of the former member at date of death exceeds that of his spouse.

(c) In the event of the death of a former member while in receipt of a retirement allowance under the provisions of G.S. 135-58, 135-60, or 135-61, if such former member is not survived by a spouse to whom a retirement allowance is payable under the provisions of subsection (a) or subsection (b) above, nor survived by a beneficiary to whom a monthly survivorship benefit is payable under one of the optional modes of payment under G.S. 135-61, there shall be paid to such person as the member shall have nominated by electronic submission in a form approved by the Board of Trustees or by written designation duly acknowledged and filed with the Board of Trustees, if such person is living at the time of the member's death, otherwise to the member's legal representatives, a death benefit equal to the excess, if any, of the accumulated contributions of the member at his date of retirement over the total of the retirement allowances paid to him prior to his death.

(d) In the event that a retirement allowance becomes payable to the spouse of a former member under the provisions of subsection (a) or subsection (b) above, or to the designated survivor of a former member under one of the optional modes of payment under G.S. 135-61, and such retirement allowance to the spouse shall terminate on the remarriage or death of the spouse, or on the death of the designated survivor, before the total of the retirement allowances paid to the former member and his spouse or designated survivor combined equals the amount of the member's accumulated contributions at his date of retirement, the excess of such accumulated contributions over the total of the retirement allowances paid to the former member and his spouse or designated survivor combined shall be paid in a lump sum to such person as the member shall have nominated by electronic submission in a form approved by the Board of Trustees or by written designation duly acknowledged and filed with the Board of Trustees, if such person is living at the time such payment falls due, otherwise to the former member's legal representatives.

(e) In the event of the death of a retired former judge while in receipt of a retirement allowance under the provisions of G.S. 135-58(d), there shall be paid to the former judge's surviving spouse, if any, an annual retirement allowance payable monthly, which shall commence on the first day of the calendar month next following the date of death of the former judge and shall be continued on the first day of each month thereafter until the remarriage or death of the spouse. The amount of any such allowance shall be equal to one half of the allowance that was payable to the former judge for the month immediately prior to his month of death, reduced by two percent (2%) thereof for each full year, if any, by which the age of the former judge at date of death exceeds that of his spouse.

(f)   There shall be paid to the surviving unremarried spouse of any former judge who died prior to January 1, 1974, while in receipt of a retirement allowance under the provisions of a previous system, a retirement allowance which shall commence on January 1, 1974, and shall be continued on the first day of each month thereafter until the remarriage or death of the spouse. The amount of any such retirement allowance shall be equal to one half of the allowance that would have been payable to the former judge for the month of December 1973, if the previous system had been in effect at his date of retirement and if he had survived to January 1, 1974, reduced by two percent (2%) thereof for each full year, if any, by which the age of the former judge at date of death exceeded that of his spouse.

(g)   Upon the death of a retired member on or after July 1, 1988, but before January 1, 1999, there shall be paid a death benefit to the surviving spouse of a deceased retired member or to the deceased retired member's legal representative if not survived by a spouse; provided the retired member has elected, when first eligible, to make, and has continuously made, in advance of his death required contributions as determined by the Board of Trustees on a fully contributory basis, through retirement allowance deductions or other methods adopted by the Board of Trustees, to a group death benefit trust fund administered by the Board of Trustees separate and apart from the Retirement System's Annuity Savings Fund and Pension Accumulation Fund. This death benefit shall be a lump-sum payment in the amount of five thousand dollars ($5,000) upon the completion of 24 months of contributions required under this subsection. Should death occur before the completion of 24 months of contributions required under this subsection, the deceased retired member's surviving spouse or legal representative if not survived by a spouse shall be paid the sum of the retired member's contributions required by this subsection plus interest to be determined by the Board of Trustees.

(h)   Upon the death of a retired member on or after January 1, 1999, but before July 1, 2004, there shall be paid a death benefit to the surviving spouse of a deceased retired member or to the deceased retired member's legal representative if not survived by a spouse; provided the retired member has elected, when first eligible, to make, and has continuously made, in advance of his death required contributions as determined by the Board of Trustees on a fully contributory basis, through retirement allowance deductions or other methods adopted by the Board of Trustees, to a group death benefit trust fund administered by the Board of Trustees separate and apart from the Retirement System's Annuity Savings Fund and Pension Accumulation Fund. This death benefit shall be a lump-sum payment in the amount of six thousand dollars ($6,000) upon the completion of 24 months of contributions required under this subsection. Should death occur before the completion of 24 months of contributions required under this subsection, the deceased retired member's surviving spouse or legal representative if not survived by a spouse shall be paid the sum of the retired member's contributions required by this subsection plus interest to be determined by the Board of Trustees.

(i) Upon the death of a retired member on or after July 1, 2004, but before July 1, 2007, there shall be paid a death benefit to the surviving spouse of a deceased retired member or to the deceased retired member's legal representative if not survived by a spouse; provided the retired member has elected, when first eligible, to make, and has continuously made, in advance of his death required contributions as determined by the Board of Trustees on a fully contributory basis, through retirement allowance deductions or other methods adopted by the Board of Trustees, to a group death benefit trust fund administered by the Board of Trustees separate and apart from the Retirement System's Annuity Savings Fund and Pension Accumulation Fund. This death benefit shall be a lump-sum payment in the amount of nine thousand dollars ($9,000) upon the completion of 24 months of contributions required under this subsection. Should death occur before the completion of 24 months of contributions required under this subsection, the deceased retired member's surviving spouse or legal representative if not survived by a spouse shall be paid the sum of the retired member's contributions required by this subsection plus interest to be determined by the Board of Trustees.

Upon the death of a retired member on or after July 1, 2007, there shall be paid a death benefit to the surviving spouse of a deceased retired member or to the deceased retired member's legal representative if not survived by a spouse; provided the retired member has elected, when first eligible, to make, and has continuously made, in advance of his death required contributions as determined by the Board of Trustees on a fully contributory basis, through retirement allowance deductions or other methods adopted by the Board of Trustees, to a group death benefit trust fund administered by the Board of

Trustees separate and apart from the Retirement System's Annuity Savings Fund and Pension Accumulation Fund. This death benefit shall be a lump-sum payment in the amount of ten thousand dollars ($10,000) upon the completion of 24 months of contributions required under this subsection. Should death occur before the completion of 24 months of contributions required under this subsection, the deceased retired member's surviving spouse or legal representative if not survived by a spouse shall be paid the sum of the retired member's contributions required by this subsection plus interest to be determined by the Board of Trustees. (1973, c. 640, s. 1; 1987, c. 824, s. 4; 1995, c. 509, s. 76; 1998-212, s. 28.27(b), (c); 2004-147, ss. 5, 6; 2005-91, ss. 5, 6; 2007-496, s. 4; 2009-66, ss. 11(c), (d).)

§ 135-65. Post-retirement increases in allowances.

(a) Commencing with the post-retirement adjustment, effective July 1, 1974, all retirement allowances payable under the provisions of this Article shall be adjusted annually in accordance with the provisions of G.S. 135-5(o).

(b) Increases in Benefits Paid to Members Retired prior to July 1, 1978. - Notwithstanding subsection (a) of this section, the increase in allowance to each beneficiary on the retirement rolls as of July 1, 1978, which shall become payable on July 1, 1979, as otherwise provided in subsection (a) of this section, shall be the current maximum four percent (4%) plus an additional one percent (1%) to a total of five percent (5%) for the year 1979 only. The provisions of this subsection shall apply also to the allowance of a surviving annuitant of a beneficiary.

(c) Increases in Benefits Paid to Members Retired prior to July 1, 1979. - Notwithstanding the foregoing provisions, the increase in allowance to each beneficiary on the retirement rolls as of July 1, 1979, which shall become payable on July 1, 1980, shall be the current maximum four percent (4%) plus an additional six percent (6%) to a total of ten percent (10%) for the year 1980-81 only. The provisions of this subsection shall apply also to the allowance of a surviving annuitant of a beneficiary.

(d) Increases in Benefits Paid to Members Retired Prior to July 1, 1982. - From and after July 1, 1983, the retirement allowance to or on account of beneficiaries on the retirement rolls as of July 1, 1982, shall be increased by four percent (4%) of the allowance payable on July 1, 1982, provided the increase in retirement allowances shall be payable in accordance with all requirements, stipulations and conditions set forth in subsection (a) of this section.

(e) Increase in Benefits Paid to Members Retired on or before July 1, 1983. - From and after July 1, 1984, the retirement allowance to or on account of beneficiaries whose retirement commenced on or before July 1, 1983, shall be increased by eight percent (8%) of the allowance payable on July 1, 1983.

(f) From and after July 1, 1985, the retirement allowance to or on account of beneficiaries whose retirement commenced on or before July 1, 1984, shall be increased by four percent (4%) of the allowance payable on July 1, 1984. Furthermore, from and after July 1, 1985, the retirement allowance to or on account of beneficiaries whose retirement commenced after July 1, 1984, but before June 30, 1985, shall be increased by a prorated amount of four percent (4%) of the allowance payable as determined by the Board of Trustees based upon the number of months that a retirement allowance was paid between July 1, 1984, and June 30, 1985.

(g) From and after July 1, 1986, the retirement allowance to or on account of beneficiaries whose retirement commenced on or before July 1, 1985, shall be increased by three and eight-tenths percent (3.8%) of the allowance payable on July 1, 1985. Furthermore, from and after July 1, 1986, the retirement allowance to or on account of beneficiaries whose retirement commenced after July 1, 1985, but before June 30, 1986, shall be increased by a prorated amount of three and eight-tenths percent (3.8%) of the allowance payable as determined by the Board of Trustees based upon the number of months that a retirement allowance was paid between July 1, 1985 and June 30, 1986.

(h) From and after July 1, 1987, the retirement allowance to or on account of beneficiaries whose retirement commenced on or before July 1, 1986, shall be increased by four percent (4.0%) of the allowance payable on July 1, 1986. Furthermore, from and after July 1, 1987, the retirement allowance to or on account of beneficiaries whose retirement commenced after July 1, 1986, but before June 30, 1987, shall be increased by a prorated amount of four percent (4.0%) of the allowance payable as determined by the Board of Trustees based upon the number of months that a retirement allowance was paid between July 1, 1986, and June 30, 1987.

(i) From and after July 1, 1988, the retirement allowance to or on account of beneficiaries whose retirement commenced on or before July 1, 1987, shall be increased by three and six-tenths percent (3.6%) of the allowance payable on July 1, 1987. Furthermore, from and after July 1, 1988, the retirement allowance to or on account of beneficiaries whose retirement commenced after July 1, 1987, but before June 30, 1988, shall be increased by a prorated amount of three and six-tenths percent (3.6%) of the allowance payable as determined by the Board of Trustees based upon the number of months that a retirement allowance was paid between July 1, 1987, and June 30, 1988.

(j) From and after July 1, 1989, the retirement allowance to or on account of beneficiaries whose retirement commenced on or before July 1, 1988, shall be increased by three and one-half percent (3.5%) of the allowance payable on July 1, 1988. Furthermore, from and after July 1, 1989, the retirement allowance to or on account of beneficiaries whose retirement commenced after July 1, 1988, but before June 30, 1989, shall be increased by a prorated amount of three and one-half percent (3.5%) of the allowance payable as determined by the Board of Trustees based upon the number of months that a retirement allowance was paid between July 1, 1988, and June 30, 1989.

(k) Increase in Allowance as to Persons on Retirement Rolls as of June 1, 1990. - From and after July 1, 1990, the retirement allowance to or on account of beneficiaries on the retirement rolls as of June 1, 1990, shall be increased by six-tenths percent (0.6%) of the allowance payable on June 1, 1990. This allowance shall be calculated on the basis of the allowance payable and in effect on June 30, 1990, so as not to be compounded on any other increase granted by act of the 1989 Session of the General Assembly (1990 Regular Session).

(l) From and after July 1, 1990, the retirement allowance to or on account of beneficiaries whose retirement commenced on or before July 1, 1989, shall be increased by six and one-tenth percent (6.1%) of the allowance payable on July 1, 1989. Furthermore, from and after July 1, 1990, the retirement allowance to or on account of beneficiaries whose retirement commenced after July 1, 1989, but before June 30, 1990, shall be increased by a prorated amount of six and one-tenth percent (6.1%) of the allowance payable as determined by the Board of Trustees based upon the number of months that a retirement allowance was paid between July 1, 1989, and June 30, 1990.

(m) From and after July 1, 1992, the retirement allowance to or on account of beneficiaries whose retirement commenced on or before July 1, 1991, shall be increased by one and six-tenths percent (1.6%) of the allowance payable on July 1, 1991. Furthermore, from and after July 1, 1992, the retirement allowance to or on account of beneficiaries whose retirement commenced after July 1, 1991, but before June 30, 1992, shall be increased by a prorated amount of one and six-tenths percent (1.6%) of the allowance payable as determined by the Board of Trustees based upon the number of months that a retirement allowance was paid between July 1, 1991 and June 30, 1992.

(n) From and after July 1, 1993, the retirement allowance to or on account of beneficiaries whose retirement commenced on or before July 1, 1992, shall be increased by one and six-tenths percent (1.6%) of the allowance payable on July 1, 1992. Furthermore, from and after July 1, 1993, the retirement allowance to or on account of beneficiaries whose retirement commenced after July 1, 1992, but before June 30, 1993, shall be increased by a prorated amount of one and six-tenths percent (1.6%) of the allowance payable as determined by the Board of Trustees based upon the number of months that a retirement allowance was paid between July 1, 1992, and June 30, 1993.

(o) From and after July 1, 1994, the retirement allowance to or on account of beneficiaries whose retirement commenced on or before July 1, 1993, shall be increased by three and one-half percent (3.5%) of the allowance payable on July 1, 1993. Furthermore, from and after July 1, 1994, the retirement allowance to or on account of beneficiaries whose retirement commenced after July 1, 1993, but before June 30, 1994, shall be increased by a prorated amount of three and one-half percent (3.5%) of the allowance payable as determined by the Board of Trustees based upon the number of months that a retirement allowance was paid between July 1, 1993, and June 30, 1994.

(p) From and after July 1, 1995, the retirement allowance to or on account of beneficiaries whose retirement commenced on or before July 1, 1994, shall be increased by two percent (2%) of the allowance payable on July 1, 1994. Furthermore, from and after July 1, 1995, the retirement allowance to or on account of beneficiaries whose retirement commenced after July 1, 1994, but before June 30, 1995, shall be increased by a prorated amount of two percent (2%) of the allowance payable as determined by the Board of Trustees based upon the number of months that a retirement allowance was paid between July 1, 1994, and June 30, 1995.

(q) From and after September 1, 1996, the retirement allowance to or on account of beneficiaries whose retirement commenced on or before July 1, 1995, shall be increased by four and four-tenths percent (4.4%) of the allowance payable on July 1, 1995. Furthermore, from and after September 1, 1996, the retirement allowance to or on account of beneficiaries whose retirement commenced after July 1, 1995, but before June 30, 1996, shall be increased by a prorated amount of four and four-tenths percent (4.4%) of the allowance payable as determined by the Board of Trustees based upon the number of months that a retirement allowance was paid between July 1, 1995, and June 30, 1996.

(r)   From and after July 1, 1997, the retirement allowance to or on account of beneficiaries whose retirement commenced on or before July 1, 1996, shall be increased by four percent (4%) of the allowance payable on June 1, 1997. Furthermore, from and after July 1, 1997, the retirement allowance to or on account of beneficiaries whose retirement commenced after July 1, 1996, but before June 30, 1997, shall be increased by a prorated amount of four percent (4%) of the allowance payable as determined by the Board of Trustees based upon the number of months that a retirement allowance was paid between July 1, 1996, and June 30, 1997.

(s)   From and after July 1, 1998, the retirement allowance to or on account of beneficiaries whose retirement commenced on or before July 1, 1997, shall be increased by two and one-half percent (2.5%) of the allowance payable on June 1, 1998. Furthermore, from and after July 1, 1998, the retirement allowance to or on account of beneficiaries whose retirement commenced after July 1, 1997, but before June 30, 1998, shall be increased by a prorated amount of two and one-half percent (2.5%) of the allowance payable as determined by the Board of Trustees based upon the number of months that a retirement allowance was paid between July 1, 1997, and June 30, 1998.

(t)   From and after July 1, 1999, the retirement allowance to or on account of beneficiaries whose retirement commenced on or before July 1, 1998, shall be increased by two and three-tenths percent (2.3%) of the allowance payable on June 1, 1999. Furthermore, from and after July 1, 1999, the retirement allowance to or on account of beneficiaries whose retirement commenced after July 1, 1998, but before June 30, 1999, shall be increased by a prorated amount of two and three-tenths percent (2.3%) of the allowance payable as determined by the Board of Trustees based upon the number of months that a retirement allowance was paid between July 1, 1998, and June 30, 1999.

(u)   From and after July 1, 2000, the retirement allowance to or on account of beneficiaries whose retirement commenced on or before July 1, 1999, shall be increased by two and six-tenths percent (2.6%) of the allowance payable on June 1, 2000. Furthermore, from and after July 1, 2000, the retirement allowance to or on account of beneficiaries whose retirement commenced after

July 1, 1999, but before June 30, 2000, shall be increased by a prorated amount of two and six-tenths percent (2.6%) of the allowance payable as determined by the Board of Trustees based upon the number of months that a retirement allowance was paid between July 1, 1999, and June 30, 2000.

(v) From and after July 1, 2001, the retirement allowance to or on account of beneficiaries whose retirement commenced on or before July 1, 2000, shall be increased by two percent (2%) of the allowance payable on June 1, 2001. Furthermore, from and after July 1, 2001, the retirement allowance to or on account of beneficiaries whose retirement commenced after July 1, 2000, but before June 30, 2001, shall be increased by a prorated amount of two percent (2%) of the allowance payable as determined by the Board of Trustees based upon the number of months that a retirement allowance was paid between July 1, 2000, and June 30, 2001.

(w) From and after July 1, 2002, the retirement allowance to or on account of beneficiaries whose retirement commenced on or before July 1, 2001, shall be increased by one and four-tenths percent (1.4%) of the allowance payable on June 1, 2002. Furthermore, from and after July 1, 2002, the retirement allowance to or on account of beneficiaries whose retirement commenced after July 1, 2001, but before June 30, 2002, shall be increased by a prorated amount of one and four-tenths percent (1.4%) of the allowance payable as determined by the Board of Trustees based upon the number of months that a retirement allowance was paid between July 1, 2001, and June 30, 2002.

(x) From and after July 1, 2003, the retirement allowance to or on account of beneficiaries whose retirement commenced on or before July 1, 2002, shall be increased by one and twenty-eight hundredths percent (1.28%) of the allowance payable on June 1, 2003. Furthermore, from and after July 1, 2003, the retirement allowance to or on account of beneficiaries whose retirement commenced after July 1, 2002, but before June 30, 2003, shall be increased by a prorated amount of one and twenty-eight hundredths percent (1.28%) of the allowance payable as determined by the Board of Trustees based upon the number of months that a retirement allowance was paid between July 1, 2002, and June 30, 2003.

(y) From and after July 1, 2004, the retirement allowance to or on account of beneficiaries whose retirement commenced on or before July 1, 2003, shall be increased by one and seven-tenths percent (1.7%) of the allowance payable on June 1, 2004, in accordance with G.S. 135-5(o). Furthermore, from and after July 1, 2004, the retirement allowance to or on account of beneficiaries whose retirement commenced after July 1, 2003, but before June 30, 2004, shall be increased by a prorated amount of one and seven-tenths percent (1.7%) of the allowance payable as determined by the Board of Trustees based upon the number of months that a retirement allowance was paid between July 1, 2003, and June 30, 2004.

(z) From and after July 1, 2005, the retirement allowance to or on account of beneficiaries whose retirement commenced on or before July 1, 2004, shall be increased by two percent (2%) of the allowance payable on June 1, 2005. Furthermore, from and after July 1, 2005, the retirement allowance to or on account of beneficiaries whose retirement commenced after July 1, 2004, but before June 30, 2005, shall be increased by a prorated amount of two percent (2%) of the allowance payable as determined by the Board of Trustees based upon the number of months that a retirement allowance was paid between July 1, 2004, and June 30, 2005.

(aa) From and after July 1, 2006, the retirement allowance to or on account of beneficiaries whose retirement commenced on or before July 1, 2005, shall be increased by three percent (3%) of the allowance payable on June 1, 2006. Furthermore, from and after July 1, 2006, the retirement allowance to or on account of beneficiaries whose retirement commenced after July 1, 2005, but before June 30, 2006, shall be increased by a prorated amount of three percent (3%) of the allowance payable as determined by the Board of Trustees based upon the number of months that a retirement allowance was paid between July 1, 2005, and June 30, 2006.

(bb) From and after July 1, 2007, the retirement allowance to or on account of beneficiaries whose retirement commenced on or before July 1, 2006, shall be increased by two and two-tenths percent (2.2%) of the allowance payable on June 1, 2007. Furthermore, from and after July 1, 2007, the retirement allowance to or on account of beneficiaries whose retirement commenced after July 1, 2006, but before June 30, 2007, shall be increased by a prorated amount of two and two-tenths percent (2.2%) of the allowance payable as determined by the Board of Trustees based upon the number of months that a retirement allowance was paid between July 1, 2006, and June 30, 2007.

(cc) From and after July 1, 2008, the retirement allowance to or on account of beneficiaries whose retirement commenced on or before July 1, 2007, shall be increased by two and two-tenths percent (2.2%) of the allowance payable on June 1, 2008. Furthermore, from and after July 1, 2008, the retirement allowance to or on account of beneficiaries whose retirement commenced after

July 1, 2007, but before June 30, 2008, shall be increased by a prorated amount of two and two-tenths percent (2.2%) of the allowance payable as determined by the Board of Trustees based upon the number of months that a retirement allowance was paid between July 1, 2007, and June 30, 2008.

(dd) From and after July 1, 2012, the retirement allowance to or on account of beneficiaries whose retirement commenced on or before July 1, 2011, shall be increased by one percent (1%) of the allowance payable on June 1, 2012. Furthermore, from and after July 1, 2012, the retirement allowance to or on account of beneficiaries whose retirement commenced after July 1, 2011, but before June 30, 2012, shall be increased by a prorated amount of one percent (1%) of the allowance payable as determined by the Board of Trustees based upon the number of months that a retirement allowance was paid between July 1, 2011, and June 30, 2012. (1973, c. 640, s. 1; 1979, c. 838, s. 104; 1979, 2nd Sess., c. 1137, s. 69; 1983, c. 761, s. 221; 1983 (Reg. Sess., 1984), c. 1034, s. 224; 1985, c. 479, s. 189(b); 1985 (Reg. Sess., 1986), c. 1014, s. 49(b); 1987, c. 738, s. 27(b); 1987 (Reg. Sess., 1988), c. 1086, s. 22(b); 1989, c. 752, s. 41(b); 1989 (Reg. Sess., 1990), c. 1077, ss. 8, 9; 1991 (Reg. Sess., 1992), c. 900, s. 53(c); 1993, c. 321, s. 74(f); 1993 (Reg. Sess., 1994), c. 769, s. 7.30(n); 1995, c. 507, s. 7.22(b); 1996, 2nd Ex. Sess., c. 18, s. 28.21(b); 1997-443, s. 33.22(e); 1998-153, s. 21(b); 1999-237, s. 28.23(b); 2000-67, s. 26.20(e); 2001-424, s. 32.22(b); 2002-126, s. 28.8(c); 2003-284, s. 30.17(b); 2004-124, s. 31.17(b); 2005-276, s. 29.25(b); 2006-66, s. 22.18(c); 2007-323, s. 28.20(b); 2008-107, s. 26.23(b); 2012-142, s. 25.13(b).)

§ 135-66. Administration; management of funds.

The State Treasurer shall be the custodian of the assets of this Retirement System and shall invest them in accordance with the provisions of G.S. 147-69.2 and 147-69.3. (1973, c. 640, s. 1; 1979, c. 467, s. 18.)

§ 135-67. Assets of Retirement System.

(a) All of the assets of the Retirement System shall be credited according to the purpose for which they are held to one of two funds, namely, the annuity savings fund and the pension accumulation fund.

(b) The annuity savings fund shall be the fund to which all members' contributions, and regular interest allowances thereon as provided for in G.S. 135-7(b), shall be credited. From this fund shall be paid the accumulated contributions of a member in accordance with G.S. 135-62, or 135-63.

(c) Upon the retirement of a member, his accumulated contributions shall be transferred from the annuity savings fund to the pension accumulation fund. In the event that a retired former member should subsequently again become a member of the Retirement System as provided for in G.S. 135-60(c) or 135-71, any excess of his accumulated contributions at his date of retirement over the sum of the retirement allowance payments received by him since his date of retirement shall be transferred from the pension accumulation fund to the annuity savings fund and shall be credited to his individual account in the annuity savings fund.

(d) The pension accumulation fund shall be the fund in which shall be accumulated contributions by the State and amounts transferred from the annuity savings fund in accordance with subsection (c) above, and to which all income from the invested assets of the Retirement System shall be credited. From this fund shall be paid retirement allowances and any other benefits provided for under this Article except payments of accumulated contributions as provided in subsection (b) above.

(e) The regular interest allowance on the members' accumulated contributions provided for in G.S. 135-7(b) shall be transferred each year from the pension accumulation fund to the annuity savings fund. (1973, c. 640, s. 1.)

§ 135-68. Contributions by the members.

(a) Each member shall contribute by payroll deduction for each pay period for which he receives compensation six percent (6%) of his compensation for such period.

(b) Anything within this Article to the contrary notwithstanding, the State, pursuant to the provisions of section 414(h)(2) of the Internal Revenue Code of 1954 as amended, shall pick up and pay the contributions which would be payable by the members under subsection (a) of this section with respect to the services of such members rendered after the effective date of this subsection.

The members' contributions picked up by the State shall be designated for all purposes of the Retirement System as member contributions, except for the determination of tax upon a distribution from the System. These contributions shall be credited to the annuity savings fund and accumulated within the fund in a member's account which shall be separately established for the purpose of accounting for picked-up contributions.

Member contributions picked up by the State shall be payable from the same source of funds used for the payment of compensation to a member. A deduction shall be made from a member's compensation equal to the amount of his contributions picked up by the State. This deduction, however, shall not reduce a member's compensation as defined in subdivision (5) of G.S. 135-53. Picked up contributions shall be transmitted to the Retirement System monthly for the preceding month by means of a warrant drawn by the State payable to the Retirement System and shall be accompanied by a schedule of the picked-up contributions on such forms as may be prescribed. (1973, c. 640, s. 1; 1983, c. 469, s. 1.)

§ 135-69. Contributions by the State.

(a)   The State shall contribute annually an amount equal to the sum of the "normal contribution" and the "accrued liability contribution."

(b)   The normal contribution for any period shall be determined as a percentage, equal to the normal contribution rate, of the total compensation of the members for such period. The normal contribution rate shall be determined as the percentage represented by the ratio of (i) the annual normal cost to provide the benefits of the Retirement System, computed in accordance with recognized actuarial principles on the basis of methods and assumptions approved by the Board of Trustees, in excess of the part thereof provided by the members' contributions, to (ii) the total annual compensation of the members of the Retirement System.

(c)   The accrued liability contribution for any period shall be determined as a percentage, equal to the accrued liability contribution rate, of the total compensation of the members for such period. The accrued liability contribution rate shall be determined as the percentage represented by the ratio of (i) the level annual contribution necessary to amortize the unfunded accrued liability over a period of 40 years, computed in accordance with recognized actuarial principles on the basis of methods and assumptions approved by the Board of

Trustees, to (ii) the total annual compensation of the members of the Retirement System.

(d) The unfunded accrued liability as of any date shall be determined, in accordance with recognized actuarial principles on the basis of methods and assumptions approved by the Board of Trustees, as the excess of (i) the then present value of the benefits to be provided under the Retirement System in the future over (ii) the sum of the assets of the Retirement System then currently on hand in the annuity savings fund and the pension accumulation fund, plus the then present value of the stipulated contributions to be made in the future by the members, plus the then present value of the normal contributions expected to be made in the future by the State.

(e) The normal contribution rate and the accrued liability contribution rate shall be determined after each annual valuation of the Retirement System and shall remain in effect until a new valuation is made.

(f) The annual contributions by the State for any year shall be at least sufficient, when combined with the amount held in the pension accumulation fund at the start of the year, to provide the retirement allowances and other benefits payable out of the fund during the year then current. (1973, c. 640, s. 1.)

Vision Books Order Form

Fax Orders:	1-980-299-5965
Phone Orders:	1-704-898-0770
E-mail Orders:	www.visionbooks.org
Mail Orders:	Vision Books, LLC P.O. Box 42406 Charlotte, NC 28215

Shipp To:
Name_____
Address_____
City_____State_____Zip_____
Phone_____Fax_____
Email_____@_____

Bill To: We can bill a third party on your behalf.
Name_____
Address_____
City_____State_____Zip_____
Phone____(_____)_____Fax_____
Email_____@_____

Pamphlet Number ($15.00 Each)	Qty	Total Cost
_____	_____	_____
_____	_____	_____
_____	_____	_____
_____	_____	_____
_____	_____	_____
_____	_____	_____
_____	_____	_____
Full Volume Set 1-92	92 Pamphlets	1,380.00

Free Shipping & Handling on Full Volume Orders
Add $1.00 Shipping & Handling per pamphlet $_____

Total Cost $_____

Thank you for your support. Management!

DID YOU ENJOY THIS BOOK?

Vision Books, LLC would like to hear from you! If you or someone you know has been fasely imprisoned, we would like to hear your story. If the 'North Carolina Criminal Law and Procedure' has had an effect in your life or if you have suggestions, we would like to hear from you. Send your letters to:

Vision Books, LLC
Attn: Staff Writers
P.O. Box 42406
Charlotte, NC 28215
Email: staff@visionbooks.org

Order Additional Copies:

Fax Orders:	1-980-299-5965
Phone Orders:	1-704-898-0770
E-mail Orders:	www.visionbooks.org
Mail Orders:	Vision Books, LLC P.O. Box 42406 Charlotte, NC 28215

www.ingramcontent.com/pod-product-compliance
Lightning Source LLC
Chambersburg PA
CBHW051629170526
45167CB00001B/121